BY THE AUTO EDITORS OF CONSUMER GUIDE®

Mercedes-Benz

The First Hundred Years

RICHARD M. LANGWORTH

BEEKMAN
NEW YORK

CONTENTS

Louis Weber, President
Publications International, Ltd.
3841 West Oakton Street
Skokie, Illinois 60076

Permission is never granted for commercial purposes.

Manufactured in the United States of America
10 9 8 7 6 5 4 3 2 1

Library of Congress Catalog Card Number: 83-62605

ISBN: 0-517-38199-0

This edition published by:
Beekman House
A Division of Crown Publishers, Inc.
One Park Avenue
New York, NY 10016

Principal Author
Richard M. Langworth

Contributing Authors
Jan P. Norbye
Graham Robson

Jacket Design
Frank E. Peiler

Graphic Layout
Herb Slobin

Photography
William L. Bailey
Daimler-Benz AG
David Gooley & Associates
Bud Juneau
Richard M. Langworth
Mercedes-Benz of North
    America
Douglas J. Mitchel
Motor Vehicle Manufacturers
    Assn.
Jan P. Norbye
Special thanks to A.B. Shuman

TOWARD THE
SECOND HUNDRED YEARS

There's a significant birthday coming in 1986, one that will be observed—and most likely celebrated—in many places around the world. Certainly there will be festivities aplenty in Germany, in towns like Untertürkheim and Sindelfingen, Mannheim and Gaggenau, the industrial heart of the Federal Republic that owes so much to the honoree. As far away as London and Paris, New York and Los Angeles, as far south as Argentina, other people will be remembering on that day, now-graying people recalling their vital roles in the story. Perhaps they were played on the misty heights of the Nürburgring or the dusty highways of Mexico, perhaps the long, fast straights of Tripoli and Le Mans or on the rally tracks of South America. Or perhaps it was in Italy, where driving is as much sport as necessity, where those privileged to witness them will lift their glasses to the great silver cars that once roared up and down their country roads on the wings of unearthly winds. A chunky auto dealer in Buenos Aires with pictures of old racing cars on his office wall will relive his memories. And at a quiet graveyard in Lugano, Switzerland, surely someone will remember to place a flower or two in memory of a German racing driver with the unlikely name of Caracciola.

Yes, 1986 marks a milestone in automotive history: the 100th birthday of Mercedes-Benz— more precisely, a century since the first Benz went chuffing down a road under its own power, an improbable rival to the horse. "In every field of human endeavor," wrote Theodore MacManus, "he that is first must perpetually live in the white light of publicity . . . The reward is widespread recognition; the punishment, fierce denial and detraction. When a man's work becomes a standard for the whole world, it also becomes a target for the shafts of the envious few." MacManus was writing of Cadillac, but the words can scarcely be denied Mercedes-Benz, preeminent builder of what many laymen and experts alike judge the finest cars in the world.

Almost every adjective you can think of has been applied to Mercedes-Benz cars at one time or another: overpriced, arrogant, overrated, understyled, heavy, unyielding, conservative. In particular, Mercedes seem to garner more than their fair share of opposites: they have been called both expensive and cheap, fast and slow, stylish and styleless, or beautiful and ugly, soul-stirring and clinical. But all this misses the point. No car has ever been—or likely ever will be—perfect, not even a Mercedes, though at times it is hard to imagine the perfectionists at Daimler-Benz capable of doing anything wrong. Still, Mercedes-Benz automobiles remain arguably the best built, best engineered, best conceived devices for moving people swiftly, safely, and in great comfort. Perfect they may not be, but few automobiles approach perfection more closely or more consistently than those bearing the proud three-pointed star.

There's a very good reason for that: the people at Daimler-Benz AG are very good at what they do. They couldn't hope to charge the prices they demand and survive very long otherwise. Besides, it's often true that the most expensive form of a commodity is usually the cheapest in the long run. So if, after parting with, say, $50,000, you feel that you can drive your new 500SEL up the side of a mountain, don't be alarmed. It's simply one of the burdens of Mercedes-Benz ownership.

These pages chronicle the first century of Mercedes-Benz. We emphasize the cars almost exclusively; the history of the equally laudable commercial vehicles awaits a future volume. The Daimler-Benz story is a record of achievement unparalleled by any other marque over a span of years that dates from the very dawn of self-propelled transport. Read it, and you will probably lift your glass at least once with the rest of us in 1986.

This book would not have been possible without the expert assistance of England's Graham Robson, who contributed the first three chapters covering Benz, Daimler, and the early years following the merger of the two. We are also grateful to France's Jan Norbye, the best technical writer in the field, who provided details on the classic prewar and postwar engines and the story of diesel engine development at Daimler-Benz. John Olson of Minnesota, publisher of the *SL Market Newsletter,* provided the chapter entitled "Collector's Choice." Bud Juneau of California was the principal photographer for many of the cars shown in the color sections.

Other color plates and much of the contemporary black-and-white photography were supplied by Mercedes-Benz of North America through the kind assistance of A.B. Shuman, public relations manager. A.B. also loaned the principal author quite a few press cars over the years, which helped foster our enduring respect for Mercedes-Benz. In one act of supreme confidence, A.B. even loaned a 600 "Grosser" to our friend Rich Taylor, whose reactions to it are duly recorded herein. The latter, as well as excerpts from Lynn Yakel's "300SL: The Legend and the Love Affair," are reproduced with the permission of The Milestone Car Society, which first published these pieces in 1973 and 1979, respectively, in its quarterly magazine.

Many books were consulted in compiling this one. The two best are sadly now out of print, but should be mentioned. One is Karl Ludvigsen's epic sporting history *The Mercedes-Benz Racing Cars* (Bond-Parkhurst, 1971), the definitive Mercedes competition history and a model of how such books should be written. The other is Alfred Neubauer's *Speed Was My Life* (Clarkson Potter, 1960), a sensitive and compelling story by the legendary racing manager of Mercedes-Benz from 1926 through 1955. Neubauer, who passed away in 1980 at the ripe age of 89, was a man with two fabulous gifts: that of managing a great racing team as no other before or since, and that of being able to write about his experiences, dramatically and well, for the benefit of those who were born too late.

Other references included *The Encyclopedia of Motor Sport* edited by G.N. Georgano, *Three-Pointed Star* by David Scott-Moncrieff, *The Mighty Mercedes* by Michael Frostick, *The Magnificent Mercedes* by Graham Robson, *Mercedes-Benz: A History* by W. Robert Nitske, *Mercedes and Mercedes-Benz Racing Car Guide* by Cyril Posthumus, *Mercedes-Benz Pocket History* by Dominique Pascal, *All But My Life* by Stirling Moss with Ken Purdy, *Racing with Mercedes Benz* by George Monkhouse, *The Golden Age of American Racing* by Griffith Borgeson, *A Racing Car Driver's World* by Rudolf Caracciola, *The Grand Prix Car* by Laurence Pomeroy, *The Rise and Fall of the Third Reich* by William L. Shirer, *Grand Prix Driver* by Hermann Lang, *Grands Prix 1934-39* by Rodney Walkerly, *The Grand Prix Mercedes-Benz Type W125* (1937) by Denis Jenkinson, *Fangio* by Juan Manuel Fangio, *History of the Brooklands Motor Course* by William Boddy, and *Adventure on Wheels* by John Fitch. Periodicals consulted were mostly contemporary with various cars and events, and are cited within the text.

The many kindnesses of Marcus Clary to this writer over the years, and his help in research projects large and small, is deeply appreciated.

Richard M. Langworth
New Hampshire, August 1983

CARL BENZ & HIS CARS: HORSEPOWER WITHOUT THE HORSE

Who built the world's first practical motor car? Who was really the founding father of the world's motor industry? And, most importantly, when did it all begin? Though historians and car enthusiasts continue to wrangle over such questions, there's little doubt that both Carl Benz and Gottlieb Daimler were in at the beginning. The Germans, as you might expect, chronicle such events rather carefully. We can be quite certain that Benz's first machine, a tricycle, began sputtering around near his workshop in 1885 and that Daimler's prototype four-wheeler was first fired up in 1886.

In Europe, historians are preparing to celebrate the automobile's centenary in 1986 around the birth of Daimler's horseless carriage. No doubt there is a "history" book in Russia claiming otherwise, but the truth is that the automobile as we know it was born in Germany: in Mannheim with Benz and in Cannstatt with Daimler. Ironically, neither inventor knew what the other was up to at first. Though they lived and worked barely 60 miles apart in the mid-1880s, they never actually met face to face.

Automotive history does not begin even with Carl Benz, for he merely harnessed the work of earlier inventors. For the record, the patent for the world's first successful internal-combustion engine was granted to a Frenchman, Etienne Lenoir, in 1860—although the fuel used was based not on petroleum but town gas. The four-stroke cycle, employing a gasoline/air vapor, was the bright idea of one Nikolous August Otto, though it was applied to huge, slow-revving engines. That patent was recorded in Germany in 1876. Otto, of course, was German, and his work was known to both Benz and Daimler. Well before the mid-1880s, "motor vehicles" and horseless carriages of various sorts had plied the roads of Europe, but all had been large, heavy, and inefficient, relying on steam power in one form or another. The real technological breakthrough—linking the "Otto cycle" to the use of petroleum fuel in lightweight, high-revving engines—had yet to be made.

Carl Benz was more than 40 years old when he built his first car—more properly, a motorized tricycle—but he had always been impeccably connected with thorough and practical German engineering. Born in 1844 in Muhlberg, near Karlsruhe in what is now the heart of industrial West Germany, Carl was the only son of Johann Georg Benz, who was an

Opposite page: the original Benz Patent Motorwagen as it likely looked in 1888 Germany. This page, left: ad touts the "new, practical" Benz in 1888. Above: Carl Benz circa 1864.

engineer on the new and very impressive Karlsruhe railway. Johann, however, died of pneumonia only two years after his son was born, so the boy had to be brought up by his mother. Frau Josephine Benz was awarded a tiny pension by the railway company, because her husband had contracted his fatal illness while laboring to re-rail an engine. She soon supplemented this income by moving into the middle of Karlsruhe where she worked as a cook, but there was never much money in the Benz household.

Even so, there was never any doubt that young Benz was destined to be a mechanical engineer. He tackled and passed an examination that enabled him to enter the Karlsruhe Lyceum (high school), which was already noted for its attention to the natural sciences—particularly physics, which soon became Carl's favorite subject. From here, he went to the local Polytechnic or trade school. It was during this period that he first encontered a Lenoir gas engine, which had been installed in the Max Eyth machine tool works in Stuttgart. After graduating in 1864, at age 20, Benz briefly worked for a locksmith, then joined the Karlsruhe *Maschinenbaugesell-schaft* as a fitter. This company had 800 employees, and was involved in all kinds of foundry and machining work for locomotives and large industrial installations.

The next 10 years were turbulent for Carl Benz. His mother died in 1870. Two years later he married Berta Ringer. In between these events, he visited Vienna briefly, then returned to Germany to settle in Mannheim. There he met up with August Ritter, and set up a small workshop with him.

This *Benz und Ritter Mechanische Werkstatte,* his first business venture, was the direct forerunner of the Benz company, but it was certainly not prosperous or widely known. In fact, throughout the 1870s Carl Benz's financial situation was precarious. By the end of the decade, he had survived potential bankruptcy more than once. But he had also managed to build his first internal-combustion engine, a two-stroke. By the beginning of the 1880s, his business was renamed the *Mannheimer Gasmotorenfabrik*

(Mannheim Gas Engine Factory), and Benz began offering a few replicas of his engine to paying customers.

Then, fate took a hand. First, Benz had commercial problems with his agent, one Otto Schmuck. As a result of this, he decided in late 1882 to start all over again. However, there were problems in freeing himself of the old business, not least because of disagreements over unfinished projects. Benz was taken to court, and ended up virtually penniless. Things looked grim until two business friends, Max C. Rose and Friedrich W. Esslinger, offered to back him in a new company, which they all decided to call *Benz und Cie, Rheinische Gasmotorenfabrik von Mannheim.* By the end of 1883,

Benz's immediate troubles were over, and he could now continue to develop his new engine ideas. He also began to think about applying them to road vehicles.

It should be noted that up to this time, road transport all over the world had relied on horse, donkey, or oxen power. Most people rarely traveled far from the town or the valley in which they were born and raised. Naturally, those in the lower economic classes walked everywhere, but upper-class folk, professional people and aristrocrats, needed to get around more quickly, so they typically either rode on horseback or used carriages of one type or another. By the middle of the 19th century, something like "mass" transportation had

appeared—for those who could afford it—in the form of horse-drawn stagecoaches and in that modern miracle of speed, the steam-powered railway train. Early visionaries of automobility, such as Cugnot and Trevethick, tried to harness steam to power self-propelled roadgoing vehicles, but their contraptions ended up heavy and unwieldy, and were often dangerous. Accordingly, horse power—courtesy of horses—reigned supreme well past the turn of the century, and long-distance travel remained a real chore for anyone not going by train.

Carl Benz was one of those forward-thinking engineers determined to produce a practical "horseless carriage" in which the new internal-combustion-type engine would

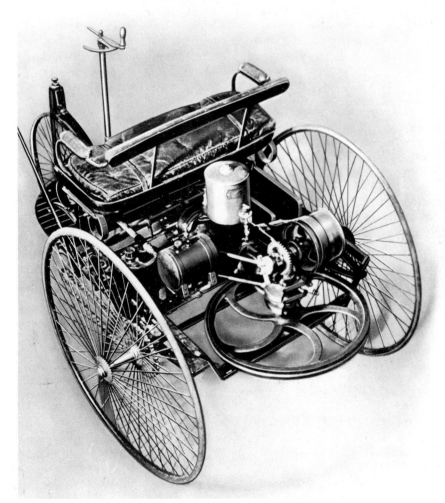

Opposite page and near left: spindly Benz three-wheeler was powered by a horizontally mounted single-cylinder engine that propelled it up to about 10 miles per hour. Note tiller steering, chain drive. Original was destroyed; this is the D-B Museum replica. Above: the Benz home workshop in Mannheim.

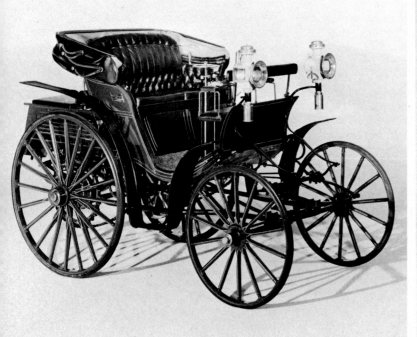

Above left: an 1893 example of the Benz Victoria, the firm's first four-wheeler, with "vis-a-vis" seating. Above right: an early two-cylinder Benz of 1899 displays a more conventional seating arrangement. Opposite page: another view of the 1899 car with its full "landaulet" bodywork in place.

substitute for the horses. Not surprisingly, most of the early efforts involved exactly what seemed so obvious: fitting an engine into what looked suspiciously like a carriage that had been shorn of the usual hitches, reins, and other horse-related gear. But Carl Benz was different. He had been so poor for so many years that he was not used to owning, let alone riding around in, a horse and carriage. Perhaps it was for that very reason that when he sat down to design his very first engine-powered vehicle, he came up with something quite unusual.

So, what should it be? A large machine or small? How many wheels? How many seats? What sort of steering? Where should the engine be placed, and how would its power be used to propel the vehicle? And, how

would the thing stop? We now know that it took Benz a long time to come up with practical solutions to these problems. Though he began work before the end of 1883, the first trials for his rig were not conducted until the spring of 1885. Happily, a replica of this Benz "car" now resides in the Daimler-Benz museum near the factory in the Untertürkheim district of Stuttgart, West Germany.

Actually, the world's first motor-driven vehicle was a tricycle with a single front wheel and a mid-mounted engine driving the rear wheels. (This brings to mind the adage that there is really nothing new under the sun. Though the mid-engine layout became common for racing cars in the mid-1960s and, later, for several roadgoing sports cars, the impecunious Carl Benz had employed it way back in 1884.) The tricycle configuration would be a feature of all Benz models built for sale until 1892.

The first Benz used a very simple tubular chassis frame, with full-elliptic leaf suspension for the rear axle and no

suspension at all for the front wheel. Steering was accomplished by manipulating a long, spindly rod, which led back from a bell crank at the top of the front wheel fork to a rack-and-pinion arrangement at the foot of the steering post. The engine was a horizontally mounted, water-cooled single-cylinder unit of 1691cc (103 cid), and produced about 1.5 horsepower. It was mounted above and a bit behind the centerline of the rear wheels, driving them by a combination of belt and chain with a single gear plus one differential gear. At first, little was known publicly about this crude but historic contraption, and today Daimler-Benz historians claim that its first run on public roads wasn't made until July 1886. Before long, however, it became almost a familiar sight on the streets of Mannheim, and Benz was soon ready to start offering replicas for sale.

Though Benz must have known about Gottlieb Daimler's four-wheeler, he made no attempt to copy or even to study it, persisting instead with development of his tricycle design. His first catalog, which illustrated an improved model, was published in 1888, the year Benz first took display space at the Munich Exhibition. By this time, the tricycle had come to look like a vehicle anyone could use instead of a mobile test bed. There were now two comfortable seats, a vertical centrally placed steering column, and full-elliptic suspension between body frame and the tube leading to the front wheel and forks support. The tires, of course, were still solid. Braking was provided, in traditional carriage fashion, by means of blocks pressing on the outside of the wheels. Since the tri-car's top speed was probably no more than 10 mph, this arrangement was perfectly acceptable.

Frau Berta Benz certainly thought so, and when development of and faith in the new Benz *Patent-Motorwagen* seemed to be lagging, she literally took matters into her own hands. In August 1888, she stole out of the Benz home at 5 a.m. along with her two teenage boys. Leaving her husband to sleep, she and her sons set out for the village of Pforzheim in one of the three-wheelers. She duly completed the 46-mile journey during the day—thanks partly to assistance along the way for pushing the underpowered machine up a few hills. The return trip was made five days later by the same intrepid trio—the world's first "durability run." Though news of this feat spread quickly in the surrounding area, it did little to spur sales. One problem was that motorized vehicles of any sort were illegal on public roads at the time. Later, the Duchy of Baden granted limited licenses to owners of Benz vehicles, but pioneer motorists were still often at the mercy of the local police, who were not inclined to look favorably on such goings on.

Shortly after his wife's sojourn, Carl Benz himself drove one of his tri-cars to Munich, an unheard-distance of some 200 miles. There, at an important trade fair, he met with much acclaim, and his invention was even awarded a gold medal. Unfortunately, only one customer could be found—and he was committed to a mental institution before he could take delivery. Some suggested buying a Benz was a good way to go crazy.

A turning point for Benz and for Daimler on the same occasion was the 1889 World's Fair in Paris, where he exhibited an improved version of his car.

Above: a one-cylinder Benz "Ideal" from 1898. Right: the 1895 version of the Benz Velo was called "Comfortable," featured a fully sealed crankcase. Below: inspired by both the Daimler Mercedes and France's Renault, the 1903 Parsifal was the first Benz with a vertical engine and shaft drive. Bottom: the two-cylinder "Spider" of 1901-02.

There, Emile Roger, a French cycle manufacturer, not only agreed to buy a car, but also to become the Benz sales agent for all of France. These machines, by the way, became known under the name Roger-Benz, and seem to have sold steadily; one or two survive to this day.

There was still much scepticism about the future of gasoline-powered cars, however. Benz's co-directors abandoned him at the end of the decade in an argument over future policies. Happily, two new financiers, F. von Fischer and Julius Ganss, moved in to support Carl Benz, who began turning to four-wheeler designs in 1891. However, beginning in 1890 and for the next few years, *Benz und Cie* concentrated on stationary gasoline engines, which were especially useful for locations where town gas was not available. In 1893, no fewer than 500 such units were completed.

The very first Benz four-wheeler was called the Victoria, and looked much more like a Daimler-style horseless carriage than any of the three-wheelers. It was finished by 1892, and the first production examples were ready for sale in the following year. The Victoria was large by Benz standards. It could be supplied in 3-, 4-, or 5-horsepower form, each using a mid-mounted, horizontally situated single-cylinder engine. One odd feature of its design was that there were two seats to the rear of the vertical steering column and two smaller, less well-upholstered seats ahead of it, facing backwards in the "vis-a-vis" position. Benz was apparently not fond of what we would term conventional seating layouts. A few years later, he designed a car in which the four seats were placed back-to-back in pairs, with a twin-cylinder engine squeezed between and under them.

It was at about this time that August Horch joined *Benz und Cie* as a technical associate. Horch believed in cars with

higher performance than Benz. As one of the motor industry's pioneers, he would go on to start up his own car-building concern at the turn of the century.

A year later, in 1893, Benz complemented the Victoria by introducing the "Velo," which history might record as the world's first compact car. In general layout the Velo was like the Victoria, but its engine was smaller and less powerful (originally a 1.5-bhp single-cylinder unit) and the whole car was significantly smaller and lighter. An interesting feature of both these models was that they employed what were really two chassis. A conventional frame in the modern sense supported the body, with full-elliptic leaf-spring suspension for both front and rear axles; a secondary tubular frame linked the front axle to the rear one. Also, both cars were equipped with two-speed gearing—the belt drive moved from one set of pulleys to the other—and even a gear for backing up. Braking was still by means of blocks pressing on the solid tires of the rear wheels only. The Velo, whose engine eventually grew to deliver nearly 3 horsepower at about 500 rpm, soon became one of the most popular cars in Europe, though it was by no means cheap. The Victoria sold for the equivalent of about $4500 in the mid-1890s, the Velo for a little less. In all probability these were the world's first series-production or quantity-production cars. Of 134 Benz cars built in 1895, there were 62 Velos, 36 Victorias, and 20 Vis-a-Vis models, the latter basically enlarged Victorias with full-sized, inward-facing seats.

Benz continued to expand its offerings, beginning in 1897 with a two-cylinder model, and sales continued to increase. However, the firm did not introduce much in the way of technical innovations, and styling of its cars was beginning to look distinctly old-fashioned, especially compared with the

latest Daimlers, their principal rivals. Even so, Benz built 572 cars in 1899 and more than 600 the following year, which must have made it one of the production leaders among early European automakers. Then Daimler introduced two winners in quick succession: first, a V-twin model, then the original Mercedes. This hit the Benz company very hard, for it had nothing as competitive. And Carl Benz himself had become something of a traditionalist by this stage, very reluctant to changing a design merely because fashion or technical developments seemed to dictate it.

Benz und Cie had become a joint stock company in 1899, and right away a great deal of dissension arose among the directors. Benz himself did not want to expand production or change his car designs, while other executives, including Julius Ganss, felt precisely the opposite. The company's founder was wrong but wouldn't admit it, even when sales slumped again in 1901 in the face of the new Mercedes' popularity. Benz was also opposed to all forms of motor racing, so he must have felt chagrin when certain of his cars began to achieve success in the new sport, thanks to the efforts of private competitors.

By 1903 there was no longer any question about the Benz company's future policy. The cars had to change, had to be more modern, for the public no longer wanted machines with belt drive and their engines tucked away at the rear. Ganss imported one of the newfangled front-engine, shaft-driven Renaults from France, handed it over to his engineers, and ordered them to produce something even better. The result was the new "Parsifal" series of 8/10, 10/12, and 12/14 models. (The figures refer to taxable and actual horsepower, respectively, and were quite commonly used in Europe from the automobile's earliest days right on through the 1940s.) All were powered by two-cylinder engines with the cylinders situated vertically instead of horizontally, mounted under and between the seats to a shaft drive. Maximum engine speed was about 1000 rpm, a real advance into the unknown for Benz, and steering columns were more stylishly raked.

Unfortunately, the Parsifals suffered many problems right from the start, and Benz sales slumped further: the 1903 total was a mere 172. In April of that year, Carl Benz and his son Eugen stormed out, abandoning the business the elder Benz founded more than 20 years earlier. Ganss, who had insisted on the shaft-driven Renault "clone," took much of the blame for the sales decline, sent his consultant engineer back to France, and resigned. Whereupon the Benz family returned to regain control.

At this point, the talented young engineer Hans Nibel joined the Benz firm, and began improving the Parsifal models. Nibel would go on to become a distinguished member of Benz (and later Daimler-Benz) management and would be responsible for the technical development of many models built up to the mid-1930s including the advanced "new generation" Mercedes-Benz touring cars of the early 1930s. In 1903, however, he transformed the basic Parsifal layout, and worked on increasing its limited performance. Carl Benz had at last been persuaded to produce a four-cylinder engine, and the first of these appeared in 1903, rated as a 14/18. In 1904 it was supplemented by a 16/20, and before long there was a version as powerful as 25/80.

Having persisted with old-fashioned engineering for so long, Benz now brought itself up to date with a vengeance. Every new Benz announced for the next two decades would be a four, the old twins being buried

as soon as decently possible. All these new fours incorporated mechanically operated, instead of atmospheric, inlet valves, a notable advance. As with so many other engines of the period, the cylinder barrels were cast in pairs and shared a light-alloy crankcase. There were two camshafts, one on each side of the crankcase, and side valves, the classic T-head arrangement. Benz appearance also improved dramatically, helped partly by competition from Daimler and partly by the advent of lower chassis with longer wheelbases.

There was no escaping some of the agreed conventions of the day, however, so Benz, like Daimler, utilized shaft drive only on its lower-powered cars at first. Engineers at that time didn't believe shafts could stand up to the greater torque of their truly powerful engines, and relied on chain drive instead. In every case, the chains were outside the main chassis members, and their primary sprockets were driven from a countershaft at the rear of the main gearbox. Naturally, the chains suffered badly from exposure to mud and debris, and needed to be cleaned and oiled every day. For that reason, almost every large-car owner employed a full-time chauffeur, part of whose job was to do just that. Benz introduced 24/40 and 25/80 chain-drive models in 1905 and 1906, respectively.

The renaissance at Benz brought with it a new interest in racing. Existing cars soon began to gain competition success, and eventually new machines with monstrously powerful engines were designed specifically for racing. Benz retained an official "factory" driver, Fritz Erle. In 1907, he was joined by Victor Hémery, who had been chief of the research division for the French automaker Darracq for the previous six years. Racing fever swept the company rapidly. The 60-hp racing Benz of 1903 was succeeded by the 70- and

80-hp models in 1907, followed by a 120-hp racer in 1908. Naturally, all these cars had chain drive, and were designed as direct competitors for the massive Mercedes models from Daimler. The racing chassis of the period employed basically the same design as that of the existing large touring cars, but bodies were lightweight and skimpy, no more than the regulations specified. These days, of course, some suggest that all racing cars tend to look very similar, but in the early 1900s as well a racing Benz looked much like a racing Mercedes and, for that matter, a racing anything else.

The next generation of Benz road cars—called "utility" models by Daimler-Benz historians—were introduced in 1908 as replacements for the 1903-1904 cars reworked by Nibel. Their design reflected lessons learned in racing, and they were thoroughly modern in all respects. There were 10/18, 10/20, and 20/35 versions. All had monobloc L-head side-valve fours, shaft drive via torque tube to a live rear axle, rear brakes operated by a foot pedal, and an externally contracting drum brake behind the transmission, actuated by the handbrake lever. The gearchange for the separate four-speed transmission was positioned outboard of the frame, and the steering wheel and other driving controls were all on the right side. The chassis design was a type that would persist into the 1920s, with channel-section side members, half-elliptic leaf spring front and rear suspension, and artillery-style wood wheels.

Benz was still building powerful chain-drive cars in these years, and in 1909 it introduced the 40/70 sports car with that transmission arrangement. But the zenith *and* the swan song of the chain-drive Benz was the formidable 200-hp "Blitzen" racing car, which appeared that year.

The Blitzen evolved from the 1908 Benz racer, powered by a huge, 12.5-liter (763-cid) four-cylinder engine. This car had notable success, setting a new distance record in a 426-mile race from St. Petersburg to Moscow. Benz racers also took second and third places at that year's French Grand Prix. The following year, a trio of these cars swept to top honors in a grueling reliability run from St. Petersburg to Riva and back. Shortly afterwards, American daredevil Barney Oldfield piloted a 150-hp version of the chain-drive Benz to set a world speed record for the standing-start mile at the 1909 Indianapolis 500: 83.8 mph. Other machines with 200-hp engines set a new record of 114 mph on the sands of Daytona Beach, Florida.

To gain even more power and speed for their next racing car, Benz engineers enlarged the engine to an enormous 21.5 liters (1311 cid), and fitted mammoth rocker arms and pushrods to operate newly designed overhead valves. Maximum speed for this leviathan powerplant was a lazy 1650 rpm. A four-speed gearbox fed power to the rear wheels through large sprockets and heavy chains, and was geared so that a calculated top speed of 140 mph could be achieved at about 1400 rpm. The 112-inch-wheelbase chassis was basically similar to that of then-current Benz road cars, but was drilled wherever possible to eliminate excess weight. Topping it was a distinctively designed streamlined body with rounded countours and a vertical radiator capped by a prominent forward-thrusting peak. After the car had been tested, one observer commented that it "actually goes like lightning" (der Blitz). It was an apt description, and it stuck.

The first outing for the Blitzen Benz was at the Brooklands track in England, where factory ace Héméry broke the world's record for the kilometer at 125.9 mph and for the mile at 115.9 mph. Next, the car was shipped to America, where Barney Oldfield got his hands on it. Running on the smooth, hard-packed sands from Daytona to Ormond Beach, he streaked to 131.7 mph in the flying mile and ran the standing mile at 88.8 mph, both new records. Oldfield then toured with the car throughout the U.S., setting record after record at many local tracks coast-to-coast.

By 1911, many thought that competition might catch up with the Blitzen Benz. But they hadn't counted on another speed merchant, Bob Burman. Once more on the Florida sands, the "white lightning" car from Germany flew to record speeds—an amazing 141.7 mph as Burman ran the measured mile in a mere 25 seconds. It was a feat that would be unsurpassed for the next 13 years. Burman ran the car at that year's Indianapolis 500, but failed to finish in the top 10. However, he took the car on another barnstorming tour, and again the Blitzen Benz was triumphant. In all, the Blitzen

Left: an imposing Benz limousine from 1911, built on the four-cylinder 14/30 chassis. Below: the amazing 200-bhp Blitzen Benz of 1909-10 set numerous speed records in both Europe and America.

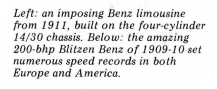

Benz was one of the most fearsome and fascinating competition machines ever built. It set the stage for the great Benz racing cars of the '20s as well as the later Mercedes-Benz racers. It was also dramatic evidence of the changes taking place at the Mannheim works.

Benz finally ditched chain drive in 1910 with introduction of the roadgoing 22/60 and 28/80 four-cylinder sports models. Benz would hang on to chain drive for racing until 1913, but from now on every touring Benz, from the 8/18 to the 28/80 would have shaft drive and what we would now call a conventional mechanical layout.

At a time when the German nation was prospering (and its expansionist ambitions becoming more obvious) so too was the Benz company. There was a quick succession of new models in the 1910-14 period covering a broad range of customers. As mentioned, the smallest Benz in these years was the little 8/18. The largest and most powerful was the 39/100. Benz also produced large sporty cars like the 25/35, 50/80, and 28/100 aimed at rallies and reliability trials such as the Prince Henry events. It was at about this time that Carl Benz drifted away from his company (he was well into his 60s by now) and moved to building Sohne-Benz models at a factory at Ladenburg. However, the cars produced by original Benz firm continued to be built at Mannheim.

In the years leading up to the outbreak of war in 1914 Benz concentrated on improving the specifications and reliability of its car chassis, while pushing ahead with trucks, built at Gaggenau, and airplane engines. Indeed, Benz was awarded the new *Kaiserpriz* for aero-engine design in a 1913 competition involving 26 competitors with 44 different designs. The Benz entry was a four-cylinder watercooled unit with overhead valvegear. It must have had some technical links with the big

Top to bottom: the big 39/100 of 1911-13, Carl Benz circa 1920, and Barney Oldfield and Ty Cobb in a Benz sports, circa 1920.

automobile racing engines of the period, for its capacity was 9.5 liters, peak output 100 bhp at 1300 rpm.

Benz was amazingly busy and successful during the First World War, though production of private cars virtually ceased except for those built for military use. However, by the time the Armistice was signed on November 11, 1918, things were different. Germany was now a defeated nation, its economy in tatters, and somehow the whole world had changed. It was as if the outbreak of war had not only killed many of those who had bought Benz (and Mercedes) cars but had also killed off the way of life that had made that possible. The fact was that by 1919, the market for Benz cars in the mold of the 1914 models had contracted considerably. And where the accent had once been on size, speed, and opulence, what few buyers remained in postwar Germany understandably wanted smaller machines with better economy. To get the show on the road

again, Benz reintroduced its smallest prewar cars—8/20, 10/30, 14/30 and 18/45—most with side-valve four-cylinder engines and all, of course, now with shaft drive and rear wheel brakes. There were touring and sports versions of each model—and once again their direct home-market competition came from Daimler. The only new postwar Benz immediately available was the 27/70, but this was merely an enlarged update of a prewar design.

Below: the 10/30 limousine of 1923. Bottom: the perky 6/18 Sports from 1921.

There was one further generation of cars to come from Benz before the merger with Daimler, and these were introduced between 1921 and 1923. The 11/40 model of 1923 had a six-cylinder engine (the 10/30 which it replaced had used a four), as did the 16/50, which was a more modern and efficient replacement for the 21/50 of 1914.

By the early '20s, a Benz was instantly recognizable, and could never be confused with its great rival, the Mercedes. Its mechanical layout, however, was entirely conventional for the period: channel-section frame, half-elliptic leaf-spring suspension, side-valve engines, four-speed manual transmission, worm-and-nut steering. And by this time there was full electrical equipment, including a starter and headlamps, plus four-wheel brakes to keep the extra performance in check. The Benz radiator, in particular, had taken on a familiar flat-faced aspect, whereas that of the Mercedes was vee'd—though some prewar Benz models also used that shape, and there were also flat-radiator Mercedes models. The circular Benz badge was in the middle of the radiator top tank, a circular motif incorporating a laurel wreath—a discreet reminder that Benz not only made good touring cars, but fine racing cars as well.

It was all very brave, but it was not enough to ensure future prosperity. Benz might have survived as an independent entity had it been able to offer more new and more exciting models, and if Germany's economy had been more buoyant. But things went from bad to worse as inflation rocketed upwards in the war-shattered country and car sales fell. There were too many makes and models chasing too few buyers. It was at about this time that Benz management, nudged by Dr. Jahr, began to think the unthinkable. Instead of squaring up to *Daimler Motoren Gesellschaft* and fighting it for every sale, Benz began to consider the possibilities of cooperation. By 1924 an agreement was ready to be signed, and the merger was completed two years later. Thus Benz, as an independent marque, had a life of 41 years, from 1885 to 1926. Founder Carl Benz had not been actively involved in company affairs for some time. He lived on, however, cushioned against economic hardship by the company's directors, to 1929, when he died at the age of 85. His indomitable widow—the lady who had attempted the world's first long automobile journey, survived until 1944 and age 95.

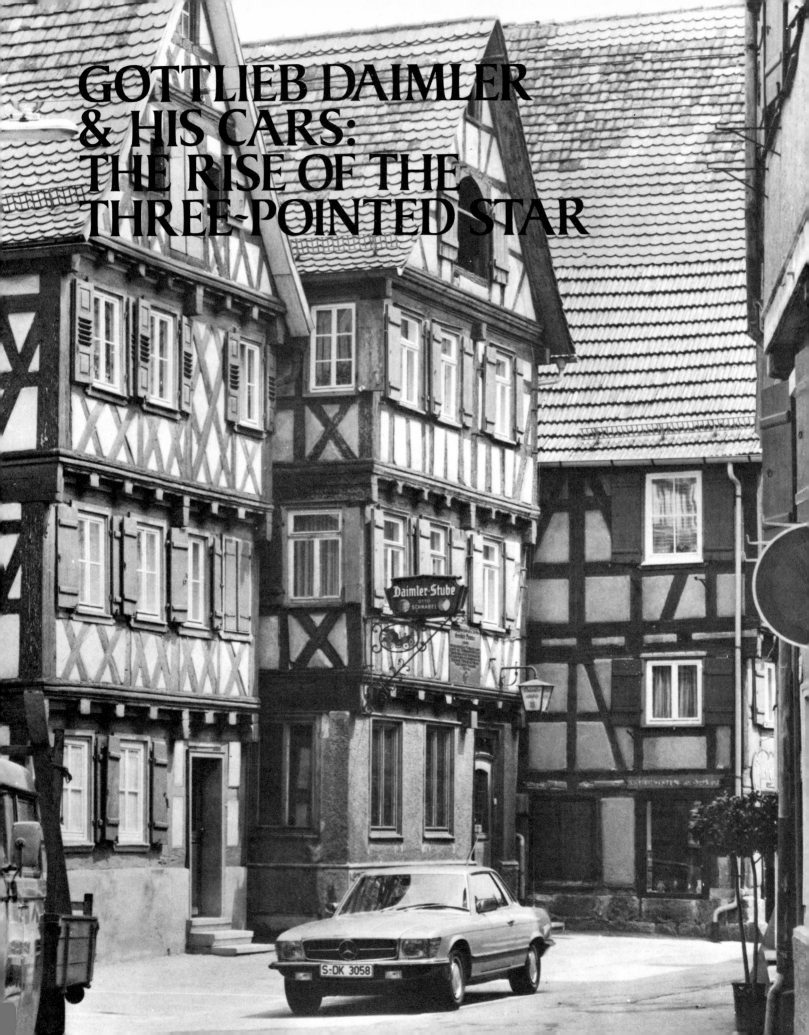

GOTTLIEB DAIMLER & HIS CARS: THE RISE OF THE THREE-POINTED STAR

Compared to Carl Benz and his immediate family, Gottlieb Daimler apparently never faced financial hardship of any kind. However, he started his automotive career even later than Benz: he was no less than 52 years old when he built his first car.

In some ways, it was amazing Daimler ever built an automobile at all. His family hailed from the Swabian provincial town of Schorndorf, a few kilometers east of Stuttgart, where for many generations they had been well-to-do tradespeople. Johannes Daimler was a baker in the town, and his son Gottlieb, born in 1834, was the second of four children. Schorndorf was quite rural and very removed from Germany's main industrial "powerhouse" in the Rhine valley. During Gottlieb's formative years there was literally no mechanical transport of any type (the country's first railway, from Nürnberg to Fürth, would not be built until the end of 1835), so life in Swabia remained much as it had been for the previous two centuries.

It is said that Johannes Daimler would have liked Gottlieb to be a civil servant. But the father foresaw a revolution requiring the raising and mechanization of armies, which in turn would require more engineers, so he decided to apprentice his son as a gunsmith. Certainly this was the way young Gottlieb began his business life, but it was several years before he started any formal engineering training. Following his sojourn at the Polytechnic, he then joined the *Werkzeug Maschinenfabrik*, at Grafenstadt near Strasbourg in the Alsace, which at that time was a part of France. This company, like the one that originally employed Carl Benz, had specialized in heavy engineering, and by this time was also involved with the design and manufacture of steam locomotives.

After three years, Gottlieb left heavy engineering and enrolled at the Stuttgart Polytechnic for concentrated technical engineering training at the age of 22. Graduating with honors in 1859, he then faced that age-old question of what to do next. He was a young man with good qualifications and, because he came from Swabia—that most-respected area of Germany—potential employers were all eager to talk to him.

Eventually, he elected to return to Grafenstadt, where he tried to persuade J. F. Messner, the managing director of his former employer, to allow him to experiment with that new, much-discussed idea, the internal-combustion engine. But Messner was not a visionary, could see no future in such things, and was happy for *Werkzeug Maschinenfabrik* to carry on with locomotives. Daimler was naturally dismayed. He soon left, moving to the next of several jobs that were to keep him active throughout the 1860s.

Helped by a wealthy patron, Dr. Ferdinand Steinbeis, young Daimler first went to Paris to see what Lenoir was doing with his gas engines. Next came a two-year stay in England that included work with the Armstrong Whitworth firm. On his return to Germany he became, at age 28, the chief engineer to the Straub & Sons metal works at Geislingen, but left there after three years when he could not interest them in developing internal-combustion engines either. Next he was appointed to manage the *Bruderhaus* engineering business in Reutlingen, but gave this up during 1869. It had been a restless decade, made bearable only by his marriage to Emma Pauline Kurz in 1867. But while working at Reutlingen, Daimler met and befriended a younger man, Wilhelm Maybach, and this would prove to be a turning point.

Daimler then served for three

Opposite page: Gottlieb Daimler's birthplace in Schorndorf, today a museum operated by Daimler-Benz AG. This page, above: Gottlieb Daimler in 1893. Below: his long-time friend and collaborator, Wilhelm Maybach.

years as technical director for the *Maschinenbaugesellschaft* of Karlsruhe—the very same company that had employed Carl Benz in the 1860s. In 1872, he moved on to become technical director of *Otto und Langen* at the Deutz Gas Engine Works. This was a vital move. Daimler was soon able to appoint Maybach as his chief design draftsman—and at 26, Gottlieb's friend was amazingly young for such a high post in the conservative German industry. Daimler also demanded—and won—complete technical freedom from Herr Langen, the major

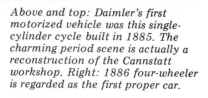

Above and top: Daimler's first motorized vehicle was this single-cylinder cycle built in 1885. The charming period scene is actually a reconstruction of the Cannstatt workshop. Right: 1886 four-wheeler is regarded as the first proper car.

stockholder. This time there was no doubt that Daimler was in the right place at the right time, for the "Otto" in the company's title would soon startle the world with his patents for the four-stroke internal-combustion engine.

In the next 10 years, Daimler worked phenomenally hard and achieved great things for his company, but he suffered what could best be described as a stormy relationship with his bosses. Predictably enough, the main source of friction was with Herr Otto, not only because he was one of the company founders but also because both men were keenly interested in engine development and were, effectively, rivals.

A split came in 1882. Daimler left Otto und Langen and moved his family to Cannstatt, a pleasant little town near Stuttgart. Eventually he induced Maybach to join him, and set up workshops in the summer house of his new home. There, he would create designs for new, high-speed gasoline engines and study their possible application to road vehicles and even boats. Daimler took out two patents in 1883-84 for a lightweight engine able to turn 750 rpm, fast by standards of the day. Not only was it fueled by *Benzin* (the German name for gasoline and not named for Carl Benz— though wouldn't it be romantic if it were), it was also a four-stroke, liquid-cooled design featuring the first-ever use of hot-tube ignition.

Daimler bore no malice toward his old employers at Deutz and,

Below left: Daimler, Maybach, and the five-ton "Phoenix" truck of 1898. Below right: a look inside the Canstatt factory, circa 1899. Bottom: the Daimler works in 1904.

according to one well-documented account, offered his new engine to them. But the directors were still wedded to large stationary engines and turned down his offer. They appear to have been revolving in their graves ever since...

Even though this was fully a hundred years ago, it is interesting to note that Daimler and Maybach had hit on the right ingredients for an automobile engine in their very first attempt. The single-cylinder unit had an enclosed crankcase, employed the four-stroke Otto cycle, and carried its liquid fuel in a small, separate container, all of which made it truly mobile. Of course, it could only run up to 750 rpm, had hot-tube and not spark ignition, and produced

negligible power—but then, it was the dawn of a new idea, and there were few precedents.

Daimler, like Benz, had long fancied the idea of a motor vehicle, for he also wanted to free people from the restrictions of owning and using horses. Also like Benz, he envisioned an inexpensive vehicle, something almost anyone could afford. Accordingly, his very first machine, built in 1885, was a motorized bicycle, undisputably a world first. One, and only one, was completed. Unfortunately, the original was destroyed in a fire, but a copy now resides in the Daimler-Benz Museum. It was, as you might expect, a crude device. Actually, it was a bike with four wheels, large ones fore and aft and two smaller

outriggers at the rear to keep the thing from falling over when stationary. All the wheels were made of wood and had steel-band rims. The single-cylinder engine was mounted vertically under a leather seat shaped like an upside-down "u," and developed 0.5 horsepower from its 264cc (16.1 cid) displacement. There was no suspension of any kind. Drive to the large rear wheel was first by belt, then by a sprocket acting on an internally toothed gear on the wheel itself. It worked—after a fashion—but it was never developed. Daimler's son Paul is known to have demonstrated the contraption on a run between Cannstatt and the Untertürkheim district of Stuttgart.

Daimler then turned to building a horseless carriage. He actually used a buggy as the basis of his first car, unlike Benz, whose three-wheeler was an original design from the ground up. The Daimler family had owned horse-drawn vehicles for many years, so it was only natural Gottlieb should order a carriage from a Cannstatt coachbuilder. It was supplied with certain areas strengthened, to stand up to the weight and stress of his engine and transmission. Daimler thus made the jump directly from two-wheel motorbike to full-fledged four-wheel "automobile." Most historians consider the machine he put on the road in late 1886 as the world's first successful car in the modern sense.

It looked for all the world like a carriage without hitching forks, which were replaced by a simple turn handle for steering on the right. Like every self-respecting carriage of the period, the body was constructed of elegant polished wood. The wheels were large, extremely narrow, and rimmed with iron. There was a rear seat, but it was rendered virtually useless—or at best uncomfortable—by the single-cylinder engine, which was vertically mounted just ahead,

sticking up through the floorboard where passengers would otherwise stretch their legs. The engine itself was a 462cc (28.2 cid) unit producing 1.5 horsepower. Like the Benz engine it had an automatic, or "atmospheric," intake valve operated by cylinder suction. Interestingly, Daimler, like Benz, had concluded that power should go to the rear wheels and that the best place for the engine was just ahead of them. Thus, he also hit upon the now-classic mid-engine layout decades before it became fashionable. Transmission was by belt to a rear-mounted countershaft, then by gear from the end of that to the rear wheels. Unlike the motorcycle, this gearing was external rather than internal. There was even a crude type of differential gear incorporating slipping leather discs. Steering was by what we would now call rack-and-pinion, and full-elliptic leaf suspension was provided, buggy-style, for each side on both front and rear axles.

Daimler's first car, though no more than a test bed, was clearly practical in concept. Soon it began making regular, though short, journeys between Cannstatt, Untertürkheim, and Esslingen. As with the first Benz, self-propelled vehicles were still not legal on public highways in Germany or any other European country, partly because the "horse lobby" was very strong. When you consider the Daimler's almost non-existent provisions for braking, it's easy to see why the first horseless carriages were denounced as dangerous.

To get around that attitude, Daimler decided to publicize his engines and thus, he hoped, stimulate demand for his new automobile. One ploy was a motorboat that he demonstrated for various high-ranking officials, including Prince Bismarck. He also gained approval to build a short public streetcar line in Cannstatt able to carry up to 12 passengers. It

wasn't long before the police changed its official position, and by the end of 1888 a Daimler taxi—another world first—was in service at Stuttgart's main station. Daimler also became involved in powered fire engines, dirigibles (blimps), and tugboats. Before the end of the decade, Daimler and Maybach had created their first V-twin engine, which must also qualify as a first. Over the next few years, Daimler made very few cars, but instead delivered increasing numbers of his successful gasoline engines. This came despite legal action from Otto und Langen, who attacked him on grounds that certain of their patents were being infringed. They lost the case.

By the start of the 1890s, Daimler and Maybach had advanced their thinking considerably, and their cars no longer looked so much like converted carriages. For example, the famous two-seat "wire-wheel" design of 1889 was altogether more integrated. Though its V-twin engine was still vertically mounted just ahead of the driven rear wheels, it was positioned behind and under a single bench seat. Its chassis was made up of steel tubing, rather like that of the earlier Benz cars, and there was a four-speed transmission and a bevel-gear type of differential built in to the rear axle on the right side. Braking, on the other hand, was still quite primitive; there were no front brakes at all, just a single drum on the left rear wheel, operated by a lever near the driver's seat. There was no front axle as such, and no suspension either. Each front wheel was mounted in bicycle-type forks, with the steering linkage at the fork tops and very close to the tiller itself.

Like Carl Benz, Gottlieb Daimler was a key figure in the birth of the world's automotive industry. As early as 1888, he had held discussions with William Steinway, owner of the famous piano company in New

York, with an eye to licensing his patents in the United States. In 1889, a successful showing at the Paris Exhibition led to licensing agreements signed between Daimler and Panhard & Levassor (for complete cars) and with Peugeot (for engines only). Both the French companies, soon to be famous in their own right, showed their first cars the following year.

The corporate parent of today's Daimler-Benz firm, *Daimler Motoren Gesellschaft,* was founded in November 1890. But it wasn't long before Gottlieb quarreled with his fellow directors. He was anxious to continue with development work on high-speed engines, while many of his associates preferred to concentrate on production of slow-running stationary engines. After more than two years of wrangling Daimler walked out, taking Maybach with him to continue his research in Cannstatt. Naturally, such a split was ludicrous, and it certainly worried those who had invested in the company. A reconciliation seemed almost a foregone conclusion, and the first moves were made during 1895. The founder unconditionally returned to the fold as chairman in March 1897.

In the meantime, one other very important licensing deal had been concluded—in England. There F. R. Simms, who became a director of the Cannstatt company in the early 1890s, set up Daimler Motor Co., Ltd. By 1895-96, British Daimlers were being built in Coventry, the first regular production cars to be manufactured in Great Britain. The significance of this was not merely as a British "first," but rather that it would ensure survival for the Daimler marque. Indeed, after a slow start the British firm became independent in the first years of the 20th century. It was later acquired by the Birmingham Small Arms group, and grew larger and more prestigious. After World War II,

it ultimately became part of the British Leyland combine by way of Sir William Lyons and a merger with Jaguar in 1960. Thus, while the Daimler marque no longer exists in Germany, it still survives—though barely—in the UK today.

Gottlieb Daimler would not live long. Years of unremitting hard work interspersed with corporate worries and distress all took their toll beginning in the 1890s. While in "exile" from Daimler Motoren Gesellschaft he had designed the Phoenix two-cylinder inline engine, notable for being the first to employ a

Top: significant 1889 "wire wheel" Daimler marked the beginnings of truly unique automotive design. Above: an 1897 Daimler "Taximeter," one of the earliest powered cabs.

spray-type carburetor. Before the end of the decade, a new automobile had been designed around this powerplant, and for it Daimler adopted the *systeme Panhard,* which would also be used for all subsequent models. This denoted a mechanical layout of front-mounted engine with the transmission behind it and a combination of shaft and chain drive to the rear wheels. After Gottlieb's return and the

Above left and near left: Emil Jellinek, the driving force behind the first Mercedes, which he named in honor of his daughter. Center spread: a four-cylinder Mercedes "Simplex" tourer from 1902.

introduction of the Phoenix, the company went from strength to strength. By the end of 1899 it had more than 330 employees. By this time, there also were four-cylinder Daimlers, and the company was already interested in that new-fangled craze, auto racing. With all this, Daimler was now too large for its Cannstatt headquarters, so the firm relocated to a new site in Untertürkheim, which remains the corporate headquarters of Daimler-Benz today. Thus, the Daimler tradition has remained unbroken for over 80 years, and not even the insistent pounding by U.S. and British bombers during World War II could destroy it completely.

Gottlieb's struggle to reconcile business matters, his family life, and his vision of the future all failed in March 1900, when a heart condition suddenly worsened. He died at home, still protesting that there was work to do. He was 65.

In the meantime, a revolution in automotive design was under way. It began in 1901 when the original Mercedes car appeared at the Nice Speed Week in France. From then on, every other car in the world would seem out of date. Daimler's reputation would soar to unprecedented heights.

The genesis of the Mercedes—quite literally—was a flamboyant and influential

Austrian businessman, Emil Jellinek. His first contact with Daimler came in 1897, when he ordered a specially built 6-horsepower phaeton. It was designed principally for speed—which in those days meant that this Daimler Model N could hit 26 mph. Jellinek was not satisfied. As French manufacturers already had faster cars, he kept on nagging Daimler for more. In his book *Three Pointed Star*, historian David Scott-Moncrieff described Jellinek as "a small, excitable, man—in the matter of cars, like Toad of Toad Hall—whatever he had, he wanted something bigger and better." The result was the 23-hp Phoenix racing car of 1899, distinguished by its watercooled four-cylinder engine.

Jellinek was not only wealthy, he was also the Austro-Hungarian Vice-Consul in Nice. And it was in that part of the world that he effectively became

a Daimler agent. As such, the cars he inspired—and sold— became progressively faster, heavier and less controllable than was desirable. By early 1900, he had joined the Daimler board of directors, and argued the firm needed to take a completely new approach with its cars. He was convinced they had to be lower, longer and, if possible, lighter. Motoring juggernauts like the 3650-pound Phoenix were wrong, he thought. What he wanted was a mechanical greyhound. And by sheer coincidence, Wilhelm Maybach and Gottlieb's talented son Paul were already at work on such a car, designed very much with racing in mind.

Though the young Daimler soon went on to manage the Daimler subsidiary in Austria, Jellinek had Maybach's support, and was able to persuade colleagues to build the new small car. He said he would purchase

the first 36 himself, provided his distributorship territory was greatly expanded—and that the cars bear a new name: Mercedes, after his 10-year-old daughter. The agreement was concluded in April 1900, and called for all the cars to be ready by mid-October. This would give the dashing Austrian plenty of time to have them prepared for the important Nice Speed Week the following March.

Unfortunately, things didn't quite go as planned. Daimler was able to complete only six cars by January, and there had been no time for shakedown runs. One car was hastily prepared for the Grand Prix of Pau in February, but the

Top: a typical chain-drive Mercedes from the 1900-1905 period. Above: a 32-horsepower tourer of 1904.

attempt was a complete fiasco. Both engine and gearbox proved troublesome in practice—and in the race itself, when the Mercedes retired after running but a few yards.

But things were different at Nice, where the Mercedes of Wilhelm Werner, a factory driver from Canstatt, completely dominated all the events. The 35 hp car was fastest in both the sprints and the hillclimbs, and also won the 393km (244-mile) Nice-Aix-Senas-Nice road race that climaxed the proceedings.

Today, 35 bhp from a 6.0 liter engine in a car weighing 2200 pounds seems very pedestrian, but it was truly sensational by the standards of 1901. The four-cylinder engine, with its camshaft-operated intake valves, was quite advanced, and gave the car a high power/weight ratio. And, the Mercedes handled better than any other car yet seen. The secret was in its squat stance. The Phoenix cars had been bulky and relatively high on a short wheelbase. The resulting instability was thought to have caused the death of Wilhelm Bauer, Daimler's professional driver, in the La Turbie hillclimb of 1899. But the Mercedes was altogether lower and sleeker. Its hoodline was little higher than the tops of its front tires, the chassis side members sat at least six inches closer to the ground, and its driver sat closer to the midpoint of a longer wheelbase and behind a considerably more raked steering column. At one stroke, automotive design had made a complete break with the horseless carriage days. By comparison with this Mercedes, contemporary Benz models seemed positively archaic.

In general layout, the first Mercedes faithfully followed the *systeme Panhard,* except for its mechanically operated intake valves (most cars still relied on "automatic" induction). The T-head layout would look familiar to any lover of early American cars. So, too, would the cast iron block, with its cylinders cast in pairs, fixed to a light-alloy crankcase. But several features made the new car a true pacesetter. These included a pressed-steel chassis (at a time when many manufacturers were using wooden flitch-plate construction), a four-speed gearbox with gated linkage, pedal-actuated internally expanding drum brakes for the back axle, and a handbrake drum on the gearbox countershaft. While not revolutionary in layout, the transmission was already used

Opposite page, top: a dashing 1902 Mercedes sports tourer, looking quite modern for its day. Note the rounded cowl and body lines and the rakish slanted windshield. Center: a bus-like six-seat sedan from 1903. Bottom: Daimler Motor Works moved from its original Canstatt factory to this facility in the Untertürkheim district of Stuttgart about 1904. Here's how things looked shortly after the move was completed. This page, clockwise from top left: this 14-horsepower Daimler-built omnibus was delivered in Berlin in 1905, and was the first gasoline-powered bus to see regular service. A chain-drive Mercedes runabout, circa 1904. Note triple foot pedals on this impressive touring Mercedes from about 1906. A "Maybach" racing Mercedes, 1903. Daimler produced a variety of trucks and commercials in its early years, including fire engines from 1907, as shown here.

by some other makers—and almost every make would adopt it in the next few years. Immediately behind this was the differential, from which two countershafts—actually driveshafts—ran to sprockets mounted outboard of the main frame members at either side. Final drive was by chain to the rear wheels, the wheel sprockets being mounted close to the drum brakes. On most cars that followed, the shift lever would also be outboard of the frame, but on the original racing Mercedes, with its skimpy two-seat body, the lever was pivoted at the base of the steering column. With all this, no wonder the performance of the new car was so outstanding. So much so, in fact, that the secretary of the Automobile Club of France, Paul Meyan, was moved to say: *"Nous sommes entres dans l'ere Mercedes."* Translation: "We have entered the Mercedes era."

The competition success at Nice and sales success that

followed throughout the year proved to be a real watershed in the affairs of DMG. Many new Daimler models had been issued in the last years of the 19th century, but after 1901 there were no more. The Mercedes name was adopted as the official marque as soon as all legal formalities were ironed out, and it has graced most every Daimler and Daimler-Benz car ever since. Purists, incidentally, should note that while Jellinek's daughter always spelled her name with accents, they have never been used on the cars. The Daimler marque, therefore, passed from the scene in Germany just a year after its founder did, though the name would survive proudly in the corporate title.

The story of the Daimler company in the next six years largely concerns the big four- and six-cylinder cars that could be called the Maybach generation. All were evolutions of the brilliant 1901 concept, and

comprised both touring and competition types. Horsepower ratings ranged from the four-cylinder 8/11 touring model of 1902 to the mighty six-cylinder Mercedes 120 racer of 1906. Of course, it was the competition variety that made all the headlines. After the original 35-bhp Mercedes came the 40-hp racer of 1902 with a higher-revving engine (though a peak of 1200 rpm can hardly be described as fast). In 1903, Daimler broke more new ground with the famous Mercedes 60 and a fearsome 90-hp machine, basically a more powerful 60 primarily intended to carry the racing colors. The 60 became even more famous than it might have been. The factory had to run customer cars in the 1903 Gordon Bennett race in Ireland because the racing 90s had been lost to a huge fire that destroyed the old Cannstatt factory on June 10th (and in any case, the 90s had failed in the earlier Paris-Madrid contest). Fate thus

Daimler would continue building its larger, chain-drive models even after the smaller, shaft-drive cars of Paul Daimler arrived in 1907. Design changed little in these years. Above: a 1905 tourer. Above right: a 40/45 American Mercedes of 1905, priced at $7500 and one of several models built in the U.S. before World War I. Right: another 1905 tourer, here with Roi des Belges coachwork on the 18/28 chassis.

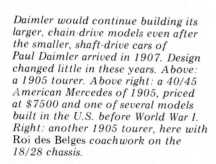

28

cast the 60-hp car into the racing limelight, even if it also paralyzed the company until the move to Untertürkheim.

The basic layout of the 60 was the same as for the 35-hp Mercedes, though wheelbase had grown to 108 inches. The big four-cylinder engine was enlarged by 50 percent—to 9292cc (567 cid), with a massive bore and stroke of 140×150mm (5.51×5.90 in.). It pushed out up to 65 bhp at 1100 rpm, and had overhead intake valves and better breathing. It was the sort of car lovers of vintage machines rave about. It was not only fast, but also very reliable. Naturally, a wide variety of coachbuilt bodies was fitted to this chassis, from stark racing types to sumptuously appointed broughams.

Personalities and personnel changes racked Daimler Motoren Gesellschaft in the early 1900s. First, Wilhelm Lorenz took over administrative control following the death of the company's co-founder, Max von Duttenhofer. In a dispute with Maybach it was Lorenz who prevailed, and he gradually pushed him out. Maybach left in 1907—only to start his own business that eventually produced many kinds of aero engines and cars (including the gargantuan Maybach Zeppelin). At the same time, DMG lost the services of Emil Jellinek, who retired after years of involvement that had left him even wealthier than when he started. Meantime, Paul Daimler, who had returned from the Austrian subsidiary in 1905, became chief engineer in 1907, and was titular head of the company's engineering division until the early 1920s. During that time, he supervised further developments of the Mercedes concept, including speedy completion of a new model lineup with shaft drive. He was also the force behind several very successful—and now legendary—racing machines. It was under Paul Daimler that the firm built a supercharged competition car—two years before Fiat fielded one in Grand Prix and some time before Dr. Ferdinand Porsche would arrive to design a new generation of supercharged Mercedes touring and sports models.

There were so many new Mercedes models introduced in the years before World War I that sorting them all out is difficult. In those days, of course, it was easy for a profitable company like DMG to produce a new car. Very little investment in permanent tooling was needed for each one, and production was quite limited. By the same token, this made prices frightfully high, far beyond the reach of most

Below: a compact runabout on an unidentified chassis, circa 1907. Note rear jump seat and curtained rear footwells. Bottom: Daimler began phasing out its older chain-drive cars about 1908, though chains were still preferred by many in larger cars, like this 1909 tourer.

Germans. So, from the first, cars bearing the Mercedes name were clearly in the realm of the privileged few. Model Ts they most definitely were not.

The Paul Daimler cars came on the scene in 1907, and were quite different from the original Mercedes design. The most obvious technical departures were in the switch from chain to shaft drive and the use of live rear axles. Another change was in marketing: all these models were smaller and had smaller engines. The Maybach cars had between 70 and 120 bhp, with construction to suit. By contrast, the first Paul Daimler line comprised 8/18, 10/20, 14/30, 22/40 and 28/60 models (the second figure denotes maximum output of their four-cylinder engines, the first a nominal output for taxation purposes). It was an obvious move for Daimler if business was to expand. It was all very well to produce massive, prestigious, expensive machines, but the fact was that real market growth could be achieved only by making cars more affordable—and to do this, smaller and more economical models were now literally the first order of business.

In the 1908-12 period the older, chain-drive cars were gradually phased out though this did not necessarily signal that the layout was completely obsolete. There was still a body of opinion that favored chains for large, powerful cars. And indeed, Daimler introduced a new series of chain-drive cars in 1910. The 22/50, 28/60, 38/70 and 37/90 models all had large four-cylinder engines, the two largest being considerably more powerful than those in the earlier shaft-drive lineup.

The same year, 1910, Daimler gave in to the "fad" then sweeping Europe by obtaining a license to build and use the sleeve-valve engine designed by American Charles Y. Knight. The British Daimler company (by now, completely independent of the German concern) had already been using sleeve-valve units, and this certainly influenced DMG's decision. Some speedy development work produced three four-cylinder models with sleeve-valve engines, plus shaft drive and live axle: the 10/30, 16/40 and 16/45. With them, the Daimler model line—still built in limited numbers, remember—was now extremely complex. Here, in order of developed horsepower, is the 1910 model group:

model	engine type	drive
8/18	poppet valve	shaft
10/20	poppet valve	shaft
10/30	sleeve valve	shaft
14/30	poppet valve	shaft
16/40	sleeve valve	shaft
22/40	poppet valve	shaft
16/45	sleeve valve	shaft
22/50	poppet valve	chain
28/60	poppet valve	shaft
28/60	poppet valve	chain
38/70	poppet valve	chain
37/90	poppet valve	chain

Bold radiator lettering marks this 1910 Mercedes phaeton, built on the 22/50 chassis and powered by a 5.6-liter four-cylinder engine. Top speed was about 50 mph.

A sample of early post-World War I models. Left: the mild 16/50 of 1921 had a 48-bhp sleeve-valve four. Above and bottom: the splendid six-cylinder 28/95, also from 1921.

Like most engines built under the Knight patents, the Daimler employed a double sleeve configuration with one slim steel tube inside another, interposed between the pistons and the cylinder block wall. But there was a problem: the sleeves not only moved up and down but had an element of rotary motion as well. Thus, they needed a lot of lubrication and this naturally meant high oil consumption. It was this factor, allied to problems brought on by the low-quality oil of the day, that eventually caused the demise of the Knight.

The First World War broke out in August 1914, and Daimler, like Benz and other manufacturing companies in Germany, turned to making weapons of war. Shortly before this, however, Paul Daimler's team had designed its first six-cylinder touring car. In the previous seven years, of course, the company had learned much about high-efficiency engines, first with the 130-bhp Grand

Prix car of 1908 and its successors, more recently with the wonderfully advanced four-cylinder 4.5-liter 115-bhp GP cars of 1914. However, this new engine was not directly related to either. And although the new 28/95 model was final by mid-1914, it went on sale only a short time before hostilities put an end to production. For all intents and purposes, therefore, it was a 1919 model, as it returned that year with the resumption of German civilian manufacturing.

The six-cylinder 28/95 engine had a capacity of 7250cc (442 cid) and in its initial form was virtually identical with the Daimler DF80 aircraft engine. Like the 1914-style Grand Prix engine, it had single-overhead-cam valvegear. This was exposed to the elements in the 1914 version, but was graced by three light-alloy covers from 1919 on. Though the new six made this the fastest Mercedes road car yet, the 28/95 had an entirely conventional chassis with shaft drive, not chain drive, plus half-elliptic leaf springs. The most prominent styling feature was a noble V-shaped radiator, which had become a hallmark of Mercedes cars in recent years. The radiator profile allowed the company to fit not one, but two of its newly adopted three-pointed star emblems, one on either side of the tank top.

World War I had meant overwhelming defeat, if not total devastation, for Germany. The country's economy was in ruins, the flower of its manhood slain, and there was general confusion and uncertainty about the future. Like every other business in the land, Daimler Motoren Gesellschaft had to start over again—if not from scratch then from a very low ebb. The trio of Paul Daimler designs was declared obsolete, and only three models initially trickled out to dealers: the splendid six-cylinder 28/95, the four-cylinder 16/50 sleeve-valve car (a development of the 16/45 of 1910-13), and a smaller 2.6-liter 10/35 with a poppet-valve four.

But there was an important technical development, though it wasn't unveiled until 1921. Daimler engineers had gained a great deal of experience in the use of supercharging for aircraft engines during the war. They decided to apply their knowledge to boosting the power and performance of car engines. The stage was set for the mighty supercharged Mercedes and Mercedes-Benz cars.

The first of the supercharged road cars bowed at the Berlin Show of 1921. These carried the official, if unwieldy, designations 6/25/40 and 10/40/65 (the first figure represented German "fiscal" horsepower, for tax classification; the second was Daimler's peak power rating with supercharger disengaged; the third figure was maximum engine output with supercharger operating). The lower-powered car used a four-cylinder engine, the more powerful one a closely related unit. To keep manufacturing complications to a minimum, Daimler designed the engines to share as many components as possible. Thus, both engines used a Roots two-blade supercharger, vertically mounted at the front of the engine and driven through small multi-plate disc clutches and bevel gearing from the crankshaft. The clutch was engaged by mechanical linkage, activated when the accelerator pedal was completely floored. Both power units had rather long and tortuous intake manifolds, and their power

Below and bottom: two examples of the supercharged four-cylinder 10/40/65 of 1922, the first blown Mercedes. Top speed for roadsters like this was over 70 mph.

Top and above: a blown Porsche-designed six, the 24/100/140, bowed in 1923.

vehicles, including smaller six-cylinder cars. Ultimately he came to blows with the major shareholder over a decision not to produce a 2.0-liter Porsche-designed engine, and stormed out. He was not out of work for long: in early 1923 he joined Daimler as technical director.

Porsche immediately settled down to work on a series of large supercharged models, his principal achievement at Daimler. They would be the last to bear the Mercedes, rather than the Mercedes-Benz, badge. It is only fair to say that, apart from their physical size and type of engine construction, these cars were not technically original. Rather, they were logical extensions of the 6/25/40 and 10/40/65 designs Paul Daimler had completed three years earlier. Porsche had developed a 2.0-liter, eight-cylinder, supercharged racer that became a class winner in 1924. The new supercharged road cars were based loosely on this engineering. Chassis specifications were typical of the early '20s: long wheelbase, channel-section pressed-steel frames, I-section front axle, live beam rear axle, stiff half-elliptic leaf springs, friction-type shock absorbers. All this combined for a very hard ride; the earliest examples, in fact, had cantilever rear suspension. There were two versions: the 4.0-liter (244-cid) 15/70/100 and the 6.25-liter (381-cid) 24/100/140. Wheelbases were huge: 142 and 156 inches, respectively.

The new engines, both sixes, were conceived at the same time, but their bore and stroke dimensions were quite different. The 4.0 unit's were 80×130mm (3.15×5.12), while the 6.25 engine had 94×150mm (3.70×5.90) measurements. Both retained the basic layout and supercharger operation established with the 6/25/40 and 10/40/65 of 1921, but they were visually quite a bit more modern and all design links with the previous aircraft-derived

output was adequate even when the supercharger wasn't engaged. But when the driver mashed the throttle it was like magically doubling power. Onlookers could always tell when a blown Mercedes blew by: the supercharger and its gear drive emitted a shrill scream—unmistakable and loud.

These first supercharged Mercedes were by no means as fast as you might think. They were large cars with spacious—and heavy—bodies. Yet they certainly were the pinnacle of achievement for Paul Daimler, who decided to retire before the end of 1922. To succeed him, company directors appointed a

remarkable man destined to change automotive history with the Volkswagen and the cars that bear his name to this day: Dr. Ferdinand Porsche.

Born in Austria in 1875, Porsche was 48 years old when he came to Stuttgart. As a youth he had been fascinated by electricity, and had gone on to design electrically powered vehicles at the Lohner Company in Vienna. In 1905 he joined the Austrian Daimler concern at Wiener-Neustadt, where his most significant contribution was the extremely successful Prinz Heinrich sports model that dominated European racing in 1910. Later, after Austro-Daimler became independent of the German parent company, Porsche designed a variety of powerplants were ostensibly gone. The block and upper crankcase were cast as a single unit from silumin, and featured wet liners. The cylinder head was made of cast iron, the crankcase and cylinder head cover of cast aluminum. A single carburetor was fitted on the small engine, twin carburetors on the other, with lengthy manifolding from the Roots blower at the front of the block. A significant change from earlier practice was that the blower "pushed" pressurized air into the carburetor before fuel was added, rather than drawing the fuel/air mixture down on the way to the engine. As with the 1914 Grand Prix Mercedes and the postwar powerplants, valves were actuated by a single overhead camshaft, driven by a vertical shaft and bevel gears from the nose of the crankshaft. The camshaft operated the valves through intermediate finger rockers.

The transmission was a massive four-speed gearbox (no synchromesh, of course: General

Two decades separate these views of the Untertürkheim plant (1904 below, 1921-22 bottom), and point up how much progress Daimler had made up to the time of its merger with Benz. Note massive chassis, vee'd radiators on cars at bottom.

Motors was still several years away from introducing this feature). Drive was taken to the rear axle through a torque tube, hinged at a universal joint immediately behind the gearbox itself. The gear lever was centrally mounted (many cars still used remote linkages on one side or the other), and the handbrake was pivoted close by. Center-lock wire wheels were fitted, along with the relatively new feature of mechanically operated four-wheel brakes. These were massive, heavy cars (over 3000 pounds even in lighter touring form), so the stopping power—or rather the relative lack of it—was often almost as exciting as the go power.

The 4.0-liter car was not a great success—it was very little cheaper than the larger-engine model and had much less performance—but the 24/100/140 was a real benchmark for Daimler. Not only was it the first of a new family that would win great acclaim for the three-pointed star in the next years, it was also the last car designed by the independent Daimler company. To be sure, the 24/100/140 had several major faults. Besides the mediocre brakes already mentioned, its chassis was quite high, and consequently handling left something to be desired. So, too, did the ponderous, heavy-handed coachwork. Even so, this car brought a new dimension to fast, open-road driving. It also exemplified Germany's growing confidence in its collective engineering ability. And, in many respects, it set standards that had other companies like Bentley scrambling to catch up.

By now, however, Dr. Porsche and his new cars were being overtaken by events. The Germany of 1923 was being consumed by roaring inflation, which led to the first hint of a tie-up between Daimler and Benz. From here on, life at Stuttgart would never be the same.

THE EARLY YEARS OF DAIMLER-BENZ: THE LEGEND BEGINS

The cockpit of the 1928 SS, one of the most exciting early models of the Daimler-Benz firm.

In the aftermath of World War I, much of German industry was at a standstill. The problems were not so much related to destruction of physical facilities as to a national economy that had been shot to pieces by the enormous cost of waging war. Now, immense reparation payments would be extracted from the defeated nation, and these Germany could not afford. Worse, her postwar economic policies were quite ludicrous, and only aggravated a deteriorating condition. Inflation began galloping almost as soon as hostilities ended, and quickly soared to triple-digit levels. The government issued more and more paper money to meet its obligations, and this only further diluted the currency in general circulation. In a few years, things had become so bad that laborers needed bags or suitcases just to carry the great chunks of paper that passed for wages. And it took about the same amount of currency just to buy a loaf of bread. Of course, only a relative few were fortunate enough to be working or earning a decent wage. There would be political consequences in all of this. As we all know now, the major one was the rise to power of Adolf Hitler and the Nazi Party in 1933.

Like so many other companies, both Daimler and Benz faced imminent collapse in the early postwar period. The government seemed unable to help much given the great need generally, so merger—or at least close collaboration with other firms—became increasingly attractive as time wore on. As early as 1919, in fact, Dr. Jahr of Benz had proposed direct cooperation between his firm and Daimler. But there was too much pride on each side, too much at stake in remaining autonomous, so for a time the idea wasn't taken seriously. By 1923, however, there seemed little choice.

Though General Motors was beginning to demonstrate what could be done by several firms working under the same corporate banner, there had been no significant company "marriages" in the German auto industry up to this point. Yet of the several possibilities that existed in the early '20s, a union between Daimler and Benz seemed, perhaps, the most natural. It was certainly necessary and long overdue. For one thing, they were direct rivals: from time to time both firms had offered similar types of cars, and both had engaged in expensive competition programs to sell them. Further, their products were aimed at the same restricted buyer group, a clientele growing ever smaller as economic conditions went from bad to impossible. If neither company could survive alone, they might survive together.

Many years later, historians for the company that resulted from the merger of these two automakers described how it happened: "In 1924, the *Daimler Motoren Gesellschaft* and *Benz und Cie* entered into an association of common interest. This was the forerunner of the complete amalgamation and constitution of the *Daimler-Benz AG* of June 28-29 1926. At that time there were 86 motor manufacturing companies in Germany who, among them, produced 144 different models. Taking into consideration the poverty that then existed in Germany as a result of the war and the period of inflation which had just been overcome, one single factory, assisted by modern manufacturing methods and mass production, would have sufficed to supply the whole of the German market." The "Agreement of Mutual Interest" was signed by the two boards of directors in May 1924. Among its provisions was a clause that ensured Carl and Berta Benz financial comfort for the rest of their lives. The director in charge of coordinating the merger was Wilhelm Kissel. One of the deal's significant aspects was a joint board that would include not one but three distinguished engineers: Nibel, Nallinger, and Dr. Porsche.

By 1924, the German government had at last come to grips with the roaring inflation and produced the Reichsmark. The country now seemed headed for economic stability. Although the market for consumer products like cars was temporarily stymied, things were generally looking up. However, it would be another two years before the Daimler-Benz merger was finalized.

Meanwhile, both companies began reorganizing some aspects of their business so that they did not compete head-on as much as before. Up to this point, both were still building cars and trucks, with their own bodywork, plus industrial engines. Thus, it was first decided to close down Benz car body operations and to center remaining production at the big modern factory at Sindelfingen, southwest of Stuttgart. Although this move would entail a lot of costly transportation to and from Mannheim, the "economies of scale" were expected to offset it. It was also decided to coordinate truck production, and to begin looking at how to eliminate duplications and overlaps in the respective automotive lines. In 1924, Benz offered the four-cylinder 10/30 sports cars and the six-cylinder 11/40 and 16/50 models, while Mercedes had its two Porsche-designed supercharged cars, the 15/70/100 and the 24/100/140. While none of these competed directly with one another, none were being built in large numbers, and the factories were working far below capacity.

Opposite page, top: unusual sports body of this late 28/95 hints at the great supercharged Mercedes tourers to come. Center: a 1924 supercharged 24/100/140 with the factory's limousine coachwork. Bottom: a more sporting 1925-26 example, bodied by Saoutchik.

Above: from 1926, a majestic town car by Farina on the Model K (24/110/160) chassis. Right and opposite page top: an early post-merger 24/100/140 cabriolet, again with Saoutchik bodywork. Opposite page bottom: the 1926 Mannheim cabriolet.

In retrospect, it's easy to see that Daimler and Benz got together only at the last possible moment. Had one or both remained independent, they would certainly have been out of business by 1925. In the wake of the drastic currency realignment following the hyperinflated "snowstorm of money" period, the country experienced severe deflation, and trade contracted seriously. As the official Daimler-Benz history put it: "The slackness of trade...
offset any advantages which should have been gained by the great attempts at rationalization. These circumstances made the amalgamation a matter of pressing necessity in order to give fresh impetus to the undertaking." At this time, there was even consideration of closing down the Sindelfingen

factory completely and concentrating on the older and smaller premises in Stuttgart and Mannheim.

Planning for new models went ahead steadily, and by the time the formal merger was concluded in June 1926, there were cheaper, more modern—and, it was hoped, more widely appealing—designs on drawing boards. The new company, with factories that seemed to be dotted all over Germany, was to be known as *Daimler-Benz Aktiengesellschaft*, usually shortened to Daimler-Benz AG. The aim was complete corporate and product integration, and less than 10

years later this had virtually been achieved.

One of the most interesting aspects of the merger was the way the company symbols or logos were combined. Fortunately, both were circular and could be married up without offending too many traditionalists. The Mercedes trademark, the three-pointed star, was first developed in 1909. It had been modified once in 1916, when the star was put in a circle, with four small stars in the two upper sections thus formed and the Mercedes name in the lower section. Another derivative with only the star and a ring appeared in 1921, and this emblem was seen atop Mercedes radiators for the first time. It was also patented. The Benz insignia had featured the company name surrounded by a laurel wreath for some time. With the merger came a hybrid symbol in which the three-pointed star sat within a circle framed either side by laurel wreaths; the names Mercedes and Benz appeared at the top and bottom, respectively, of the circular motif. This emblem and the noble radiator design developed soon afterwards have become among the most recognizable, respected, and durable symbols in the automotive world. Today, it would be as hard to accept a Mercedes without the three-pointed star as it would a Rolls-Royce without the linked double-R badge and "parthenon" radiator.

Technically and commercially, there was little doubt that Daimler came out of the union on top. Although the existing Benz factories would continue building cars for years to come, those cars would eventually be designed wholly at Stuttgart. And although their name survived, existing Benz models were soon dropped to make way for the first new D-B generation. The supercharged Mercedes cars conceived by Dr. Porsche were merely renamed Mercedes-Benz, and intensive development work on them was continued.

An important decision taken by both companies as early as 1924 was not just to get rid of slow-selling models as soon as possible, but to develop new middle-class models to take their place. Nowadays, we would say this was timely product planning. The supercharged Mercedes were beautifully engineered, but they were costly, so their market was very limited. The familiar Benz models were more affordable but very old-fashioned. By 1925, two new models looking more like evolutions of Benz than Mercedes design were on the way. These were launched in October of the following year—just three months after the merger, which confirmed that engineering work had been started much earlier. Both had six-cylinder engines. To signify where they were built, they were dubbed Stuttgart 200 and Mannheim, respectively. Naturally, both employed separate chassis with channel-section side members, and there was a full range of available body styles from sedans to tourers. Styling was simple but severe and upright. The new Mercedes-Benz insignia was prominently displayed on radiators, which were flat-faced and clearly reminiscent of earlier Benz models such as the 16/50, which they replaced in the revised model hierarchy.

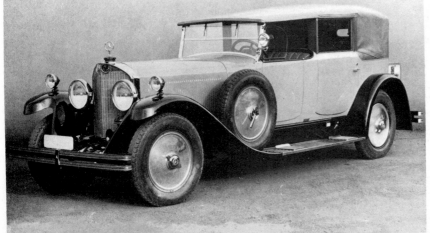

Anyone who knows mid-1920s GM cars will have no difficulty appreciating these Mercedes-Benz designs, though they had many German—and specifically Benz—touches. Although the two cars differed in many important respects, such as wheelbase length and engine size, they had clearly been developed in parallel. Both employed sturdy, though conventional, frames, with stout pressed crossmembers, a rigid Mercedes-style front axle, and "banjo" type rear axle. Other shared design points included artillery-style steel road wheels, three-speed gearbox in unit with the engine, ball-and-socket joints in the gearbox top cover, and torque-tube drive with ball joints at the rear of the gearbox. Half-elliptic leaf springs were used,

and there were four-wheel mechanical brakes.

The Stuttgart 200 was the smaller of this new duo. It ran on a 112-inch wheelbase and 56-inch tracks front and rear. As its designation suggests, engine displacement was 2.0 liters (65 × 100mm/2.56 × 3.94 in). The crankshaft was supported in seven main bearings, the block and head were made of cast iron, and the crankcase was in light alloy. The valve arrangement was a conventional L-head, with the valves placed side by side and operated by a camshaft mounted low down at the side of the engine. In typical Daimler and Benz parlance, the Stuttgart 200 was designated an 8/38 (fiscal power rating/actual horsepower).

By contrast, the Mannheim

(built at the Benz factory, hence its name) was altogether larger and more expensive. Though its general chassis layout was the same as the Stuttgart's, it sat on a long 137-inch wheelbase. The engine was also more substantial, with a swept volume of 3.1 liters (189 cid vs. 122), and it employed light alloy for the upper cylinder block as well as the crankcase. The company's rating was 12/55. The Mannheim was also distinguished by use of a four-speed gearbox.

All this was a good basis for the new marque, but it was just the start. Two years later, in 1928, engines were enlarged, to 2.6 liters (159 cid) and 3.5 liters

Below left: 1927 Model K four-seat touring. Below right: 1925-26 Type 24/100/140 by D'Iteran Freres. Bottom: 1928 Suttgart 260 sedan.

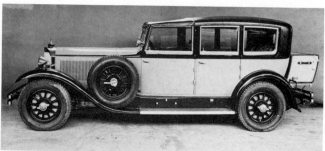

(214 cid) respectively, with corresponding ratings of 10/50 and 14/70. Model names were adjusted to Stuttgart 260 and Mannheim 350, thus inaugurating the long-standing Daimler-Benz model numbering system of engine capacity in liters multiplied by 100. The Mannheim power unit was uprated to 3.7 liters (226 cid) in 1929 for the 15/75 Mannheim 370, and a sports version was developed from it in the early 1930s.

The next new Mercedes-Benz was built along the same conventional lines as the Stuttgart and Mannheim, but was altogether larger, faster, and

Below: a more imposing Mannheim was this six-passenger pullman-limousine from 1929. Styling was very much in the contemporary Detroit idiom.

more expensive. Called the Nürburg 460, it has been described by Daimler-Benz as the last of the "classic models"—in other words, the last series-production design to employ the old channel-section frame and solid-axle suspension. There was little noteworthy about the Nürburg apart from its status as the first eight-cylinder Mercedes-Benz road car. (The 2.0-liter supercharged racer of 1924 was also an eight, but the Porsche-designed sports cars used overhead cam sixes.) Bore and stroke (80 × 115mm/ 3.15 × 4.53 in.) were shared with the Mannheim 350, but two extra cylinders meant swept volume of 4624cc (282 cid) and an 18/80 power rating. Construction and valvegear were related to the Mannheim six,

though the Nürburg's crankshaft ran in no fewer than nine main bearings, and coil ignition had now been adopted in place of the outmoded magneto. The chassis featured central lubrication, and there was a Bosch-Dewandre vacuum brake servo mounted on the side of the gearbox. The Nürburg's 121-inch wheelbase was shorter than that of the original Mannheim, but its I-section front axle, torque-tube rear axle, half-elliptic leaf springs, and Houdaille shock absorbers were all thoroughly familiar.

Ferdinand Porsche, meanwhile, parted company with Daimler-Benz in 1928 following a disagreement with senior colleagues over future model policy. The ostensible reason was Porsche's insistence that a

Above: Daimler-Benz built this 1930 Type 770 Grosser for Kaiser Wilhelm II. Right: an early-'30s Type 770 with pullman-limousine body. Bottom: 1930-31 Type 770 Cabriolet F.

radically new rear-engine design he had conceived be built. Porsche was premature, of course. There would be rear-engine Mercedes-Benz cars in the '30s, but for now he would return to realizing his lifelong dream of designing a "people's car," a *volkswagen*. With Porsche's departure, ex-Benz engineer Hans Nibel assumed the post of technical director, and it was he who is credited with the next new Mercedes-Benz, the eight-cylinder *Grosser* model of 1930.

The Type 770 *Grosser* was an amazing machine that appeared at exactly the wrong time. As with the contemporary V-16 Cadillac, there was really no rhyme or reason for expensive multi-cylinder giants in the depths of the Depression, and they were more or less indulgences for their makers. The *Grosser* was Daimler-Benz's way of saying to the world: "We are still here, we are confident about our future, and here is the finest automobile we can build to prove it." The name *Grosser* (German for "grand") was appropriate. It was a very large car both in physical size and engine size and output. Indeed, Daimler-Benz put it all in perspective by rating it a 30/150/200 (the last figure being nominal peak power with the optional supercharger engaged). The 770 was not intended as a series (or even serious) production car in the usual sense. Rather, it was to be built by hand in tiny numbers for heads of state, civic dignitaries, entrepreneurs, celebrities, anyone who craved prestige—and who were approved as worthy by Daimler-Benz.

The Type 770 sat on a massive, rigid box-section chassis. There was no independent suspension, the solid front and rear axles being suspended on half-elliptic leaf springs. Wheelbase stretched to no less than 148 inches, and track width was a noble 59 inches. It was the sort of majestic machine that only formal sedan, limousine, or convertible coupe bodies would suit, and Daimler-Benz was quite happy to build them itself. As a result, the *Grossers* not only looked magnificent and imposing, but they were all very heavy and, frankly, ponderous to drive. The chassis alone weighed more than 4000 pounds, and it's very doubtful that all-up curb weight was less than three tons. When you recall that power steering had yet to be invented, it's easy to see why Type 770 chauffeurs had to have a lot of stamina.

The first *Grossers* were powered by an entirely new straight eight designed for this model alone. Unlike the totally unrelated Nürburg engine, this unit had overhead valves operated by pushrods and rockers. It was normally supplied with a vane-type

supercharger that could be "clutched in" by flooring the accelerator, the same well-proven system used in Porsche-designed supercharged sixes. Bore and stroke were 95x135mm (3.74 × 5.31 in.) for a swept volume of 7655cc (467 cid). What power it actually produced at peak revs with the blower engaged is not certain (most carmakers were delightfully vague about such things at the time), but historian David Scott-Moncrieff has suggested that 280 bhp was available. Like the newer Daimler-Benz side-valve engines, this one had "vintage" construction, with cast-iron cylinder head and block and separate light-alloy crankcase. Sending all this power to the rear wheels was a six-speed gearbox—more accurately, a conventional three-speed transmission with a special two-speed auxiliary box mounted ahead of it, sandwiched between the engine and the main gearbox. This assembly was provided by Maybach (the old link between Daimler and Maybach persisted, even though the Maybach company now had its own large cars in competition with Daimler-Benz), and had been seen at motor shows for the past two years. To keep the performance in check—and to reduce physical demands on the

chauffeur—there were power assisted brakes, with a vacuum servo of the same basic type as that used in the Nürburg 460.

The *Grosser* was sold as a strictly limited-production hand-built exotic for seven years, when it was replaced by a much more advanced model. In all, just 117 of the 1930-37 cars were built, mostly for German customers, The most prestigious foreign orders came from Emperor Hirohito of Japan, who bought seven of them, which he used into the 1960s. Several *Grossers* were naturally supplied to high-placed officials in Hitler's Third Reich, which in recent years has led to confusing claims that almost every surviving Type 770 was *Der Führer's* personal car.

The magnificent supercharged six-cylinder sports cars conceived by Dr. Porsche continued—and continued to make history—in the early years of Daimler-Benz. Their development and racing exploits are treated in the next chapter. Production of the 6.25-liter 24/100/140 carried on at Stuttgart, with bodies built at Sindelfingen, but the smaller 4.0-

Below: one step below the Grosser was the Nürburg 460, a rather dull model introduced in 1928.

liter 15/70/100 did not survive the merger and the model realignment that followed.

By the end of the 1920s, a great deal had been done to ensure a more expansive and more profitable future for Daimler-Benz AG. Production had reached a new high, there were no longer any clashing Benz and Mercedes models, and the company's image as a builder of powerful, solidly engineered cars was being firmly established. In 1930, the firm offered the six-cylinder Stuttgart 260 and Mannheim 370 touring cars along with the straight-eight Nürburg 500 range, a higher-displacement version of the original Nürburg 460. All these were "bread-and-butter" models. For glamour and prestige, Daimler-Benz had a new line of blown six-cylinder sports cars, the S, SS, and short-chassis SSK machines, plus the enormous Type 770 *Grosser*.

Though Daimler-Benz exported very few cars at the time (it's doubtful more than a handful were delivered in North America), the company did promote its wares overseas. Prices advertised at the Olympia Motor Show held in London that October ranged from £720 (about $3500 contemporary) for the Stuttgart 260 to a whopping £2785 ($13,400) for the *Grosser*. The latter was in the same league with the Rolls-Royce Phantom, which sold for perhaps $1500 *less*, and the new Cadillac V-16, which was much cheaper than that. The Type 770, in fact, was the most expensive car at the show and, apart from the near-mythical Bugatti Royale, was probably the world's most expensive car at the time.

But all this was no more than a prelude for the future German colossus. As with General Motors, the joining of Daimler with Benz had touched off much change and new-model development right away, even if no far-reaching innovations were immediately apparent. Behind the scenes, a heated debate was going on about the direction the new company should take. As mentioned, this had led Ferdinand Porsche to resign in 1928 shortly after the debut of the new supercharged Model S. By that time, management had pretty well determined that Daimler-Benz should move more aggressively into the volume car market in the '30s with less expensive, more versatile models. But though they had confidence in the way Europe's economy was developing, they did not forsee the Depression that followed the Great Crash in 1929. To say the decision to move downmarket was fortuitous is something of an understatement, and it may well have been the difference between survival and failure for the new company.

Accordingly, an entirely new family of cars with smaller engines was ordained, along with

Below: only 117 Type 770s were built over seven years. This 1931 example was created for King Faisal of Saudi Arabia. Bodywork is by Holl & Ruehrbeck.

installation of modern factory tools and equipment that would allow tailoring the product mix to meet changing market conditions. At the same time, management decreed the end of the traditional chassis and body construction used in the 1920s. Channel-section frames and beam front axles were on the way out, to be replaced by independent front suspensions and box frames. For the fiery Dr. Porsche, this didn't go far enough. He wanted to push further into the future: even smaller cars with rear-mounted engines, unit construction, advanced styling—and all the commercial risks this entailed. With Porsche now gone, it would all be up to Hans Nibel, and his Mercedes-Benz designs would be startling enough. The acid test came in the spring of 1931, when Europe's economy was at its most gloomy. With the radical new Type 170, Daimler-Benz would open a new era in automotive history—no mean feat for a company that already had so much history behind it.

THE CLASSIC MERCEDES-BENZ 1926-39: POWERFUL INNOVATIONS

Below and right: two typical late-1926 examples of Saoutchik bodywork on the massive Model K chassis. These cars bear consecutive commission numbers; the one below was built first.

The years beginning with the supercharged six-cylinder Mercedes Model K and ending with the outbreak of World War II could well be termed the golden age of Daimler-Benz. But in a way that's not fair. There have been so many great years in D-B history—including the present—that somehow the description becomes hackneyed. Nonetheless, it was an extraordinary period, dominated by the most magnificent road cars and racing machines the motoring world had ever seen. They were the sort of cars that for many reasons Daimler-Benz would never be able to build again.

The story of these years is also very much a tale of great men: Wilhelm Kissel, who directed the new company created by the Daimler-Benz merger; the trio of engineers—Porsche, Nibel, and Nallinger—responsible for the cars themselves; a stable of racing drivers—Caracciola, Fagioli, von Brauchitsch, Lang, and Seaman—second to none; and, not least, the increasingly familiar figure of racing manager Alfred Neubauer, who appeared at Solitude on September 12, 1926 "for the first time," as he later recalled, "guiding the drivers through the race with invisible strings." It is the engineering triumvirate and their creations that are the subjects of this chapter.

Ferdinand Porsche and Fritz Nallinger had come from Daimler, Hans Nibel from Benz. This combination had enormous potential, but it would not last. Even in those early years, the mercurial Porsche was consumed by a desire to realize a "people's car" (he'd already attempted one for Austro-Daimler in 1920, the ill-fated Sascha). But the managers of the new Daimler-Benz concern were conservative, and looked on Porsche as something of a dreamer. The closest they came to his ideal was in 1928 with a proposal for a medium-price model called the

Stuttgart. Late that year, management asked Porsche to prove that he'd finally licked his prototypes' cold-start problems by firing up any one of the 15 that had been left outside overnight. Porsche failed, flew into a fury, and resigned on New Year's Day 1929. Overall engineering responsibility then passed to Nibel, assisted by Nallinger. But it was Porsche who conceived the six-cylinder supercharged Mercedes-Benz cars that today rank among the immortals.

As described elsewhere, the first of the line was the Mercedes 24/100/140 of 1924, which originated at Daimler and was also known as the Type 630. This large, powerful touring car of little aesthetic merit quickly evolved into a series of progressively lighter, more powerful, and more rapid sports tourers, most of them capable of

well over 100 mph. The ultimate descendant, the mighty SSKL (*sehr schnell, kurz, leicht*—very fast, short wheelbase, light) developed 300 bhp, and was good for an astounding 120 mph. It was the fastest sports car of the era.

The blown sixes that powered these cars all stemmed from Porsche's original Daimler design, created largely for the carriage and export trade and not drawn up with sporting purposes in mind. This powerplant, as Karl Ludvigsen observed in *Car Classics* magazine, "kept such hallmarks of Porsche's predecessor, Paul Daimler, as a single overhead camshaft and a Roots-type supercharger, mounted vertically at the front of the engine and driven through a multi-disc clutch that was engaged when the driver pressed his foot all the way down on the throttle

pedal. This kind of supercharger was used on every top-line Mercedes-Benz built before World War II."

But the Type 630's ponderous chassis was not up to the technical sophistication of its engine. Ludvigsen, in his book *The Mercedes-Benz Racing Cars*, wrote that the power unit was "far more satisfactory," and Leonard Setright, in *The Engineers*, flatly declared that Porsche "was utterly hopeless on chassis design." The enormous channel-section chassis that was stretched over a huge 147.5-inch wheelbase was very high slung, and had semi-elliptic leaf springs at all corners, cantilevered at the rear. Handling was definitely not this car's forte. One of its distinctly curious features was two sets of shoes for the rear drum brakes, one actuated by the brake pedal, the other by a handlever. If D-B

was going to make a sports car out of this rig, it would have to make considerable modifications.

These were duly carried out. The first one made was the most obvious: a shorter wheelbase. At 134 inches it was still not short by any means, but the new Model K thus created was a step forward. Oddly, the letter K stood for *kurz* (short). The official type designation was 24/110/160, a clue to its larger and more powerful engine, now at 6246cc (381 cid) on a bore and stroke of 94 × 150mm (3.7 × 5.9 in.). This big six exhaled through an exhaust system that became a Mercedes-Benz hallmark in these years. Instead of traveling modestly under the floorboards and ducting out quietly at the rear, it was ostentatiously led through the side of the hood as three enormous tubes of flexible, corrugated metal, usually polished or plated. These merged

into a single pipe after vanishing under the front fenders. This arrangement would be widely imitated—often mainly for appearance sake—by many cars with performance pretensions, including many of today's replicars (which shall remain nameless). The feature was said by some to be essentially un-German, while others said it couldn't have been more characteristic, particularly for the 1930s. No matter. It gave all these supercharged cars a recognizable and romantic look.

The Model K was lighter than the 24/100/140, but not much: the rolling chassis still weighed nearly 1.5 tons all by itself. However, the K had more conventional suspension (the cantilevered semi-elliptic springs were discarded), and it had more power: 110 bhp at 2800 rpm nominal, 160 bhp at 3000 rpm with supercharger engaged. Although the fully equipped car weighed almost exactly two tons, it would easily do 95 mph. And it would have almost certainly been developed into a serious racer had management not then decreed a ban on competition research activities. But engineers like Porsche, Nibel, and Nallinger were not to be denied, and in 1927 they unleashed the Model S (Sport), an even more serious effort.

The Model S is often overlooked by both historians and enthusiasts, overshadowed as it is by both its SS and SSK contemporaries and by the 380/500/540Ks of later years. But it was a tremendously impressive machine in its own right.

The S was mounted on a new and much lower channel-section frame of the "cow belly" style, dipping very low between the

Low-slung Model S was well suited to a variety of stylistic approaches. Opposite page, top: a 1927 standard-body car. Bottom: a 1928 model with coachwork by Papler. This page, top: a 1928-29 four-place cabriolet by Erdmann & Rossi of Berlin. Bottom: an early-'30s factory-body Model S.

47

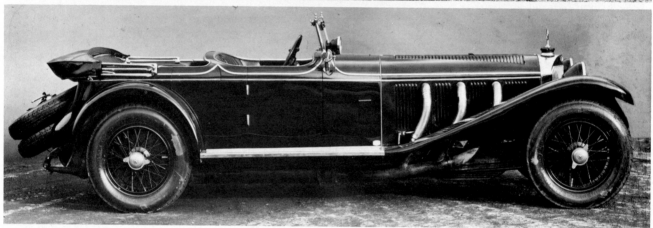

Top: a racing Model S from 1927, but note four-seat body. Bottom: coachwork on this handsome 1928 Model S is attributed to Zietz of Geneva, Switzerland.

axles and rising at each end, so that the rear leaf springs passed under the axle. The engine was moved 12 inches rearward from its Model K position; the vast radiator moved back with it. The result was a lower center of gravity, greatly improved front/rear weight distribution, a lower profile, less wind resistance, and splendid looks. The chassis featured torque-tube drive and a strong four-speed gearbox. The Model K's twin rear brake shoes, an artifact of the 24/100/140, were eliminated, and the handbrake now operated simply as an override to the foot pedal, which on some cars was assisted by a Bosch vacuum booster. A bore increase to 98mm (3.86 in.) boosted engine displacement to 6789cc (414 cid),

and the factory fitted tubular connecting rods with double big-end bolts, aluminum pistons, and larger valves. Sans supercharger, power output was 120 bhp; with supercharger engaged it went up to 180, hence the factory's official 26/120/180 model designation. With higher compression ratios and using special fuels, the racing versions put out 200-220 bhp, truly phenomenal power for the period.

Pause for a moment and consider the figures we've been casually reeling off. They would seem ordinary for the 1950s or '60s. Yet this was 1928: the mighty SJ Duesenberg had yet to appear, and the hottest American car of the day was the 120-bhp McFarlan.

Because it was conceived with competition strongly in mind, the Model S was extremely low for these years. As a result, most chassis were fitted with rakish open bodies, their hoods clearing the huge engine by only a couple of millimeters. Former race driver and now columnist Phil Hill, recording his impressions of a 1927 tourer in 1979, spoke of remarkably flat handling with just a trace of oversteer, combined with a surprisingly smooth ride. Phil's restoration shop had rebuilt this

continued on page 65

48

Pioneer efforts of the automobile's founding fathers. Above: the replica Benz three-wheeler of 1885 with 1.5 horsepower. Below: Gottlieb Daimler's experimental motorized cycle, 1885.

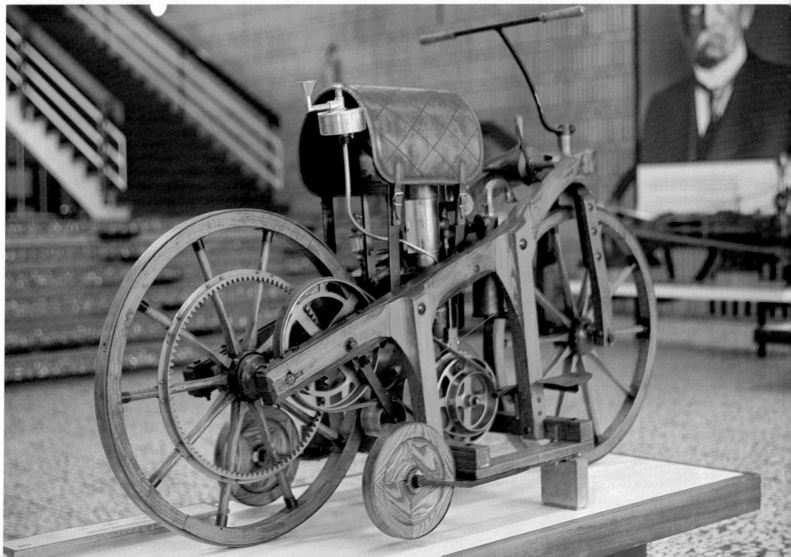

Above: The first four-wheel Benz was the Victoria, which went on sale in 1893. It was available with a choice of 3-, 4-, or 5-horsepower engines, all single-cylinder. Near right: A modified horse-drawn carriage served as the basis for Gottlieb Daimler's 1886 four-wheeler, considered by many to be the world's first true automobile in the accepted sense. Opposite page, above: Another first for Daimler was this 4-horsepower taxicab. It carried the citizens of 1897 Stuttgart. Below: the famous 1889 Daimler "wire wheel" V-twin car was an important step toward automotive design as a distinct entity.

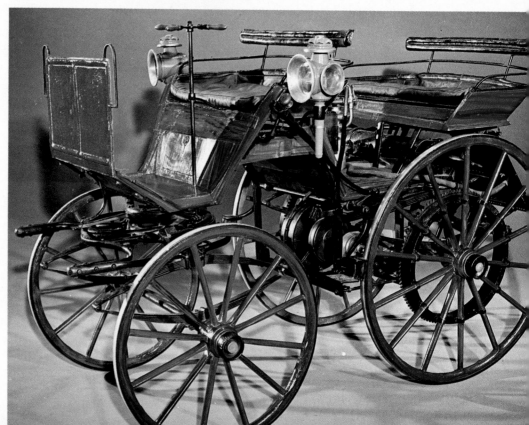

Opposite page, above: by 1902, Benz automobiles had become quite conventional and staid. Shown here is the 15-horsepower "Spider" open model, typical of the firm's designs in this period. Below: this 1908 Mercedes Grand Prix racing car was powered by an enormous 12.78-liter (779.9-cid) four-cylinder engine rated at 150 horsepower. It won that year's French GP at Dieppe, piloted by Christian Lautenschlager. The basic design dated from the highly successful original Mercedes of 1901. This page, above: typical of early-1900s Daimlers is this 1904 Mercedes-Simplex touring car, designed by Wilhelm Maybach. Below: this 1906 Mercedes racing car had 125 horsepower, and was amazingly fast for its day.

Above: a 40-bhp Mercedes touring car from 1910 with sleeve-valve engine. Near right: the 200-bhp "Blitzen Benz" set many speed records in 1911. Opposite page, top: perhaps the most successful pre-World War I Mercedes racer was this 1914 4.5-liter GP car. Below: a later 48-bhp sleeve-valve Mercedes from 1921.

Another look at the highly successful Mercedes Grand Prix racing car of 1914. Designed principally by Paul Daimler, son of the firm's founder, it ran a 4.5-liter (273.6-cid) four-cylinder overhead cam engine developing 115 horsepower. Though it won several major events in the final year before World War I, its most notable victory was a 1-2-3 sweep in the 1914 Grand Prix of Lyons in France. Bodywork on this beautifully restored example typifies race car design practice of the early 1900s. Note in particular the high cowl, nearly full-length external exhaust pipe, long rear leaf springs, and the twin spare tires. Prominent vee'd grille was by this time a Mercedes hallmark.

The Mercedes 28/95 marked the birth of supercharging for both road and competition cars. Shown on these pages is a fully restored 1924 example of the type that won that year's Targa Florio open-road race in the hands of Christian Werner. The production 28/95 had a normally aspirated 7.25-liter six, virtually identical with the Daimler DF80 aircraft engine. A Roots blower was originally adapted for it by engineer Paul Daimler for racing use. In this form it developed 120 horsepower.

Lack of any Benz insignia on this Model 24/100/140 marks it as a pre-merger Mercedes. Also referred to as the Type 630, this model was powered by a 6.2-liter (381-cid) supercharged six designed by Dr. Ferdinand Porsche. Together with its 4.0-liter running mate, this was the direct forerunner of the glorious supercharged S-models of the late '20s. All 24/100/140 cars had custom-built bodies fitted to their very ponderous 3400-pound chassis.

The combined Daimler-Benz company wasted little time in showing what it could do by unleashing the potent supercharged Model S in 1927, just a year after the merger. Shown here are two 1928 developments of Ferdinand Porsche's concept. Opposite page, bottom: the Model SS, a lighter S with a more powerful 7.0-liter (427-cid) six producing up to 200 horsepower. All other pictures: The short-chassis SSK arrived with the SS, and developed up to 225 bhp. Both models were built in very small numbers.

Another example of the 1924 Mercedes Type 28/95 as used at that year's Targa Florio. Body and fenders are all-aluminum and original. Note the practical rear rumble seat.

continued from page 48

car, and he'd seen it taken down to the last nut and bolt. "It was very obviously a car of the early school," he said, "big and heavy with a massive engine. This was in a time when a lot of American cars had already gotten away from this and were getting quite reliable power out of smaller, lighter, side-valve engines.

"Other than the usual German passion for quality...the great feature of the Model S is the supercharger, which allowed, if only for a short period of time, exceptional output. That would obviously have meant nothing if the cars weren't tremendously reliable, which they were, and that stemmed from the excellent manner in which the Mercedes were (and still are) built... [They] are all very Teutonic in

Top and above right: a very Germanic Model SS tourer from 1928. Above left: a more graceful SS, with body by D'Iteran Freres of Brussels.

the sense of things being husky..."

But there was more to come. The Model SS (Super Sport) debuted in 1928, officially rated a 27/140/200. Displacement went to 7010cc (427 cid) due to another bore stretch (to 100mm/3.94 in.). Maximum horsepower of 110 nominal/200 supercharged was developed at 3300 rpm, with higher compression and larger valves and ports doing their part to increase output. The lighter SS chassis was fitted with graceful closed bodies as well as touring coachwork, and some of the

loveliest were produced at D-B's own shops at Sindelfingen.

Along with the SS appeared the most sporting Mercedes-Benz yet, the SSK (super sport short). Mounted on a wheelbase of only 116.1 inches, it packed the SS drivetrain but used a bigger blower and was thus more powerful, having the designation 27/170/225. Most typically, these were seen with tiny cockpits and a mile-long hood announced by the most imposing radiator of the 1920s. Most SSKs built were roadsters, though the occasional and rather unsuccessful cabriolet was attempted. If *Herr Doktor* Porsche was as inept at chassis design as Setright claims, he must have had help from his teammates on the SSK chassis. Making extensive use of aluminum, it weighed 2680

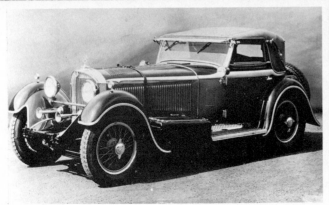

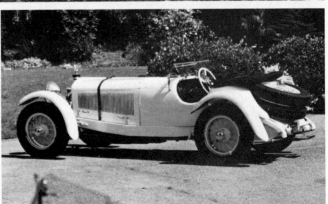

pounds, comparatively a welterweight for a Mercedes, and most road-ready examples with roadster bodywork just nudged over 3700 pounds at the curb. It was an astonishing car for its time. And it remains so today.

And there was still more: the fearsome SSKL. The work of Hans Nibel and Max Wagner and designed after Porsche had left Stuttgart, it appeared in 1931. Wagner was a chassis specialist, so his job was to make the SSK chassis as light as possible. To do this, he had holes drilled everywhere he could without compromising structural integrity. He ended up with a frame that weighed 250 pounds less than before and looked like it had been carved from Swiss cheese. Meantime, Nibel was tweaking the sturdy six. The engine had now reached its displacement limit, so he resorted to a larger supercharger, plus special components and fuel. Unsupercharged, the SSKL developed 170 horsepower. With the blower, it produced a staggering 300 bhp at 3200 rpm, and was good for an equally remarkable 120 mph.

All the variations on the Model S were uncommon—and uncommonly fine examples of the automotive art. Each was built mostly by hand from the ground up. Though sources do not agree on exact production, the figures are miniscule: 111-114 for the SS, 33-42 for the SSK, and a dozen or less for the SSKL, the last example of which was produced in 1932. Such rarity—plus splendid engineering—is the main reason these cars occupy the top echelon of old-car values today.

Opposite page: the magnificent SSK appeared in 1928 with the SS engine in a shorter, lighter chassis. Most built were roadsters, though the occasional cabriolet (bottom left) was also tried. This page, top: the ultra-rare SSKL in pure race trim. Center: the roadgoing SSKL. Bottom: a low-slung SSK roadster from 1928-29, with D'Iteran Freres bodywork.

Though the Sports were undoubtedly the most exciting Mercedes-Benz models of the 1930s, they were by no means the most exclusive. As previously noted, the Type 770 *Grosser,* introduced in 1930, continued to be built through most of the decade in extremely limited numbers—only 117 total. Of course, far fewer than this survive today. Since many of the cars were originally provided to prominent members of the Nazi Party, and because the *Grosser* was so rare to begin with, every one that surfaces now seems to be touted as the "Hitler Mercedes." In fact, *Der Führer* used cars from a motor pool, so no single example can be accurately represented as "his" car.

In 1937, a new *Grosser* arrived with the same basic straight-eight engine but with output raised to 155 bhp unblown and 230 bhp blown. It rode a titanic 155-inch wheelbase spanning a more modern frame with tubular construction along the lines of the latest small passenger models. The solid-axle front suspension now gave way to a fully independent arrangement with coil springs, and De Dion rear geometry was employed. These astonishing cars weighed close to four tons, yet they could, when the occasion arose, easily exceed 100 mph. Most observers put their top speed at upwards of 110 mph.

However impressive they were, sports cars and limousines were only a tiny fraction of Daimler-Benz production. The amalgated company had grown rapidly into the 1930s, largely on the strength of the Stuttgart and Mannheim series of side-valve six-cylinder cars. Much less important was the fast-aging Nürburg straight-eight models. Some 3500 of these were built, which was quite something given their antiquated specifications. The Mannheims are significant as the forerunners of the memorable 380/500/540K sports tourers. But the car that

Left and center: 1931 Mannheim 370S standard cabriolet. Bottom: Type 200 debuted in 1932 as a larger-engine companion to the significant Type 170 introduced the year before. Styling was the same on both models.

cars they could. Daimler-Benz was affected as much as anyone, and must have missed Ferdinand Porsche at this point—how the new realities would have suited him. Still, the 170 was quite advanced.

Perhaps the 170's most notable feature was its all-independent suspension. The front was via transverse leaf spring, the rear courtesy of swing axles and coil springs. That rear-end geometry would become characteristic of Mercedes-Benz cars, and would not entirely disappear until the latter half of the 1960s! Perhaps the company stayed with it too long. Certainly, as performance levels rose in later years the disadvantages of geometry that permitted such wide camber variations became increasingly apparent—and required increasingly complicated countermeasures. But on a car of the 170's size, power, and price it was a remarkable advance, doing much to improve ride and handling, and leapfrogging other manufacturers by many years. (The swing axle was soon widely accepted on the continent. However, the British didn't employ it until the '60s and we Americans never did, with one exception: the 1960-64 Corvair.)

All-independent suspension wasn't the only thing advanced about the Type 170. It also had central chassis lubrication, four-wheel hydraulic brakes, and pressed-steel wheels. None of these were genuine "firsts." Triumph had been using four-wheel hydraulic brakes since 1929, and many upper-class American makes had earlier offered steel wheels and central chassis lubrication. But again, for a lower-priced car they were important pluses, and hydraulic brakes were as desirable on small cars as on large ones. So,

Opposite page, top and center: the original Type 770 Grosser gave way to a more modern successor in 1937. Most examples had this flowing pullman-limousine bodywork. Bottom: the 370S Mannheim Sport of 1930.

carried Daimler-Benz through the hard times of the 1930s was the Type 170, undoubtedly the firm's single most commercially important product of the decade.

Introduced in 1931, the 170 was a Nibel-designed six-cylinder car of modern specification and much smaller size. It would spawn a wholly new design family in the '30s, and would help D-B recover in the early postwar period. In concept there was nothing mysterious about the Type 170. The Depression had arrived with a bang in Germany, as elsewhere, during 1929, and for most automakers the obvious response was to field the cheapest, smallest-engined the 170 was technically impressive, disappointing only in its performance. It could barely reach 60 mph, not surprising as its 1.7-liter engine produced just 32 DIN horsepower. An evolutionary linemate, the Type 200 arriving in 1932, was better, with 40 horsepower and a top speed of close to 70 mph. Through 1936 over 30,000 of these two models were sold despite the difficult market, a tribute to the excellence of their basic engineering.

These modern six-cylinder Mercedes evolved through the '30s in two steps. The first came in 1933 with introduction of the Type 290, which featured its own special front suspension with transverse leaf spring and twin coil springs. The second appeared in 1936-37 in the form of larger-displacement versions of the original 170/200. These were the Type 230, powered by a 2230cc (140-cid) unit, and the Type 320, with capacity of 3208cc (195.3 cid). But the decade's really startling developments were the world's first diesel-powered passenger car, the 260D of 1936 (described fully in another chapter), and the *heckmotor*, the rear-engine Mercedes.

The rear-engine chassis first appeared in 1934, and eventually became the basis for three variants, all four-cylinder models carrying the H designation. The initial 1.3-liter 130H used a puny 26-bhp side-valve unit. A sports-bodied rendition, the 150H, had 55 bhp and an overhead-cam head. Last in the series was the 170H, which arrived in 1935 with a 38-bhp 1.7-liter engine. All these engines were watercooled units mounted together with their gearboxes aft of the rear suspension, along with a radiator and header tank. A large fan placed ahead of the engine drew air down through slots in the top of the deck and directed it through a casing to the top of the radiator block. The blower also doubled as a "heat-forcer": a bypass from the

casing ducted some air past the exhaust manifold, where it was warmed before being routed into the passenger compartment. This was controlled by a dashboard valve that opened or closed the separate heat ducts. To keep the driver apprised of coolant level, a sort of "tea kettle" whistle was built into the header tank. If the two-gallon system ever became dangerously low, escaping steam would activate the whistle, warning the driver to add more water.

The rear-engine cars were mounted on frames consisting of a central tube with several right-angle braces, plus a fork at the rear embracing the engine/gearbox assembly. Beefy

outriggers led from the suspension units, which were the established transverse-leaf-spring ifs and swing-axle irs. Hydraulic shock absorbers were fitted all around. The 130H and 170H carried full five-seat sedan and convertible bodies not unlike those of the early Volkswagens. The 150H was offered only as a cabriolet. On all, the trunk was up front under the "hood," but unlike the Bug's this was extremely roomy, capable of holding a couple of suitcases.

The 170H was more acceptable than the original 130H because of its better performance. Its conventional side-valve engine was a "stroker," measuring 73.5 × 100mm (2.89 × 3.93 in.). A

A sampling of the middle-range six-cylinder Mercedes of the '30s. Above: the 1933 Type 290 with factory-built two-seat Cabriolet A body. Right: the 1936 Type 200 sedan, here to UK specification. Below: the four-place Cabriolet D version of the Type 230 from 1936.

four-speed transmission was geared for direct drive (1.00:1 ratio) in third and for overdrive in fourth, against an overall final drive ratio of 4.00:1. Remarkably for a car of its limited power it would do over 70 mph. In a test session at the Nürburgring, Britain's weekly magazine *The Autocar* "had to remember to keep the engine pulling on a corner to get the best results, but that is also true of any car, whether with front or rear engine. The steering was light, yet not unduly so, and the absence of weight in the front has made it possible to use higher-geared steering than usual." On the rough, potholed inner test track a Mercedes

driver "sailed over the gullies in an extraordinary manner. It would be an exaggeration to say that one did not feel the bumps—they were far too bad for that—but one could certainly say that one felt no shocks at all."

Very few 150H sports models were made, but Daimler-Benz did turn out over 10,000 of the larger-engine cars. This was hardly abject failure, as these

Below: 1937 Type 230 Cabriolet A. Center left: the ungainly Type 150H sports roadster, 1936. Center and bottom right: Mercedes mainstay in the years immediately before and after World War II was the Type 170V, introduced in 1936. Bottom left: the rear-engine Type 170H sedan of 1935.

cars have often been pronounced in retrospect. An improving economy was probably more to blame than low buyer acceptance for their cancellation in 1939, although they were handily outsold by their front-engine compatriots.

The rear-engine chassis influenced the last of the low-line front-engine Mercedes of the prewar years. First in this series was the popular Type 170V, which appeared in 1936. It marked a major change from the original 170 in that the old-style box-section chassis was replaced by a tubular backbone frame as in the rear-engine cars. Fully independent suspension was retained, using 290-like

coil/transverse leaf springs up front. Daimler-Benz also fielded an upmarket 2.3-liter six-cylinder derivative of the new chassis. But the 170V was clearly the star of the show, outselling its rear-engine counterparts by 12 to one. It was the bread-and-butter model for six full years, and close to 100,000 were built through 1942, when the war brought production to a halt. Later, it was the obvious choice for resuming production postwar, and it filled a big void until newly designed successors could be readied.

Capping the story of the classic Mercedes-Benz is a line of beautifully conceived sports tourers, the noble K-models. These were machines of immense strength, power, and presence, a manifestation of the pomposity for which Germany was known in that decade. They rank among the greatest automobiles that have ever put rubber to road.

The first of the series was the 380K, introduced in Berlin in February 1933, just after Adolf Hitler came to power as chancellor of Germany. Designed by Hans Nibel, who died in November 1934, the 380K was really the spiritual successor of the SS, though it owed its technology to the *Grosser* and formally superceded the outmoded Nürburg 500 in the M-B lineup. Nibel designed a new straight eight for this model along Type 770 lines, with a simplified version of the *Grosser's* pushrod-operated overhead valves, but the block was cast as a single piece rather than two pieces. It was a "stroker" at 78×100mm $(3.07 \times 3.93$ in.), and its 3823cc (233 cid) produced 120 horsepower with supercharger.

The 380K was a glorious-looking car—and certainly potent— but its chassis also has historical significance. This was, in fact, the world's first production car with independent front suspension by means of parallel wishbones and coil springs. Notwithstanding

the advent of the later MacPherson-strut arrangement, this remains the most acceptable, durable front suspension design. The massive box frame of the 380K carried the typical Mercedes swing-axle rear suspension, and there was a tremendously strong forged front crossmember to help carry the bodywork, which comprised closed coupe and sedan styles as well as open types.

Only 60 of the Type 380Ks were made. The reason was that the model was phased out the very next year, 1934, for something better: the 500K. Displayed at Berlin as an exotically styled streamlined coupe, it was also available as an open sports tourer, a conventional coupe, a soft-top cabriolet, and a four-door sedan. The 500K rode a 129.5-inch-wheelbase chassis that weighed over 3400 pounds alone. As most bodies added 2000 pounds to that, a larger engine with more power was essential. Accordingly, the 3.8-liter straight eight was bored and stroked to 86×108mm $(3.39 \times 4.25$ in.) for 5019cc (306 cid) and 160 bhp supercharged. Daimler-Benz built 354 of these magnificent cars through early 1936.

The 500K was schizophrenic as only blown cars can be. Cruising along at moderate speeds with the blower idling, it was surprisingly quiet, docile and easy to handle. In this mode, given the space, it could build up to 100 mph, thanks to its top-gear overdrive; yet the indirect gears would enable it to cover the quarter-mile rapidly. But when the supercharger kicked in, as *The Autocar* recorded, "it becomes another machine altogether. The control is such that the first light-moving part of the throttle pedal motion has no effect upon the blower; a clean-cut pressure of the right foot beyond that point engaged a multi-plate clutch mounted on the front of the crankshaft, which applies the

drive to the supercharger rotors through the gears. Upon releasing the pedal, a multi-disc brake had precisely the opposite effect to that when engaging the blower, stopping the supercharger drive and rotors instantly." As the blower engaged, "an almost demoniacal howl comes in...The rev counter and speedometer needles leap round their dials. There is perhaps no other car noise in the world so distinctive as that produced by the Mercedes supercharger...Flashing climbs are possible up considerable gradients—50 mph, for instance, on a 1 in 6½ hill, even though baulked by other traffic." The magazine's timed performance figures were astounding. From dead stop to 60 mph in this 2.5-ton beast took only 16.5 seconds; another 14 seconds and the 500K was doing 80. At 100 mph it had pretty much reached its limit, but this was a mind-boggling speed back in the 1930s. And as for acceleration, there was little else that could stay with it.

Equally noteworthy, the 500K had good handling despite its tremendous weight. "This car controls magnificently," said *The Autocar.* "Its very weight gives it a solidity that helps toward safe road holding, and the independent suspension... though extremely comfortable, does not permit any disturbing degree of roll or side sway... safe [cornering] limits are not easily discovered...There is a wonderfully firm 'feel' about the steering for absolutely accurate control when traveling very fast...3¼ turns of the wheel are needed from lock to lock. [The brakes] are oversensitive and can be too easily applied with extreme results."

The magazine also observed "a host of interesting details" that further placed this car in a class by itself: "The radiator is a fine piece of work, with the now very rare real honeycomb block. There are abutments under the running boards for a side jacking system." The test concluded with the opinion that "this is a master car for the very few. The sheer insolence of its great power affords an experience on its own."

An even more thrilling experience awaited in the 540K, introduced in 1936 as the 500K's successor. It was designed by Gustav Rohr, who took over for Hans Nibel in 1934—and who himself would pass away in 1937, leaving the engineering helm to Max Sailer and Max Wagner. Stroke on the Daimler-Benz straight eight went to 111mm (4.37 in.), bore remained as before. The result was 5401cc (329.5 cid), 115 bhp standard, and 180 bhp supercharged. *The Motor,*

Britain's other automotive weekly, tested this car in 1937, recording 0-60 mph in 15.5 seconds and a top speed of 160 mph, both astounding for the day.

Most 540Ks were fitted with coachbuilt bodies from Sindelfingen in the 380/500 styles. Only a handful were shipped to the U.S., where they sold for about $12,000 apiece. That was close to double the price of a Packard Twelve or a Cadillac V-16, and a king's ransom in 1936 dollars—perhaps equivalent to the cost of one and a half Rolls-Royce Camargues today. A very few 540Ks were fitted with custom bodies. One of these, a roadster by Erdmann & Rossi of Berlin, was tested by

Don Vorderman for *Automobile Quarterly* during 1970. "The car runs as well as it looks," he wrote. "By modern standards the 540K's performance is not very startling. But one should really bear in mind that they were not meant to be high-performance cars. Their best feature was a sense of style, even flamboyance—both curiously un-German characteristics—that set them apart from anything else on the road in the Thirties...My most

Below: the Type 380K was the first of the legendary supercharged sports touring Mercedes of the prewar era. Shown here is the very rare sedan model. Bottom: more powerful Type 500K arrived in 1934. Cabriolet A shown was one of many bodies offered.

memorable impression of the car, apart from its glorious looks, was one of enormous strength and rigidity—two qualities, by the way, that you can also find in any modern Mercedes. Some people, it seems, do build them the way they used to..."

The big Ks have their critics, of course. A variety of adjectives have been used to describe them, including over-engineered, overrated, decadent, effeminate and "Goeringesque." Writing in *Car Classics* magazine, Karl Ludvigsen quoted the preeminent English collector E.L. Mayer: "...they seem to my mind rather too 'gentlemanly' and not so ultra Mercedes as the [SS and SSK.] The independent springing of the wheels is very fine on bad roads. I had a short run in one

Stunningly beautiful streamlined Special Roadster body was offered in both 500K (below left) and 540K (below right) series. Style dates from 1936-37, and commands sky-high prices at auctions today. Bottom left: the 1936 540K in its more sober Cabriolet B form. Bottom right: also from '36, the 540K Cabriolet A two-seater.

of the first to come over, with Herr Neubauer driving, and he put the nearside front wheel on and off the pavement in a quiet street to show how good the springing was."

How has history treated the 380/500/540K? Ludvigsen's description is most apt: "As we see them from a later perspective...they display a glorious flamboyance of shape and style that has never been equalled. The recipe...has many ingredients. One was that the chassis, so modern in other respects, kept an engine position well to the rear. This let the radiator remain nestled well back between the front wheels, contributing to the classic look. Another was the evolution at Sindelfingen of a rhythmically curving and sweeping fender line that was simultaneously sporty and elegant. Yet another ingredient was bold use of chrome for flash and fittings that always seemed to accent the basic shape in an effective way. During the 1930s others sought to ape the extravagant glories of these cars, but none

came close. The few that were made, including 406 540Ks, are the royal peacocks of the cars of their day."

Royal peacocks would be seen again from Mercedes in the 300S and the fabulous 300SL. After the war, Fritz Nallinger, who had spent the early '40s in the aircraft division, replaced Max Sailer as technical director, while Max Wagner was in charge of passenger-car designs. Nallinger would continue to be one of the great technical forces at Untertürkheim in the '50s.

But, great as they were, the 300S and 300SL clearly belonged to the postwar era. World War II brought an end to many fine things, and among these were the larger-than-life Superclassics: Stutz, Duesenberg, and these great Deutschlanders. Those who never knew them should be glad there are still a few around to admire, a few that occasionally bellow their own kind of Wagnerian song through the rotors of wide-open superchargers. For we will never see their like again—from Daimler-Benz or anywhere else.

MERCEDES-BENZ ENGINEERING: PIONEERING THE SUPERCHARGER

Below: superb engineering made the 1928-32 Model SS/SSK 7.1-liter supercharged straight six amazingly powerful for its day. Left: the 1928 Model SS standard tourer.

At the halfway point of the 1930 Le Mans 24 Hours, a lone Mercedes-Benz SSK driven by Rudolf Caracciola and Christian Werner had built up a comfortable lead over the raucous Alfa Romeos and the steady Bentleys. After a pit stop for fresh fuel and a tire change, the Mercedes refused to start. According to team manager Alfred Neubauer, the generator had failed during the night. Now the battery was flat, and putting in a new one—unless it had been carried in the car since the start of the race—would mean immediate disqualification. Push-starting was also against the rules. There was no legal way to get the white giant back in the race. The valiant challenge by Mercedes-Benz had failed, its supercharged 7.1-liter engine paralyzed for want of electric power.

Such failures were few in the competition history of the SSK, as indeed it was for its part-time stablemates, the S and SS. They were usually triumphant wherever they ran.

The Model S made its racing debut in the inaugural event on the new Nürburgring circuit in June 1927. This was a true road course, conceived as a dual-purpose project to alleviate unemployment and to stimulate tourist business in the nearby Eifel mountains. Two of the new Sports were entered, one for Rudolf Caracciola, the other entrusted to Adolf Rosenberger, and they finished first and second in the sports car class. Caracciola's average speed was 62.82 mph—considerably faster than Christian Werner's 2.0-liter supercharged straight-eight Mercedes (built in 1925) that won the racing class. With the same drivers and others, the S quickly proceeded to score a number of hillclimb victories, such as the Klausenpass, Semmering, and Freiburg-Schauinsland.

The first outing for the SS also came at the Nürburgring, in the sports car category of the German Grand Prix in July 1928. Three cars were entered, and they took the top three places. Caracciola also won the Irish Tourist Trophy with an SS in 1929. Perhaps the most memorable drive of all came in 1931, when Caracciola and Sebastian in their specially prepared SSKL romped home to an overall win in the gruelling Mille Miglia.

As stated previously, the engines in all these cars were related, as they stemmed from a common base. Their origin deserves to be examined at some length, since it involved major changes in engineering philosophy at Untertürkheim. The starting point for the technology that blossomed in the mid-'20s was the Mercedes 28/95 of 1914. There was no Benz ingredient in it at all.

Although derived from an aircraft engine, the 28/95 unit was a slow-running, long-stroke powerplant with an understrength four-bearing crankshaft. The engine and the car it powered had been designed under the direction of Paul Daimler, son of the company founder. This was after he returned from Austro-Daimler and was named technical director to succeed Wilhelm Maybach, who resigned and moved to Friedrichshafen to design engines for Count Zeppelin's airships. Paul Daimler was an innovator in many ways. He had steered Mercedes from chain drive to shaft drive, and had adopted the Knight sleeve-valve engine design for a number of models as early as 1910. He also introduced the worm-and-peg steering gear, with a hollow steering column, in 1908, and invented the double-cone clutch that became typical of Mercedes cars beginning in 1910. He simplified driving controls, and ceaselessly improved the honeycomb radiator, engine lubrication system, wheel construction, springs, and shock absorbers.

In 1913, Daimler Motor Works fielded a Mercedes team for Le Mans—not the 24-hour race, but a Grand Prix of much shorter duration. These cars were powered by six-cylinder, 90-bhp, 7.3-liter (445-cid) engines originally designed for aircraft use, the DF80. Among its notable features were an overhead camshaft driven by a vertical shaft and skew gears at the rear of the engine, crossflow cylinder head with splayed valves, individually cast cylinders with integral heads and welded-on water jackets, and two-piece cast aluminum crankcase. This design was chosen as the basis for a new six-cylinder powerplant destined for a high-performance touring car to replace the four-cylinder 37/90 that had been around since 1910.

This new 28/95 engine closely followed the DF80 valve arrangement and camshaft drive, but differed in having the cylinders cast in pairs. Cylinder heads remained non-detachable, and water jackets were still welded on. With a 105mm (4.13-in.) bore and 140mm (5.51-in.) stroke, displacement totaled 7250cc (precisely 442.25 cid), and maximum output was rated at 95 bhp at 1800 rpm. The 28/95 came on the market in 1914—just in time for World War I. Though production was resumed after the war in 1919, the car was, for a variety of reasons, outmoded by 1921.

Paul Daimler had won universal acclaim for the Grand Prix racer that won at Dieppe in 1908 and the 4.5-liter (274-cid) four-cylinder car, built on aircraft-engine principles, that won at Lyon in 1914. But his greatest fame lay ahead with the advent of the supercharged Mercedes engines. His first supercharger arrangement consisted of a gear on the flywheel driving a Roots-type blower shaft via a multi-disc clutch that permitted engagement and disengagement at will. This system had been proven on Daimler aircraft engines, where it had been used since 1915 to compensate for power losses at high altitudes. The first supercharged auto engine was road tested in October 1919. By 1922, it had developed into the production 10/40/65, a 2.6-liter (158.5-cid) four-cylinder unit of 80mm (3.15-in.) bore and 130mm (5.12-in.) stroke. Architecturally, it was quite similar to the 28/95 six. In the meantime, Paul Daimler had adapted the Roots compressor to the 28/95 engine, raising maximum output to 120 bhp. It was never installed in a production model, but it did help Mercedes return to international racing in May 1921 at the Targa

Florio. There, Max Sailer drove a prewar 28/95 equipped with the new supercharged unit to second place behind Count Giulio Masetti in a Fiat. Sailer also won that year's Coppa Florio with a blown 28/95. Sailer, who hailed from Esslingen, had been an engineer with *Daimler Motoren Gesellschaft* for three years beginning in 1902, returning in 1910 after nearly five years with the Dixi Company, later to become BMW.

Below: exposed SS/SSK chassis shows strong, heavyweight construction and "front/mid-engine" layout. Note kicked-up rear frame rails. Bottom: the romantic 1928 Model SS roadster.

During the winter of 1921-22, Paul Daimler also supercharged the 1.5-liter (91-cid) 6/25/40 engine, which did find its way into a production model the following spring. Two of these in racing trim were entered for the 1922 Targa Florio, but the results were mediocre. The next year, displacement was increased to 2.0 liters (121.5 cid), but the car remained an also-ran. Even the 2.6-liter 10/40/65 did not take the world by storm. Supercharging had thus failed, so far, to do its job.

On the last day of 1922, Paul Daimler resigned, and signed up with Horch of Zwickau in Saxony as technical manager.

(That firm never produced a supercharged model in the time he worked there.) Before leaving, however, he had prepared a new supercharged four-cylinder Grand Prix car of 2.0-liter displacement, and even laid out an eight-cylinder supercharged racing unit of the same capacity. His successor was charged with developing both engines into race winners. That man was a young Austrian engineer, Ferdinand Porsche. He had succeeded Paul Daimler once before, at Austro-Daimler in 1906. Now, 17 years later, he followed him again to Stuttgart.

Porsche went to work on April 30, 1923. Although just 48, an age considered quite young for an engineer, he had already accumulated a great deal of experience. That included designs for a number of Austro-Daimler aircraft engines in 1910-17 and the very advanced Prinz Heinrich trials car of 1910, with an overhead-cam engine delivering 86 bhp at 2700 rpm from 5.7 liters (349 cid).

The production-car line Porsche inherited had serious weaknesses, but Paul Daimler's racing engines were masterpieces. The 2.0-liter four had a 70mm (2.76-in.) bore and 129mm (5.08-in.) stroke, following the long-stroke fashion of the period practiced by Bugatti and Alfa Romeo. There were four valves per cylinder, tilted at an included angle of 60 degrees and operated by dual overhead camshafts. The exhaust valve stems were mercury-filled, probably the first application of cooled valves. Both camshafts were driven by spur and bevel gears from a vertical shaft at the flywheel end. Cylinders were individual machined forgings, with integrated heads and sheetmetal water jackets welded on. The crankcase was a very large aluminum casting, bolted to the lower end of the block. The crankshaft was a built-up structure running in three roller

bearings. Connecting rods were steel forgings with roller-type big-end bearings. The supercharger was mounted vertically at the front of the engine, driven at 1.78 times crankshaft speed via the multi-disc clutch and bevel gears, and engaged on kickdown as on earlier models. Compressed air was forced through an updraft two-barrel carburetor.

Three 2.0-liter supercharged racers were sent to Indianapolis in 1923, but they did not do well. They were down on power—only 110 bhp at 4500 rpm—and suffered from insufficient testing for the particular conditions of the 500-mile race. By the end of the year, however, Porsche had pushed output up to 120 bhp at 4500 rpm.

The 1924 racing season opened with two major events. The Königsaal-Jilowischt hillclimb outside Prague was then no less important than the Targa Florio. The latter would take place on the new Madonie circuit, four laps of a 67-mile road course zigzagging through some of the most savage hill country in Europe. Since the contests were staged just one week apart, there was no time to get the cars from Prague down to Sicily, so the Mercedes team had to be split up. Otto Salzer and Otto Merz went to Czechoslovakia, while Porsche accompanied

Above: D-B's first move toward a sports car was the 1926-27 Model K (sports touring shown). Opposite page: though shorter, Model K chassis was still too heavy and unwieldy.

Christian Werner, Christian Lautenschlager, and Alfred Neubauer to Sicily. Salzer won the hillclimb, with Merz second, while Werner beat the Fiat, Alfa Romeo, and Peugeot teams in the road race, Lautenschlager finishing 10th and Neubauer 15th. Werner's time was 6 hours, 32 minutes, 37.4 seconds, for an average speed of 66.018 km/h. In recognition of these twin victories, the Technical University of Vienna rushed to confer an honorary doctor's degree on Ferdinand Porsche, blithely ignoring Paul Daimler's contribution. But the worth of supercharging had now been thoroughly established, and the *kompressor* became an indispensable part of all Grand Prix racing cars up to 1950.

On his return from Sicily, Porsche began development work on the supercharged straight eight. It made its first appearance in the 1924 Italian Grand Prix at Monza, but instead of running away from the red cars of Portello, the Mercedes entries were roundly beaten by the Alfa Romeo team. However, the defeat was due more to insufficient testing than

faulty design. In architecture and construction the new eight was similar to the blown four in most respects, such as use of individual steel cylinders with non-detachable heads, twin overhead camshafts, and four valves per cylinder. The built-up crankshaft ran in nine roller bearings. One of the big differences was in cylinder dimensions, still undersquare but with the stroke much shorter at 82.9 mm (3.26 in.). Bore was also reduced, to 61.7mm (2.43 in.), sufficient for the desired displacement. Another vital difference was full-time engagement for the Roots blower. And instead of a vertical timing shaft, both camshafts were driven by a train of spur gears. Originally the blown eight delivered only 130 bhp, but Porsche managed to push it up to 150 bhp and, finally, to 165.

Mercedes raced both four- and eight-cylinder cars in 1925 and 1926. The greatest success for the latter came at Avus in July 1926, when Caracciola won the sports car class in the German Grand Prix.

One of Porsche's first assignments in Stuttgart was a new family of powerful six-cylinder touring cars. He was assisted mainly by Otto Kohler, who had worked with him at Austro-Daimler. For this project the pair effectively ousted engine specialists Albert Heess and Otto Schilling. (Heess, who had joined the company under Gottlieb Daimler, would remain active in the engine design office until 1944, however.)

The lesser of Porsche's new creations was a 4.0-liter or 400 engine, a Roots-blown 15/70/100 with bore and stroke of 80 × 130mm (3.15 × 5.12 in.) giving 3920cc (239 cid) and maximum output of 100 bhp at 3100 rpm. The larger one was the 6.3-liter or 630 unit, also Roots-blown and rated at 24/100/140 with bore and stroke of 94 × 150mm (3.70 × 5.90 in.), 6240cc (381 cid), and maximum output of 140 bhp at 3000 rpm. Both engines were of similar construction, size being the principal difference. Both had a single overhead camshaft resting on four bearings and driven by a vertical shaft with skew gears. In this, Porsche followed Paul Daimler (the single overhead camshaft on the big Porsche-designed Austro-Daimler engines was driven by a train of helical gears). Two valves per cylinder stood vertically in line with the cylinder axis. They were opened by finger-type followers and closed by double coil springs. The cylinder blocks were huge one-piece aluminum castings with wet cast-iron liners. The cylinder head was detachable, thus bringing head gaskets to Untertürkheim, and was also a single piece of cast iron. Both engines used a compression ratio of 4.7:1. Crankshafts were made of chrome-nickel steel, and ran in four main bearings fitted with bronze-backed shells. Connecting rods were tubular with plain big-end bearings. The main oil pump was gear-driven from the vertical timing shaft, which assured pressurized circulation throughout the engine. The block contained a separate reservoir for a fresh oil supply, which was metered as needed by a tiny piston-type pump and was intended to keep oil level in the sump more or less constant.

The compressor on both power units was located on the lower right side. Again, it was driven from the front of the crankshaft via a multi-disc coupling that engaged on demand by throttle kickdown or disengaged on releasing the pedal. Also as before, the Roots supercharger contained a pair of two-lobe rotors. At the time, there were no specialist producers offering blowers "off the shelf," so Daimler had to build its own.

The company also produced its own special carburetors. These were designed to work under pressure, as Paul Daimler had chosen to mount the carburetor downstream of the blower. At the time, virtually all other supercharging applications favored the carburetor positioned upstream of the blower, which would then be compressing an air/fuel mixture instead of pure air. Daimler Motor Works took out many patents on its pressure-carburetor, and carefully guarded those details that weren't patentable so as to preserve what management saw as a technological lead over the competition. In a way this was curious. Though we do not know why Paul Daimler chose this arrangement, it became apparent by about 1935 that it simply wasn't as effective as the best of the "upstream" layouts. And nobody ever tried to copy the Daimler setup, other engineers feeling they obtained better results.

The 630 engine was enormous, about 58 inches long, and it must have weighed over half a ton. The naked Model 24/100/140 chassis it powered weighed 3418 pounds. These were hardly ideal starting points for a high-performance machine— which makes the achievements

of the cars built around them even more amazing.

Fast touring cars had always been Mercedes' stock in trade, but since the demise of the 28/95 in 1924 the lineup had lacked a worthy replacement. Also, makes like Audi, Horch, Maybach, and Stoewer were beginning to challenge Mercedes in this class. It was now up to Dr. Porsche to stave off the threat.

His first steps were to shorten the Model 24/100/140 chassis and to find more horsepower. The result was the Model K ("short") introduced in 1926 as a Mercedes (not a Mercedes-Benz). Chassis weight was pared to 3153 pounds. Compression ratio was bumped to 5.0:1, which increased maximum output to 110 bhp at 2800 rpm without the blower or 160 bhp with the blower engaged. Thus the K was rated a 24/110/160. An important change was made in the cylinder head so as to allow the use of two spark plugs per cylinder, one fired by magneto ignition, the other by coil and contact breaker.

The Model K was equipped with the same four-speed gearbox specified for the basic 24/100/140, but final drive ratios were numerically lowered to reduce engine revs in relation to road speed. The three available ratios were 3.50:1; 3.28:1; and 3.00:1. In all cases, top speed was about 93 mph.

In all, the Model K was an admirable touring car, but with its strangely tall stance and upright styling, both penalties of the chassis design, it was certainly no sports car.

But its successor most definitely was. It arrived in 1927 with the appropriate designation, Model S (Sport). A direct derivation of the K, this new Mercedes had impressively low construction and looked far more modern—and potent.

And indeed it was. Though the S engine was identical with the K unit, its bore was stretched out to 98mm (3.86 in.), which

raised displacement to 6789cc (414 cid). The Roots blower was gear-driven from the crankshaft and set to run at three times crank speed. Owners were advised to avoid long periods of running with the supercharger engaged, the factory suggesting 15-20 seconds as the practical limit. All this boosted maximum power to 120 bhp without blower, 180 bhp with blower, thus giving the S a 26/120/180 rating (the extra displacement also raised the taxable horsepower figure). A new close-ratio four-speed transmission was adopted, and final drive gearing was altered to permit considerably higher cruising speeds relative to rpm. The standard ratio was 2.76:1, though some cars were built with 2.5:1 and 3.08:1 gearing. Chassis weight for the S was reduced to 2867 pounds, and the roadster body was engineered for lightness. Top speed rose to 103 mph, with corresponding gains in standing-start acceleration.

The impact of the S on the racing world was tremendous, as we noted at the outset. During its competition career this model racked up 53 race victories plus 17 speed records, including a German national mark of 110.3 mph. It was never a high-volume item, of course. The most authoritative estimate puts the total at 149, all built in 1927-28.

At the end of 1928, Ferdinand Porsche left Daimler-Benz in a huff, and moved to Vienna to take over as chief engineer for Steyr. That lasted only 12 months, however. At the start of 1930 he returned to the Zuffenhausen district of Stuttgart and opened his own engineering consultant firm, thus beginning the Volkswagen saga that ultimately led to the cars bearing his name. As for his replacement at Untertürkheim, there was no need for a major search and no thought of going outside the company. The obvious choice was the former engineering director for Benz, Hans Nibel, who had worked as Porsche's second-in-command since 1926.

A Bohemian by birth, Nibel had studied engineering in Munich. He had joined Benz in 1904, and was named chief engineer four years later. His credentials were impressive and well-respected. They included the 200-bhp "Blitzen Benz" speed-record car of 1910, which held the world's record up to 1919. He had also been responsible for such fine touring cars as the 10/30 Type GR of 1912, the 27/70 Type E of 1923, and the 16/50 DS and DSS of 1924.

Dr. Porsche was still at the engineering helm when an even more formidable sporting Mercedes went into production in late 1928. This was the SS (Super Sport), basically a lighter version of the S (by some 66 pounds) packing a more powerful engine. Bore was taken out to 100mm (3.94 in.), which raised displacement to 7010cc (427 cid). Stroke remained at 150mm (5.12 in.). The blower, providing 8-psi boost, was shared with the S, but compression ratio was raised to 5.2:1, and there were larger

Below and bottom left: two distinct yet similar body treatments by Castagna on the SS chassis, circa 1929. Bottom right: SS had lighter chassis, more power than Model S.

valves and ports. Maximum output rose considerably, going to 110 bhp nominal and 200 bhp supercharged, both at 3300 rpm. Top speed took another jump, this time to 115 mph, and 0-60 mph acceleration improved to under 15 seconds.

The SS remained in production up to 1933, but very few were constructed after the end of 1929. Total production is estimated at only 109 cars.

An even hairier development was the SSK, a short-wheelbase derivative of the SS that arrived with it in 1928. As with the 1926 Model K, the letter denoted *kurz* (short). Its chassis was lighter still, 2680 pounds compared with the 2800-pound

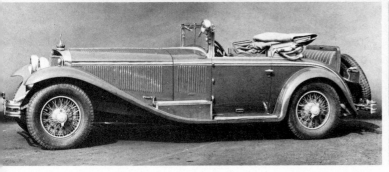

SS frame. Mainly due to the use of a bigger blower delivering 10-psi boost, the SSK engine was somewhat more powerful. It was rated at 27/170/225, meaning that with the blower engaged it put out 225 bhp (at 3200-3300 rpm), good for a sizzling 120-mph top speed.

The SSK enjoyed a brilliant competition career. Caracciola scored its first victory in August 1928 by winning the Gabelbach hillclimb. Then he repeated the Model S wins at Freiburg and Semmering with the SSK. In 1930, he won the Irish Grand Prix at the wheel of an SSK against a lot of open-wheel racers.

On the track and open road alike, the SSK was truly a supercar. Britain's automotive weekly *The Motor* published a test report in its issue of June 16, 1931. The results—a timed top speed of 103.2 mph and 0-90 mph acceleration of 45 seconds—fell somewhat short of expectations. Considering the state of the art in the early '30s, the magazine's editors must have expected a great deal, for such performance was virtually unequalled by any other car in the world. The number of SSKs built is estimated at 31, all constructed from 1928 to 1931.

It was in 1931 that a lightweight SSK made its appearance, not as a production item but as a special reserved for the factory racing team. Only six of these cars, known as the SSKL, are said to have existed. The L stood for *leicht* (light),

because the frame and many other components were drilled to remove excess metal. Chassis weight accordingly went down to about 2640 pounds. At the same time, horsepower went up. The major modification was adoption of an "elephant" compressor delivering 12-psi boost, but the SSKL also boasted lighter crankshaft and flywheel, special valves, high-lift camshaft, and high-compression pistons. The factory recommended using a 50/50 mixture of gasoline and benzole to avoid local overheating in the cylinder head. Maximum output with the blower engaged soared to 300 bhp at 3300 rpm.

One measure of the SSKL's performance was provided much later, in November 1960 by *Road & Track* magazine. Geared with a 2.76:1 axle, the subject car's top speed was about 120 mph. Out of deference to the car's age, acceleration figures were calculated on the basis of power/weight ratio. The magazine came up with 9.5 seconds for the 0-60 mph test, 41 seconds from rest to 100 mph. Even 25 years later those numbers still look good. A special streamlined single-seater was built on an SSKL chassis in 1931 for Manfred von Brauchitsch to drive at Avus. It was by far the fastest car present, completing the race at an average speed of 121.6 mph. And its top speed was not far short of 150 mph.

Speedy and sensuous, rare and nearly unattainable by mere

Above left and right: the bare 1928 SSK chassis was as hefty as it looked despite weight and size reductions over the previous S and SS.

mortals, all these Mercedes-Benz Sport models—from S to SSKL—were among the most glamorous machines of their era. But the fact is that their basic engineering represented something of a dead end by the early '30s—not to mention their tiny niche in the market. As competition cars their performance would be bettered by the W25 *monoposto* and its developments from 1934 on. As road cars they had no direct successors; that would have been difficult at best. Besides, there was really no longer any place for such rarified beasts in the chaotic, poverty-stricken Germany of the early Depression years. Also, there was the need for Daimler-Benz to trim its production costs to meet the new economic realities, and the Sport models were a luxury the company could no longer afford.

Ferdinand Porsche, as we have pointed out, was above all an engine man. That fact is not obvious if you only consider his five years with Daimler-Benz, though it is when you look at the later Auto Union V-16 racers and, of course, the air-cooled Volkswagen. This was not true of Hans Nibel. Of course, he had designed engines and the cars built around them as technical director at Benz, but engines were not his main interest. At least, they were no longer what he concentrated on, if they ever had been. In the late 1920s, Nibel began devoting himself very deeply to chassis studies, and designed a variety of independent front and rear suspension systems. While he did keep an eye on engine development after he succeeded Dr. Porsche, he generally left the task of working out details to his assistants, and often bowed to economic pressure when management had to decide whether to build a new engine or continue with an old one. New engines in the Nibel period tended to be low-budget projects anyway, making maximum use of tooling and components with existing units.

If this doesn't exactly sound like a formula for great and exciting cars, then consider the 540K. Though it did not begin a new era in design and engineering, it was definitely the culmination of one. If the separate Daimler and Benz models had established a reputation to live up to, then it was the first products of the new

Below: a look at the intake side of the supercharged SS/SSK six. With blower engaged, maximum output was 200-225 bhp DIN, good for 110-120 mph.

combined company that had to maintain and extend it. By the time the 540K appeared, Mercedes-Benz was firmly established as one of the world's most respected marques.

It all began in 1926 with two new mid-range models, the 200 Stuttgart and the 300 Mannheim. The former was comparable with the contemporary Dodge, the latter with Oldsmobile in size, price, and buyer appeal. Overall responsibility for these cars rested with Dr. Porsche, but their engines really originated with Benz. These side-valve sixes really reflected U.S. thinking rather than the state of the art in the Benz drawing office. One reason American cars tended to have simple engineering like this was the concern with profitable mass production. Benz, on the other hand, knew it would never build engines in such high volume, but liked the L-head layout for its relatively quiet valvegear and its easier maintenance requirements for jobs like valve grinding.

The 200 and 300 engines were an identical design realized in two sizes. In America they would have been a production engineer's nightmare. They had different bores (65 vs. 74mm/ 2.56 vs 2.91 in.), so they could

not share pistons, rings, or valves. Because of different strokes (100 vs. 115mm/3.94 vs 4.53 in.), they could not share crankshafts. The blocks also employed dissimilar cylinder spacing and bearing width, leading to different manifolds and cylinder heads. Both had a 5.0:1 compression ratio, but the 200 crankshaft ran in seven main bearings while the 300 was carried in four mains only. The Stuttgart unit delivered 38 bhp at 3200 rpm, the Mannheim 55 bhp at 3500 rpm, figures that suggest that working parts were subjected to only very light stress. No doubt this was intentional in the interest of longevity.

Two years later, in 1928, the 3.0-liter unit became a 3.5, the cars it powered still called Mannheim. This was not just a bore job, as retention of the 115mm (4.53-in.) stroke would indicate, but a brand-new design with a seven-main-bearing crankshaft. In fact, it was a six-cylinder version of the straight eight developed for the Nürburg 460, a prestige model intended to fill in for the defunct Benz 27/70 E-Type.

The Nürburg eight had the same cylinder dimensions as the 350 Mannheim unit. Displacement was 4592cc (280

cid) and, on a 5.0:1 compression ratio, maximum output was 80 bhp at 3200 rpm. The chassis weighed a hefty 3275 pounds, and with formal sedan bodywork the car tipped the scales at a portly 4410 pounds. Not surprisingly, the Nürburg 460 could run no faster than 68 mph. This was pitiful performance for a car that had the majestic good looks of a Cadillac or a Marmon, so in 1930 the eight was bored out to 82.5mm (3.25 in.) for 4918cc (300 cid). At the same time, compression was raised to 5.75:1, and maximum output for the renamed 500 Nürburg climbed to 110 bhp at 3200 rpm. Top speed went to 77.5 mph, still not enough against many lighter, smaller-displacement rivals.

The 630 series evolved into the magnificent and costly Mercedes-Benz Sports models, but the new Daimler-Benz concern still lacked a serious prestige car leaving Maybach and Horch to till that field. The 500 Nürburg was not a contender. Ferdinand Porsche had made plans for something he called the *Grosser* Mercedes, but the task of finishing them fell to Hans Nibel. The result was the Type 770, introduced in 1930 with a giant-size straight eight featuring pushrod-operated overhead valves. This engine had nothing whatever in common with the 7.1-liter SS/SSK overhead cam sixes, which were Daimler contributions, but rather was another Benz inspiration. Its gear-driven camshaft was located low in the side of the block, just as on the flathead engines, so the big differences were the pushrod galleries and the new cylinder head with its rocker-arm shaft above the valves. With a 95×135mm (3.74×5.31-in.) bore and stroke, displacement was an enormous 7655 cc (466 cid). And just to make sure the car had adequate power, Nibel added a supercharger blowing through twin Daimler pressure carburetors. Compression ratio

was held at 5.5:1, which resulted in 150 bhp nominal/200 bhp supercharged, both developed at 2800 rpm. It all worked: the 770 had a top speed of 100 mph, remarkable for a car of its leviathan proportions.

Once engine production began to be coordinated following the Daimler-Benz merger, a lot of juggling in cylinder dimensions was made in the Benz-generation blocks. Thus, the 3.5-liter Mannheim six was bored out to 82.5mm, which matched the tooling setup for the 500 Nürburg, and became the 370 Mannheim. In 1931 a 370S Mannheim Sport series appeared with coachwork reminiscent of the earlier S/SS. These cars had a truly modern chassis and an even lower, more rakish stance, but they did not live up to their looks. There was only 75 bhp on tap, so top speed was limited to 75 mph. But they were lovely cars, and important as a stepping stone to the 540K.

The first of the supercharged Mercedes-Benz sports tourers was unveiled in 1933. This was the 380K, powered by a new engine that was sort of a scaled-down *Grosser*. Bore and stroke of this straight eight were 79×100mm (3.07×3.94 in.), giving swept volume of 3822 cc (233 cid). (Incidentally, the same bore and stroke appeared on the Type 290 side-valve six that same year, further proof that engines were at last being sorted out.) Other features were a gear-driven camshaft in the side of the block, roller tappets (as on the 770), and 6.0:1 compression. Maximum output was 90 bhp nominal/120 bhp supercharged, and the typical 380K was good for 87 mph. It turned out to be only an interim measure, however; no more than 134 examples were built before the model was discontinued in 1934.

Hans Nibel died suddenly that year, at age 54, felled by a stroke. This time, Daimler-Benz managers refused to promote from within. Instead, they hired 40-year-old Hans Gustav Rohr,

the brilliant chief engineer at Adler, which had recently introduced two exciting front-wheel-drive cars. Foremost among his lieutenants were Max Sailer and Fritz Nallinger. This team not only completed the product-renewal cycle left unfinished by Nibel, but also expanded research activities and explored the technical feasibilities of mid- and rear-mounted engines as well as front-wheel drive. Tragically, Rohr died of lung inflammation just three years later, in 1937. Now, D-B chairman Wilhelm Kissel insisted Sailer be appointed technical director, a post he would occupy through 1939. Sailer's imprint was found on many cars of earlier times but, paradoxically, his influence waned because of added responsibilities. So it was mainly Nallinger's ideas that marked the last of the prewar models.

Nallinger was the son of a longtime Benz executive, and received his engineering diploma from the Karlsruhe Polytechnic Institute in 1922. Later that year he joined Benz, and in 1924 went on loan to Daimler in Untertürkheim, where Dr. Porsche made him head of the experimental department four years later. He was Nibel's closest assistant during his tenure, and would become chief engineer after World War II.

The short-lived 380K sired the fabled 500K in 1934 and the 540K two years later. The 540K was not a replacement for the 500K, as they continued as companion models up to 1939. Their production figures are totally overshadowed by their fame: only 760 in all were made. Both were powered by overhead valve straight eights with Roots blowers, and shared the same roller-tappet arrangement and blower drive, the latter featuring on-demand operation via a coupling with no fewer than 70 discs.

Bore and stroke of the 500K were 86×108mm (3.39×4.25 in.), for 5020cc (306 cid).

Compression ratio was 6.0:1. Without the blower, maximum output was rated at 100 bhp at 3400 rpm. With the blower working, it was no less than 160 bhp. A 4.88:1 final drive ratio was specified, giving a top speed of 100 mph. The 540K engine used the 5.0-liter block bored out to 88mm (3.46 in.), and had a new crankshaft with a longer throw to lengthen stroke to 111mm (4.37 in.). Displacement thus worked out to 5401cc (329 cid). Maximum output was 115 bhp at 3300 rpm or 180 bhp at the same crankshaft speed with the blower engaged. Top speed was 110-112 mph.

Both these sterling supercharged Mercedes certainly had enough performance to become eminent racing machines. *The Autocar*, for example, tested a 540K at the Brooklands circuit in England in 1938, and recorded 0-60 mph acceleration of 15 seconds—not SSKL swiftness, but still quite fast for the late 1930s. But the 500/540K never made it to competition. Like their illustrious S-series forebears, they were meant more for high-speed touring than hillclimbs and circuit races—touring with flamboyant, almost arrogant style.

The 1936-39 Type 540K used these underpinnings, designed largely by Fritz Nallinger. Note outsize twin rear coil springs.

In fact, they were the sort of cars that suited the style of one Adolf Hitler, arrogant beyond words but an automotive aficionado—and one in a position to create roads for them. The world's first superhighways, the *Autobahnen*, were one way Hitler intended to demonstrate German superiority in everything. That included racing, of course, and Daimler-Benz was his chosen standard-bearer. Backed by a continuing flow of government funds in the '30s, the company produced a juggernaut that would dominate Grand Prix racing as no other single team had ever done. It's an amazing story, and it's told in the next chapter.

MERCEDES-BENZ
IN COMPETITION 1900~1939:
THE GLORY YEARS

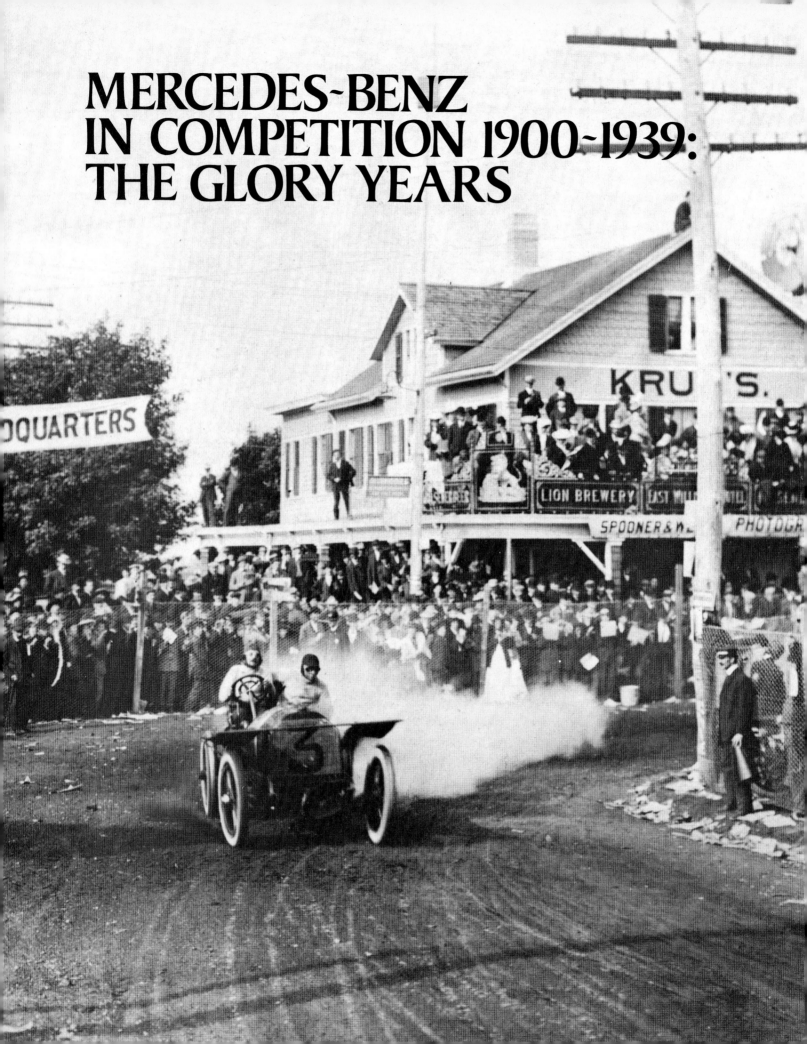

Even with the aid of contemporary photographs it is hard to imagine what automobile racing was like before World War II. The sport had a special, vital intensity in those days: the cars were much different, of course, and their drivers were prominently visible, manhandling them through the chicanes of the 'Ring, down the long straights at Tripoli, through the darkness of Le Mans, and around the vast saucers of Brooklands and Indy.

Today it's all so different. There is disagreement about when the sport began to change; some say the late '50s, others the 1960s. But there is no doubt the changes came with a rush. Today, writes William Boddy, racing is "such a money-grabbing, professional business that most of the light-heartedness has vanished from it. Now it's all a matter of clinching the sponsorship, insuring that safety factors are observed, and traveling like the jet set from one circuit to another...a purely professional rat-race, tough, intense." But before the war, Boddy says, while motor racing "was the fastest, most demanding and most dangerous sport of them all, it was also *fun.*"

Both Daimler and Benz stepped into this now-vanished milieu early on. For example, Emile Roger, the Benz agent in France, entered a belt-driven car in the Paris-Rouen Trials of 1894, and the marque scored high in the Chicago *Times-Herald* competition in 1895. The 8.0- and 9.0-liter twin-ignition cars, the favorites of Prince Henry of Prussia, ran spectacularly in 1907, winning the Herkomer Trophy in their first season and finishing 2-3 in the Coppa Florio.

The Benz company itself become seriously involved in racing in 1908. That year, Victor Héméry, its contract driver, won the grueling 440-mile Moscow-St. Petersburg road race. Héméry was also runner-up in

the Savannah Grand Prize race at 64.9 mph in a Grand Prix Benz. The monster 21.5-liter, 200-bhp "Blitzen Benz" was capable of well over 100 mph, and Héméry ran one in the flying kilometer at Brooklands at over 125 mph.

Cigar-chomping Barney Oldfield bettered this mark with 131.72 mph in 1910, and two 150-bhp cars romped home 1-2 at Savannah the same year. Benz also produced an advanced 7271cc (444-cid) racer with 16 overhead valves and radical streamlining for the Prince Henry trials—and it was a good 5 mph faster than the winning Austro-Daimlers. Before World War I, Hornsted's Blitzen Benz held the world standing-start kilometer record at 73.47 mph, while Bob Burman's Blitzen ran an unofficial flying-start mile of 140 mph at Daytona in 1911.

Benz's last Grand Prix effort as an independent came in 1923 with a rear-engine car designed by Dr. Edmund Rumpler and powered by a 2.0-liter twincam six. Packing 80 bhp, this was the famous *Tropfenwagen* or

"teardrop" car, with four-wheel brakes (mounted inboard at the rear) and swing-axle rear suspension. It appeared only once in a GP, scoring fourth and fifth place finishes at Monza, before quietly disappearing from the scene. But the Blitzen was still being heard from long after the Daimler-Benz merger: Cyril Paul lapped one around Brooklands at 115.82 mph in 1930, some two decades after the car had first taken to the tracks!

Daimler had been active, too. In 1901, the 35-bhp Mercedes, the first car to bear the name, won a 244-mile round-robin race between Nice and Salon in France. This was followed by a win at the La Turbie hillclimb. A 60-bhp racer driven by Camille Jenatzy won the 1903 Gordon Bennett Trophy event. Other models of that type, including a 9.2-liter (561-cid) four with 65

Opposite page: Camille Jenatzy and his racing Mercedes in the 1906 Vanderbilt Cup. This page, below: Barney Oldfield in the Blitzen Benz at Ormond Beach, 1910. Bottom: Benz GP car at 1910 Savannah Grand Prize.

bhp, were victorious the next year at Nice and La Turbie, as well as in the Semmering mountain contest in Austria. Technically formidable but less successful was the derivative 120-bhp 14-liter (854-cid) Mercedes. It won a Belgian closed-circuit race in 1905 and broke the Semmering mountain record, though it proved disappointing in the Gordon Bennett contest. However, a heroically engined 12.8-liter (781-cid) version proved unstoppable at the 1908 French Grand Prix.

After these early forays, Daimler took a leave of absence

before World War I, they finished 1-2-3 at the Lyons Grand Prix. In 1915 they were victorious at Indianapolis, and were capable of winning a world-class event postwar, Sicily's Targa Florio, in 1922.

Aircraft engine experience greatly influenced Daimler engineers in the design of the Le Mans and GP cars, as it would during the 1920s and 1930s. The centrifugal supercharger—in simple terms, an engine-driven compressor that forces a high-pressure mixture into the cylinders—had its origins at Daimler in the engines that powered the Kaiser's *Luftwaffe*.

supercharging formula was rigidly followed: a twin-rotor Roots blower mounted ahead of the engine. Incidentally, the Roots name stemmed from Philander H. and Francis H. Roots, who perfected the design in pumps long before superchargers per se were ever heard of, although somebody in England had had the same idea before, in 1848. The brothers had simply discovered that a pump would have greater internal volume if its gears had most of their teeth removed, were shaped for close mating, and were synchronized by external gearing. The concept

from competition. It did not return until 1913, when an aero-engined chain-drive car was entered at Le Mans. It was both the last chain-drive Mercedes racer and the first to bear the now-legendary V-shaped honeycomb radiator, and the two-car team took fourth and sixth places. For 1914 the factory fielded its now-classic Grand Prix cars: four cylinders, single overhead cam, four inclined overhead valves, three spark plugs per cylinder, twin Bosch magnetos. On displacement of 4483cc (273.6 cid) from 93×165 mm (3.66×6.49 in.) dimensions, these mighty fours developed 115 bhp at 3200 rpm. In the final year

As planes began to fly higher, the blower provided the necessary extra performance. Thus, it was natural for Daimler to apply supercharging to competition cars after the war.

Everybody else did, too. In fact, it was the only way to go. Except where they were banned, supercharged cars won all but one of the major international events from 1924 through 1939. The governing bodies that made the rules did not distinguish between blown and unblown cars as far as displacement was concerned until 1938—and the blown cars could beat their normally aspirated foes every time.

Once established, Daimler's

Though Jenatzy's 1906 Vanderbilt drive came in the twilight of his career, he managed to place fifth in the event with this Mercedes.

translated easily from gas and liquid pumps to superchargers.

The car that bridged Daimler's racing efforts before and after World War I was the Mercedes 28/95, a production model based almost entirely on the 1913 Le Mans car. As noted in the previous chapter, its 7.25-liter ohc six was virtually identical with the DF80 aircraft engine. Max Sailer, then one of the best drivers in Germany and later one of D-B's leading engineers, built a sports racer on the 28/95 chassis that was good enough to place second in the 1921 Targa

Florio. It was this showing that got *Daimler Motoren Gesellschaft* interested again in racing.

The next step on the path to racing greatness appeared at the Berlin Auto Show in late 1921. This was the 1922 Model 10/40, powered by a 2.6-liter aircraft-based engine that, before it entered production, acquired a supercharger to become the 10/40/65. A year later it was joined by the 1.6-liter 6/25/40,

Below left and right: the highly successful 1908 Mercedes GP car, photographed at Indianapolis in 1983. Car packed 150 horsepower from a huge 12.78-liter four.

Another racing venture was doomed to failure: the Indianapolis 500. Daimler thought a victory here would promote sales of Mercedes cars in North America. A long-stroke, normally aspirated 2.0-liter engine with twincam head and aircraft-style construction was prepared for Christian Lautenschlager, Werner, and Sailer. Sailer ran as high as third, but the best team finish was only eighth—they were just outclassed. At the of 1922, chief engineer Paul Daimler left the company his father had founded, and Ferdinand Porsche arrived as the new engineering chief

plagued by lack of low-end torque, but it looked competitive at Monza, where Count Masetti had worked it up to second spot after the first lap. Unfortunately, Louis Zborowski, the famous "Mad Count" of England, was killed when he crashed his Mercedes, and the other factory cars were withdrawn. The new eight did prove itself, however, in 1926, winning at Solitude and in the first German Grand Prix run at Avus. The driver at the latter event was a young German with an Italian name who would become a legend in his own time: Rudolf Caracciola.

Caracciola was born in 1901 in

which differed from the larger unit in that it had been purposely designed for supercharging. Almost immediately, engineer Otto Schilling, who would create a long line of great racing engines, was asked to develop a 1.5-liter version of "the highest possible performance" for the just-established *voiturette* class. Though this racer had 79 bhp at 4500 rpm, it was saddled with an inadequate, overly long chassis, and failed to do well. Happily, the more potent 28/95s did better, Sailer's supercharged car finishing a respectable sixth in the 1922 Targa Florio, with Christian Werner eighth (running without a blower).

with the assignment to make the racing cars more competitive.

Daimler would not contest Indy again, but Porsche's revised Mercedes dominated the 1924 Targa under the sure hand of Christian Werner. Porsche, however, had yet bigger fish to fry: he was at work on the first GP Mercedes of racing's glory years. Its engine was a new monobloc straight eight featuring welded steel water jackets, dual overhead cams, four valves per cylinder, and Roots direct-drive supercharger. It drove through a four-speed gearbox, and sat in a strong chassis with full-elliptic leaf-spring suspension. The first car rode like an oxcart and was

Remagen, and from about the age of 14 he cared only about racing cars. He broke in as a trainee with the Fafnir company in 1918, and drove an NSU motorcycle to a win at Cologne in 1922. He moved to Dresden to become the Fafnir dealer there, but sold only one car. Later, he set himself up as a Mercedes dealer and with as little success: he didn't care about anything except competition.

After an impressive win in a 4-bhp Ego light car at Berlin in 1923, Rudi met the local Daimler agent and joined that firm as a salesman and sometime racing driver. He was a reserve pilot for the tragic Monza GP of 1924,

but came into his own just two years later. Driving one of Porsche's eight-cylinder cars, he scored a tremendous victory at Avus, overcoming a torrential downpour to vanquish everything in sight. This performance earned Caracciola front rank on the factory racing team. Only the Depression would force him to relinquish it, and then only temporarily.

The advent of Caracciola and the success of the eight-cylinder cars were heartening

fabulous screaming banshees that would soon dominate the Grand Prix scene. As we have seen, the Model 24/100/140 led to the K, S, SS, SSK, and SSKL road cars that could take to the track without breathing hard. The final ingredient for greatness was Alfred Neubauer, who took over as team manager in September 1926.

As a competition machine, the original Model K was not impressive. Though Otto Merz led the Mercedes team home to a class win at the San Sebastian 12 Hours in Spain, he was outdistanced by smaller-displacement rivals, and tire failure was a serious problem. The team switched to

trouble besting the field in one of these cars (along with co-driver Werner) at the 1928 German GP—then for the rest of the year contented himself with winning hillclimbs. In 1929, Caracciola had a spectacular rain-soaked drive in the Irish Tourist Trophy, but his Grand Prix efforts were plagued by bad luck. At Monaco, for example, he lost the lead because of a fuel stop, and had to settle for third. He was leading again at the 'Ring, only to suffer a broken rod.

Things went better for Caracciola in 1930. He won the Irish Grand Prix, the Semmering and Shelsley Walsh hillclimbs for sports cars, and went on to become the European hillclimb champion—all with SSKs. "Mercedes' trust in its ace driver was now total," wrote Doug Nye. "He decided where and when he should race outside Germany." Caracciola and Christian Werner would also have certainly added Le Mans 1930 to the SSK's credits had they not been forced out with generator trouble halfway through the Rheims classic.

By now the Depression had set in, forcing the Daimler-Benz racing program into temporary hibernation, at least officially. The company at first unhappily shelved Rudi's contract for 1931, but the faithful Neubauer convinced chairman Wilhelm Kissel to support his best driver as a privateer. Neubauer knew the firm potentially had an even greater car in the SSKL. Sure enough, Caracciola teamed with Wilhelm Sebastian to win that year's Mille Miglia—the first non-Italian drivers ever to capture this most rugged of all European public-road contests. This feat would be repeated only once—by Stirling Moss and the 300SLR in 1955—but never before and never again would a German driver and car win the 1000-mile grind.

The SSKLs were admirable competitors and, coming from a company that ostensibly wasn't

Above: factory pilot Christian Werner won the 1924 Targa Florio and Coppa Florio with this supercharged Model K Mercedes racer, powered by the Porsche-designed 24/110/160 six.

developments in the year that Daimler and Benz joined forces. Porsche went to work almost immediately on new machines— the cars from which virtually every Mercedes racer through 1933 was derived. These were the supercharged "big sixes," the 3.9-liter (239-cid) 15/70/100 (Type 400) and the 6.3-liter (381-cid) 24/100/140 (Type 630), the latter replacing the 28/95.

These were the first of the

the Model S for 1927, and this low-hooded speedster was a decided winner. Caracciola blitzed the opening-day event at the new Nürburgring, and S-type racers finished 1-2-3 at the German Grand Prix a few weeks later. Also, Adolf Rosenberger won the Semmering hillclimb, while Caracciola did over 120 mph in a Belgian speed trial.

The SS (Super Sport) appeared in 1928. It was ostensibly designed for better passenger accommodation, but its real attraction was 200 bhp in what was essentially the Model S chassis. Caracciola had no

racing anymore, they were tangible proof that D-B's enthusiast engineers just weren't giving up. Wrote Karl Ludvigsen in describing the car's construction: "[Max] Wagner attacked the chassis...The side members were lightened, with the exception of the section between the firewall and the radiator. In addition to the drilling, the side rails were pared down in the width of their flanges as seen in plan view. The drilling crew continued on the rear frame crossmembers, gusset plates and fuel tank brackets. With smaller bits they went after the pedal pads and arms, even the inboard fins of the brake drums...some 250 pounds were pared from the SSK. [The German Grand Prix] saw the introduction of the quick-lift racing jack, an invention of Wilhelm Sebastian and Willy Walb."

The 1930s would be a decade of contrasts in racing because of the difficult, up-and-down economic conditions and, in Europe, ominous political developments. In the early years, technical developments were few and manufacturer support dwindled. With the withdrawal of Daimler-Benz, Caracciola signed with Alfa Romeo in 1932, driving the new Type B *monoposto* to victory in four Grands Prix. Then Alfa Romeo bowed out, so Rudi formed a private effort, the Scuderia CC, with his longtime friend Louis Chiron. But Mercedes would require his services again.

The 1932 season was the year of the privateers. Young Manfred von Brauchitsch, an aristocratic ex-Army officer of means, campaigned a radically streamlined SSKL with good success. At Avus in May he dogged Caracciola's Alfa until the final lap—then simply left Rudi in the dust, his car a good 10 mph faster. Another independent racer, Hans Stuck, drove an SSKL prepared with some help from D-B to win the Czechoslovakian GP and the European Hillclimb Championship, as well as setting a new 128-mph speed record in Brazil.

The factory prepared a streamliner of its own for Avus in 1933 and, without Caracciola, handed the drive to aging Otto Merz, who had pleaded for one last chance at glory. Alas, it was one chance too many: the car hit a bumpy section in practice, slid, crashed, and poor Merz was dead. It was a sad finale to the SSKL's career, one of the finest ever compiled by a single model.

The regressive technology and low-level competition that had marked the early part of the decade disappeared in 1934. "No examples today can provide meaningful parallels to the way the Germans went Grand Prix racing from 1934 through 1939," wrote Karl Ludvigsen. "Their dominance, especially in the last three years, was total. As one example of many, both Mercedes and Auto Union brought five cars each to the starting line of

the German Grand Prix in 1937. During the race, Bernd Rosemeyer in an Auto Union set a lap time which was not bettered in competition again until 1956. And, back at their factories, both firms had duplicate teams of cars being prepared for the next event, plus two engines for each car!"

Daimler-Benz' full-bore return to racing was prompted by two events. The first came in late 1932 when the governing body of motor racing, the *Association Internationale des Automobile Clubs Reconnus* (AIACR), declared an unlimited formula for 1934-36, except for weight, which was 1650 pounds (750 kg) maximum. It was more or less an open invitation for a company whose specialty was light-alloy, supercharged engines.

The second event occurred in January 1933 with the coming to power of the one-time Adolf Shicklgruber, whose grandiose promises of a new Germany dominant in every form of human endeavor most definitely included motorsport. Hitler's interest in cars was intense, but the man who focused it on Daimler-Benz was Jacob Werlin, the Nazi chieftain in Munich, home of Hitler's party. Werlin arranged for the Ministry of Transport to subsidize D-B to the tune of RM450,000 per year, with bonuses of

RM20,000/10,000/5000 for first/second/third-place finishes. This looked pretty useful, as it took about three million Reichsmarks a year to finance a successful racing program at the time. Unfortunately, the promised funds didn't materialize, because Auto Union—in the guise of Ferdinand Porsche—had argued for the same plum. Hitler decided to divide the pot between the two companies.

Today, some historians find it difficult to believe that the Austrian ex-corporal could make this undoubtedly shrewd move. But it was completely in character, and it worked. Over the next six years, Daimler-Benz and Auto Union vied for supremacy of the Grand Prix circuits to the betterment of racing and the automobile in general. The fact is that Hitler

Below: Caracciola climbs aboard the new W25 before the Internationale Klausenrennen *in Switzerland in 1934. Below right: Von Brauchitsch in the W25 as seen at the 1935 German GP.*

did something positive here in pitting one company against the other. As it turned out, the Mercedes cars always did better than the Auto Unions, though both cars and drivers were often quite evenly matched. The reason for D-B's success probably lies with Alfred Neubauer. Auto Union had nobody remotely like him.

The Mercedes GP car that resulted from all this was the Type W25, powered by a traditional dohc straight eight that made ample use of light alloys and light steel water jackets. Originally producing 354 bhp from its 3360cc (205 cid) (78×88 mm/3.07×3.46 in.), this power unit eventually grew to 5660cc (345 cid) (94×102 mm/3.70×4.02 in.) and as much as 646 horsepower. Reflecting D-B's by-now customary approach to suspension design, it employed coil springs up front and half-shaft swing axles at the rear. With the 750kg weight limit in mind, it was fitted with a light yet structurally sound

Above left: Rudolf Caracciola (driving) in the 2.0-liter straight-eight car after winning the rain-soaked 1926 German Grand Prix at Avus. Above: "Caratsch" drove the SSK to capture the 1931 Brescia 1000-mile road race.

alloy body on a rather conventional box-section frame. Official weighing found the prototype one kilogram overweight. The wily Neubauer thus ordered its German racing white paint be sanded off, which made the difference—and revealed the gleaming silver color for which the W25 and its successors would be known as the "Silver Arrows."

The W25 won its first time out, at the 344km Eifel race, where von Brauchitsch drove smoothly at a 76-mph average. But the German GP fell to Auto Union, and Luigi Fagioli had to settle for second. He later brought the W25 home to win the Spanish and Italian GPs, however (the latter with Caracciola co-driving), but Hans Stuck's Auto Union topped him

Right top, center, and bottom: the 5.7-liter W125 appeared in 1937, the final year for the 750kg GP formula, which indicated how serious D-B was about winning. Engineered largely by Rudolf Uhlenhaut, this 646-bhp bullet dominated the GP circuits that season.

in France, Switzerland and Czechoslovakia.

The 1935 campaign was more successful. For one thing, Caracciola was back. He had been through a couple of depressing years, losing his first wife in an avalanche and, in 1933, smashing his thigh at Monaco. Rudi was being nursed back to health by pretty Alice "Baby" Hoffman, who became Mrs. Caracciola in 1937 and remained his greatest companion and fan until his death. Neubauer wanted "Caratsch," healthy or no. He was duly signed in time to share the 1934 Monza drive with Fagioli. Now, Neubauer had not only the one driver who could compare with Nuvolari but also a new W25, with a 4.0-liter (244-cid) 400-bhp engine and a new ZF limited-slip differential. This combination was extremely hard to beat. The W25s won at Monaco and Tripoli, took the *Eifelrennen*, Avus, and captured the Grands Prix of France, Switzerland, Spain, and Belgium. Caracciola won five GPs, four other events, and the German and overall European driver's championships.

The only break in Mercedes' skein of dominance during 1935 was an ironic and amusing one: Tazio Nuvolari's inspired drive in the obsolete Alfa P3 in none other than the German Grand Prix. Starting from sixth place, the great "Nivola" overhauled Auto Unions and Mercedes one by one, finally putting so much heat on race-leader Brauchitsch that Manfred pressed too hard and blew a tire. Tazio romped home an easy winner. It was supposed to have been a great day for the Nazis. The Nürburgring was awash with swastikas, and *Korpsführer*

Top: a trio of W25s head the grid at the 1935 Monaco GP. Luigi Fagioli won in car 4. Above: the D-B team relaxes before the 1937 German GP. (L to r): Von Brauchitsch, Neubauer, Seaman, Lang, and winner Caracciola.

Hühlein—"head" of German racing—was on hand to congratulate the victor. "Deutschland Über Alles" was already on the public address system turntable. But a smiling Nuvolari just happened to have with him a recording of "Inno de Mameli," which he kindly proffered the nonplussed Nazis. It was Tazio's day, but the year clearly belonged to Mercedes-Benz.

It was just as well, because 1936 proved a catastrophe for D-B. The revised W25/1936 had a lower chassis with De Dion rear suspension and a 4.7-liter (287-cid) engine with 474 horsepower. Caracciola debuted to win handily at Monaco, but the rest of the season was a catalog of near total disaster. Auto Union and Alfa Romeo piled up a batch of victories between them, spoiled only by Rudi's win at Tunis—and that only after the leading Auto Unions had crashed or burned. Toward the end of the year "Caratsch" ran a record 228.05 mph in a 12-cylinder 5.5-liter (336-cid) streamliner, which was one of the few bright spots.

A determined Daimler-Benz roared back in 1937 with the now legendary W125, one of the most important cars in Grand Prix history. Doug Nye called this screaming *Silberfeile* "the ultimate expression" of the 750-kilogram formula, then in its last year. (Actually the formula had been extended a year as a courtesy to the manufacturers, because the AIACR had announced its replacement too late and had thus decided not to apply the new rules until the 1938 season.) That Daimler-Benz created a new car around a formula with only a year left to run is an indication of how determined the company was.

A key figure in the W125 project was a 30-year-old engineer who would be heard from a great deal in future years: Rudolf Uhlenhaut. "He was held in the highest esteem by drivers," wrote Phil Hill, "because he was an engineer who could drive...All those stories you and I read about Uhlenhaut being able to drive Mercedes GP cars at competitive speeds around circuits such as the Nürburgring were true, and that's no mean feat."

One of the factors Uhlenhaut and his colleagues had to wrestle with was weight. The potent eight-cylinder engine had now reached 550 pounds, light alloys notwithstanding. The obvious place to begin paring pounds was the chassis, specifically the heavy box-section frame. D-B's experience with tubular chassis design in production cars now came into play, and the W125 was given an oval-section tube frame braced with tubular cross members. Parallel A-arm front suspension was retained, but the arms were longer, resulting in more wheel travel. The De Dion rear suspension, held over from the 1936 car, had a tube that bent behind the transaxle and was located laterally by a ball, which allowed it to move vertically behind the axle casing. The magnificent GP engine now reached its maximum (5.7-liter/349-cid) size, and pumped out 646 bhp at 5800 rpm. The four-speed gearbox was mounted in the rear axle.

Hermann Lang started off the season with a fine win at Tripoli's fast circuit, averaging over 134 mph. At Avus, also a very quick course, he and Caracciola were given streamlined versions with more slippery bodywork patterned after that of the 1936 speed-record car. Lang was the winner at a stupendous average speed of 162.6 mph—and he ran one lap at 171.63 mph. At the *Eifelrennen* and again in the U.S. Vanderbilt Cup race, Auto Union triumphed thanks to Bernd Rosemeyer, the only driver who could really master those tricky rear-engine behemoths. But Mercedes ran 2-3 in the Vanderbilt as Caracciola gave Rosemeyer a terrific challenge, falling back only when his supercharger failed. "Caratsch" and Von Brauchitsch led Rosemeyer home at the 'Ring, and again at Monaco where they finished in reverse order. Brauchitsch was second at Pescara. Then came a Mercedes parade: 1-2-3-4 in the Italian GP at Livorno, 1-2-3-4 in the Czech GP at Brno, 1-2-3 in the Swiss GP at Berne. At Donington Park it was Rosemeyer's turn again, with the W125s close behind.

Beginning in 1937, Neubauer's stable of drivers was further enhanced by Richard Seaman, "Der Englander" who finished second to Rosemeyer in the 1937 Vanderbilt. Born in Sussex in 1913, Seaman was possibly the leading example in the prewar period of the sporting English amateur turned professional: a smooth, skillful driver capable of winning races even in obsolete machinery. At first the potent W125s proved a handful for him, but he soon had their measure.

For 1938's new 3.0-liter supercharged formula Daimler-Benz fielded mainly unaltered chassis fitted with a new engine. This was a 420-bhp V-12 with four overhead cams. Known as the M163 unit, it was angled into the frame with its rear end slanting downwards and coupled to a five-speed gearbox. Auto Union was now very vulnerable. Bernd Rosemeyer had been killed while making a speed run in a record attempt, and engineer Porsche

had left the firm to direct Hitler's KdF (Volkswagen) project. The season opener at Pau saw challenge from an unexpected quarter, however, as René Dreyfus won with his unblown 4.5-liter Delahaye. After that, the Silver Arrows had it all to themselves, running 1-2-3 at Tripoli and Rheims. The team was confident of success in its "home" event at the Nürburgring, and Herr Hühlein and his brown-shirts again turned out expecting to award the trophy in honor of the "master race." Again, the *Korpsführer* was to be disappointed: this time he had to fish for a recording of "God Save the King." It was Dick Seaman's finest hour.

It started at 10:59 on July 23, 1938. While the world pondered Hitler's designs on Czechoslovakia, the collapse of the Republican front in Spain, and the Arab threat to make war in Palestine, Alfred Neubeur raised his index finger and drew circles in the air. The Mercedes drivers switched on their ignitions. The white flag dropped, and 22 cars shot away in a roar of thunder and a cloud of dust at the first turn. Trouble developed promptly. Lang, initially in the lead, had engine problems and pitted. On lap nine, Caracciola came in complaining of stomach trouble. The idle Lang leaped into Rudi's car and took off again.

Seaman was now in the lead, driving beautifully, and Neubauer gave the signal for his teammates to hold their position. Brauchitsch didn't. Now, Manfred led Richard, but "Der Englander" dogged his tracks giving no quarter, no let-up. "I knew the background to this," Neubauer recalled in his autobiography, *Speed Was My Life.* "It was sitting up in the reserved seats behind me in the shape of an extremely attractive young woman, Erika Popp, daughter of the managing director of BMW..."

The two silver cars flew

through the twisty circuit in full cry. "...This crazy duel made my hair stand on end," Neubauer wrote, yet "I had to admire the coolness and elegance of Seaman's driving. I could see that Brauchitsch was beginning to lose his nerve."

The two cars pitted at almost the same instant, Manfred shouting at Neubauer, "I've had enough! This damned fellow Seaman's driving me mad sitting on my tail." Neubauer said he'd have a word with Dick, who sat in his car frowning angrily, his knuckles white around the steering wheel. "For my sake, Dick, leave Brauchitsch alone for today," Alfred said. Seaman said he would do so. But fate intervened. A careless mechanic had over-filled Brauchitsch's fuel tank. Unknowingly, Manfred switched on and his car was engulfed in flames. Neubauer seized him by the collar and yanked him out while the car was doused in foam. But Seaman's car was still in the pits! Neubauer rushed back to the Englishman. "What are you standing there for? Why haven't you started?" he roared. Seaman gave his chief a seraphic smile. "I thought I was to let Brauchitsch keep his lead," he said innocently. Neubauer told him to stop thinking—just drive.

The balance of the race was a virtuoso performance by the British pilot. "He drove like a dream," Neubauer remembered. "His feet were burning; the soles of his shoes were smouldering. The palms of his hands were blistered and bleeding after 1144 gear changes in 22 laps, but he drove the race of his life to win the German Grand Prix of 1938 with a lead of three minutes from Hermann Lang."

At the victory banquet that night, Neubauer noticed that one chair, next to the beautiful Erika, was still empty. "Suddenly Dick Seaman appeared and there was a burst of applause. He walked straight

continued on page 113

A pristine-condition Mercedes-Benz SSK from 1929. Only a handful of these classic roadsters were built through 1931.

An early Type 540K from 1936, with special rumble-seat cabriolet body designed at the Daimler-Benz works in Sindelfingen. This particular style shows the influence of the streamlining movement that took hold throughout the auto industry in the mid-'30s. The 540K was built on the Type 500K chassis, but the supercharged six was enlarged to 5.4 liters (329.5 cid) for this model to produce 180 horsepower with supercharger engaged. In the U.S., the 540Ks sold new for a minimum of $12,000, equivalent to some $100,000 now, and specimens like the one shown here routinely command that much or more today on the collector market.

A rare example of an uncommon car. This Type 540K carries the true roadster body without roll-up side windows that was briefly offered early in the model's life. Compare the scooped-out door line here with the straight-topped doors on the car shown in the pages immediately preceding. Not readily apparent in these views is the car's immense size, a tribute to its styling. The radiator proudly stands more than a foot aft of the front bumper. This British-registered car has the twin rear-mount spare tires that could be specified on both open and closed two-seat body styles in the 540K catalog.

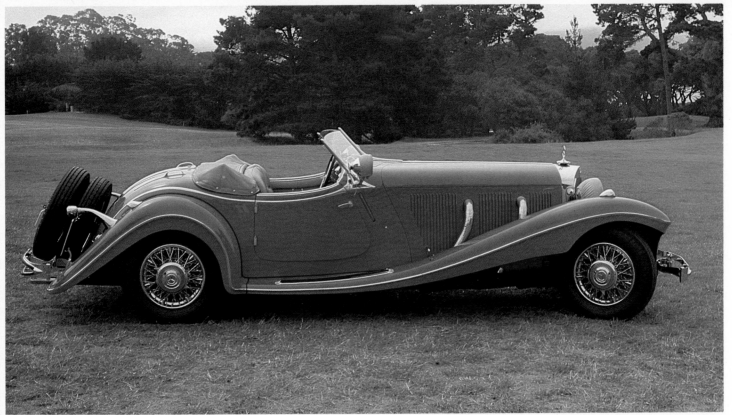

Top: another look at the 1936 Type 540K, here with the 4/5 seat Cabriolet B body. Center: created for the last year of the 750kg GP formula, the 1937 W125 racer was powered by a 5.7-liter supercharged straight eight packing 646 horsepower. This car returned D-B to the competition forefront. Above: the 3.0-liter W154 GP car of 1939 had a supercharged V-12 rated at some 480 bhp. Its career was cut short by the outbreak of World War II. Opposite page, top: the 1937 Type 230 cabriolet. Bottom: the 1939 version of the Type 770 Grosser limousine.

The first sporting Mercedes-Benz of the postwar era was the Type 300S or Super, introduced during 1952. Shown is the 1953-model cabriolet with the heavily padded folding top and functional landau bars characteristic of German convertibles. Some 344 open cars were built through 1955, plus 216 of the companion fixed-roof coupe. The 300S powerplant was a tuned version of the newly designed 3.0-liter ohc six introduced with the Type 300 sedan in 1951. Higher compression and multiple carburetors boosted output from 115 bhp to 150 bhp on the Super. The fitted luggage shown was an option.

Another example of the 1952-55 Type 300S cabriolet. Traditional Mercedes-Benz radiator dominates the frontal aspect. Note high-mounted turn signal indicators above rear fenders.

continued from page 96

to the end of the table and Erika Popp raised her glass. Then with a gesture of her hand she invited him to take the empty chair. I knew then that these two delightful young people were in love and I was glad. What I could not know was that their love idyll had exactly 330 days to run . . .''

Mercedes' banner year continued. Lang's was the only W125 left at the end of the Coppa Ciano—but he was in first spot. At Bern it was another 1-2-3 parade of *Silberfeilen* in the Swiss GP. Caracciola was the sole Mercedes survivor—and the winner—in the Coppa Acerbo. Auto Unions won the Italian and Donington Park GPs, but the W125s finished close behind.

For 1939, Daimler-Benz readied its ultimate weapon. This was the Type W154, with a two-stage supercharger that raised output on the M163 engine to 480 bhp. Lang won at Pau and took the *Eifelrennen*—though Nuvolari, now driving for Auto Union, almost stole the latter by running the entire race without a tire change.

Seaman had married Erika Popp the previous December. Halfway through the Belgian GP at Spa he held the lead, averaging over 94 mph in the wet, apparently a sure winner. He was aiming at the fastest lap of the day two-thirds through the race as he neared the bend at La Source. "He went into the bend at almost 140 mph, which was very fast on a wet macadam surface," Neubauer wrote. "But this time he was travelling too fast. As Seaman's car went into a skid, Lang braked. He saw the other car turn on its axis, leave the track and crash sideways into a tree. As Lang passed he caught a glimpse of flames shooting up . . .'' Seaman struggled to get out, but he was trapped. Two Belgian officers bravely risked an explosion to pull him out. He died of his

burns on the 26th of June, 1939. One of the wreaths at his funeral was from Adolf Hitler—possibly *Der Führer's* last public tribute to an Englishman.

Seaman's death was an irreparable loss for the Mercedes team, and much more would soon be lost as well. But the indomitable W154s, perhaps the most elegantly engineered racers in history, went on to the end. Again Mercedes finished 1-2-3 at Berne, and Lang won the difficult Grossglöckner hillclimb. At Belgrade in September—the last prewar Grand Prix—Von Brauchitsch closed the W154's career with a second-place finish—and almost died. Desperate under steady pressure from Nuvolari, Manfred skidded off course, stopped pointing the wrong way, then drove back onto the track in the path of Nivola's hurtling Auto Union. "Had it been anyone else but Tazio Nuvolari that would probably have been the end of both of them," wrote Neubauer. "With incredible coolness, Nuvolari gauged the distance between Brauchitsch's Mercedes and the

stone wall at the side of the track. It was just wide enough! Brauchitsch had lost the race, but thanks to Nuvolari he was still alive."

The last achievement for the W154 came at the Dessau *autobahn*, where "Caratsch" and a pair of streamliners recorded the standing kilometer at 107.9 mph and the flying kilometer at 247.44 mph. The Tripoli GP had been altered to a *voiturette* event in an attempt to stop the three-pointed star, but Uhlenhaut fielded a 1.5-liter V-8 car, the W165, based on the M163 engine and the W154 chassis. It qualified, and Lang won at 122 mph. Finally, a six-wheel Land Speed Record car designed by none other than Ferdinand Porsche was prepared for the record attempt. This was the Type 80, nearly 30 feet long and powered by a Daimler-Benz V-12 aero-engine with 3000 horsepower. Though it's on display today at the Daimler-Benz Museum, it never

Below: Neubauer, Caracciola, and Uhlenhaut at the 1938 Coppa Acerbo. Bottom: the W154 GP car for 1938.

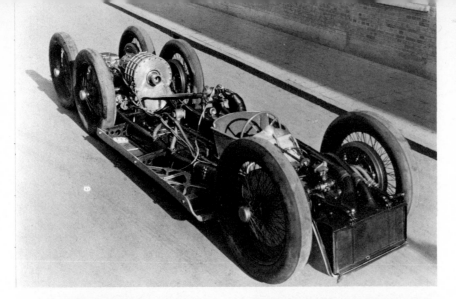

ran. In September 1939, Hitler attacked Poland, and the curtain crashed down on a glorious era.

War was declared on September 3 as a subdued Mercedes team drank to Von Brauchitsch's survival at Belgrade. "It all seemed much less important that evening," Neubauer recalled. "We knew as we made our way home that, if anything was at all certain, it was that we would not be meeting, much less racing, again for a very long time . . . if at all . . ."

Top and center: the Type 80 was to set a new Land Speed Record but never ran because of the start of World War II. Above: Caracciola after winning the Tripoli GP in 1935.

The Mercedes-Benz racing story is one of cars, yes—wonderful cars, the likes of which had never been encountered or even dreamed of by most engineers outside Stuttgart. But it was also a saga of people, as we have seen. They were giants in their time, larger-than-life figures who, like their cars, were part of a breed

that somehow vanished. Perhaps it was inevitable given the rise of global electronic communications after World War II. A world in which 100 million people can examine flaws in the character of any man or woman—close up and in the twinkling of an eye—has little room for giants.

Which driver was the greatest? Those who have studied the sport tend to be noncommittal. For many it was Nuvolari. For others, including Neubauer, it was Rudolf Caracciola: "He combined to an extraordinary degree single-mindedness, concentration, physical endurance and intelligence. No other driver I have known could, in my view, have triumphed over disability as Caracciola did. [Remember, he drove his greatest races with an injured thigh.] I felt then, as I feel now, that of all the great drivers I have known—Nuvolari, Rosemeyer, Lang, Moss or Fangio—Rudi Caracciola was the greatest of them all."

"Caratsch" returned to racing in the postwar years, but only sporadically—and only until a decisive crash in 1952 injured his good leg and ended his career. He joyfully continued working for Daimler-Benz though, supervising sports car demonstrations at NATO installations throughout Europe. He died at the age of 58 from an infectious jaundice that developed into incurable cirrhosis. For his wife, "Baby," it was "as if the world had stopped breathing."

And so it was for Daimler-Benz. Unlike most hard-bitten auto companies, this is a firm with feelings and a sense of history. It paid a special farewell to Rudi at the proving grounds, with two great silver racing cars flanking a company of mourners—engineers, mechanics, drivers. The pallbearers were led by Karl Kling and Herman Lang. Today, Rudi rests in Lugano.

MERCEDES-BENZ IN THE 1950s: THE RETURN TO EMINENCE

Below: D-B resumed production after World War II with the prewar Type 170V, shown here in 1949.

In the early spring of 1945, crack French regiments marched into the ruins of Stuttgart. Most recently the headquarters for *Ausland Deutschen,* the foreign intelligence department of the Third Reich, Stuttgart and its environs now presented only the forlorn face of near total ruin. The French did not come as liberators: they had scores to settle. "Many," wrote one reporter, "were famous native regiments who did not lose much time in demonstrating how the vanquished are dealt with in the less civilized places of the Asiatic and African deserts."

Innumerable bombing raids had reduced the facilities of the city's two famous auto-related companies, Robert Bosch and Daimler-Benz, almost to rubble. Barely 30 percent of each factory still stood. The outlying D-B plants at Sindelfingen and Gaggenau were in even worse shape, and the great aero-engine plant at Berlin-Marienfelde had been so badly hit that what was still standing had to be pulled down. Only the truck works at

Mannheim had survived largely intact. By early 1945, the company whose screaming silver racers once dominated motorsport in prewar Europe had, as its directors said, "ceased to exist."

An Englishman touring Untertürkheim four years later for *The Autocar* magazine noticed that "a substantial number of heaps of debris... have not yet been cleared." Yet he could not help feeling as he entered the D-B main plant that "the greatness of this once famous automobile has not passed. Reconstruction, as far as materials permitted, has gone on at breakneck speed since May 1945, and by now some 14,000 people are employed on a very substantial production program."

"Substantial production program" was an understatement in view of what Daimler-Benz had accomplished since V-E day. Before 1945 was out a few hundred workers were already clearing rubble from the plant and offices. Others were fetching critical bits of

machinery that had been spirited to safe hiding places as the war closed in around Germany; many hauled it back to the factories in handcarts. By February 1946, a hand-built 170V sedan prototype, based entirely on prewar tooling, had been completed. "The attention and care which is being paid to the training of the coming generation at Mercedes-Benz is worth while observing," wrote *The Autocar* observer in 1949. "...Some 200 apprentices are being coached in the finesse of the trade by former racing mechanics, who have the grey look of under-nourishment on their faces and who are dressed in clothes held together by patches. Their attitude, however, still breathes precision, speed and a pride in their work. The youngsters are keen, and much of their work is done with files and scrapers, which shows that they are following in the footsteps of their ancestors."

These early efforts went on with only the begrudging acquiescence of the occupation forces. "Whilst good progress

Opposite page: the Sindelfingen line in 1946. D-B built only 214 cars that year, all 170Vs. This page, top: the 1949 Type 170V. Above: the externally identical 1949-53 170D.

was made at Untertürkheim, Sindelfingen and Mannheim, which were in the American zone, it was impossible for a time to tie in the Gaggenau plant near Baden-Baden in the French zone, on whose

management Daimler-Benz had only a very limited influence in the early postwar period," wrote historian David Scott-Moncrieff. Similarly, the Allies temporarily forbade development of a 1.5-liter diesel engine for the 170, although Daimler-Benz would eventually get a 1.7-liter car into production.

At first, factory employees engaged in repair work on old

cars while cleaning up and attempting to bring order to the bombed-out plants. This brought in money and employed a small but growing workforce. Hard work and persistence paid off, and Type 170 production was underway again by June 1946. German currency reform two years later set the economy of the Western zones on a firm footing. Revisionist historians who have equated Western occupation with that of the Soviets have failed to examine such indicators as this: Mercedes-Benz production was 214 units in 1946; 1045 in 1947; 5116 in 1948; 17,417 in 1949; and 33,906 in 1950. The phoenix was rising from the ashes.

The Type 170 was the logical choice to get the company rolling again. It was the least complicated to build, and it was appropriate for its time. Its forbears, the original front-engine 170V and the rear-engine 170H, had been around since 1936, and D-B had built close to 100,000 Type 170Vs by 1942 in various body styles including two- and four-door convertibles and a cabriolet-limousine. However, 1946 production consisted almost entirely of commercials—panel trucks, ambulances, fleet and police cars. The 170 would continue through 1953 in two successive variations. The 170Va of 1950-52 employed a slightly larger 1.77-liter (108-cid) version of the original four with 45 bhp (DIN), and was about 10 mph faster. It also rode better thanks to adoption of tubular shock absorbers, and had larger brakes with 114 square inches of drum lining area instead of 87.4, a significant improvement. The second development was the 170Vb of 1952-53, which introduced a hypoid rear axle and had a wider track, more glass, and revised hood styling.

Daimler-Benz was gradually conquering chaos at Untertürkheim and its outlying plants, and by 1949 the firm had recovered sufficiently to add a second gasoline-powered model, the 170S. Like the 170V, this car's styling and bodyshell were entirely prewar (actually that of the previous Type 230), but the 170S was available in a greater array of body styles—touring sedan, two-seat tourer, and convertible sedan. It was also more expensive: about $2400 for the sedan vs. $1860 for the 170V

sedan. The S chassis followed 170V practice with tubular, oval-section cruciform chassis and tubular outriggers to carry the body, plus coil-spring/swing-axle rear suspension. Up front, however, the V's transverse-leaf suspension was abandoned in favor of coil-and-wishbone geometry similar to racing-car layouts. The front wheels were interconnected by an anti-sway torsion bar, which yielded a considerable improvement in roadholding. The 1767cc four was the same as for the 170V a/b, but produced 52 bhp (DIN). Though it looked larger and heavier, the 170S weighed only about 100 pounds more than the 170V and was therefore livelier. The factory's claimed acceleration figure was 0-100 km/h (0-62 mph) in 32 seconds, against 36 seconds for the V-model. An improved version, the 170Sb, appeared in 1952, sporting a stronger heater, hypoid rear axle, wider track, a dashboard-mounted starter button, and a gearlever relocated from the floor to the steering column. The final variant was designated 170S-V, and was built in 1953-55. It reverted to the 45-bhp 170V engine specification and leaf-spring front suspension in order to sell at a lower price, about $2000.

Despite some reluctance by the occupation powers, it was inevitable that Daimler-Benz would resume building diesel passenger cars. The company had been a pioneer in this field, introducing its first diesel car, the 260D, in 1936, and these were still widely seen in taxi service in the late '40s. Even today, Mercedes-Benz continues to give more emphasis to compression-ignition engines for passenger cars than any other automaker.

Postwar diesel design was predicated on two goals: light weight for optimum performance, and as much parts interchangeability as possible with the gasoline powerplants to reduce manufacturing cost and

complexity. Accordingly, the 170D was announced in 1949 as the diesel double of the 170V. It was powered by a 1.7-liter pushrod ohv four of 38 bhp (DIN), not dissimilar in basic engineering from the 1.7 gasoline unit. The new diesel followed prewar practice of injecting fuel into a pre-combustion chamber, which also housed an electric glow plug to assure easy starting. "The system ensures combustion with the minimum of smoke under a wide range of loads or speeds, apart from operating well on all kinds of diesel fuel," the factory stated.

Britain's weekly magazine *The Autocar* tested a 170D in late 1949: "On the road the car gave a pleasant ride, being slightly slower in acceleration than with the comparable petrol engine, but the performance on winding hilly roads left little to be desired. Although it was not possible to measure independently the claimed maximum speed of 62 mph, an average speed of 37.6 mph on a 127-mile journey, partly on the *autobahn* and partly on normal provincial roads, was achieved. The engine was reasonably silent, chiefly owing to the large rubber mountings which also absorb a considerable proportion of the vibrations...The four-wheel independent suspension gave excellent roadholding, even over bad pavé roads, with a full complement of passengers. The measured fuel consumption on the 127-mile journey worked out at 37 mpg [29.6 U.S.] which is most economical considering the price of the fuel and the unladen weight of the car."

Not surprisingly, engineering and equipment revisions for the 170D paralleled those made to the gasoline-engine line. Thus appeared the 170Da (1950-52) with the larger 1.77-liter displacement, 40 bhp (DIN), tubular shocks and bigger brakes. The 170Db (1952-53) had the wider track, hypoid rear axle, altered hoodline, and larger

windshield of its 170Vb
counterpart. The 170DS
(1952-53) and 170S-D (1953-55)
were the diesel variations of the
gas-powered 170S series.
Altogether, the first postwar
diesel line accounted for over
60,000 units, the total nearly
evenly divided between the
170V- and 170S-based models,
with final production in
September 1955.

West Germany (the Federal
Republic of Germany after May

*Above: the diesel-powered 170S-D
sedan of 1953. Right: the handsome
Type 170S Cabriolet A, offered in
1950-53. Below: the Cabriolet A
version of the significant Type 220,
introduced in 1951.*

1949) proved a quick reviver from World War II. In some cities, bombed-out areas were simply left alone as new blocks of offices and factories rose around them. The need to produce was acute, but the Federal Republic did not, at least immediately, attempt a major export drive for the sake of earning "hard" foreign currency like the dollar. Hence, the 170V was designed more for the German buyer and his pocketbook than for any particular overseas clientele. The 170S, of course, was a step toward the export market, but the first really significant move in that direction did not appear until the Frankfurt Automobile show in April 1951. Here Daimler-Benz returned to its prewar tradition with out-and-out luxury cars led by the stately Type 300.

The Type 300 and its Type 220 linemates were the first Mercedes to employ entirely new postwar styling: an envelope body with headlamps integrated into the front fenders. The 300 was also the first Mercedes designed with an eye to the American market. The U.S. was, at that time, the best place in the world for an automaker to be doing business. The demand for cars was 20 million deep, and even the most pessimistic predictions were that this market would not be satiated before 1953. But America at that time was also a competitive car exporter to lucrative areas like Switzerland and the "ABC" countries of South America, Argentina, Brazil, and Chile. Though sales in those areas were not numerically large, they were certainly sufficient to attract firms like D-B with relatively limited production capacity.

As John Dugdale wrote at the time, it was realized "that in equipment, the American cars leave little to be desired and their latest power units are very good. German manufacturers, like the British, cannot afford to develop [the] automatic

*Opposite page, top: the 1957-62
Type 300d convertible sedan. Center
and bottom: the 300d hardtop sedan
and its spaciously elegant cabin.
This page, top: only 51 of the
300c cabriolets were built. Above:
the wood-bedecked 300d dashboard.*

transmission on the scale achieved in America. Attention was therefore focused on the suspension to score a vital sales point...Mercedes-Benz concentrated on producing a rear suspension which could accommodate the considerable variations in load encountered on a modern five/six-seater car with large luggage accommodation while maintaining full comfort and roadholding in all conditions." The result was the swing-axle/

coil-spring rear suspension, introduced with the 170V but now combined with hydraulic damping. With a heavy load, Dugdale continued, "the driver presses a switch which brings into action an auxiliary torsion bar. Normally the bars turn freely in their bearings, but there are stops mounted on screw threads which can be driven out by an electric motor working through a reduction gear...the torsion bar takes over part of the work of the suspension system. The effect is to change the rate of suspension from 55mm per 100kg to 40mm per 100kg. An adequate range of deflection can now be obtained under all load conditions without using a total deflection range which would produce undesirable geometric effects. In fact, negative camber is avoided almost completely... the [300] offers an extraordinary combination of top-class stability and superb riding comfort."

Equally intriguing was the 300's hydraulic steering damper. A characteristically German device, this item would one day find its way into even the lowly VW Beetle, but it was new and different in 1951. The principle was simple: a telescopic shock absorber mounted between the frame and middle section of the three-piece steering linkage. This absorbed road shocks that would normally be transmitted from the frame through the steering linkage to the wheel. One road tester drove a 300 across a plowed field attempting to prove otherwise, but reported "no reaction could be felt." Yet road feel and steering precision remained very good. The Type 300 also featured one-shot chassis lubrication via a cockpit control.

The single-overhead-cam six in the Type 300 was the progenitor of the great 300SL sports car powerplant, and was engineered and built with a high level of precision. Its bore and stroke were near square at 85 × 88mm

(3.35 × 3.46 in.), and total displacement was precisely 2996cc (182.8 cid). With twin Solex carburetors it initially developed 115 horsepower (DIN). Jaded observers now tend to take Mercedes craftsmanship for granted. But given its introduction, with D-B just barely recovering from the war, the 300 engine was astonishing. The block was a simple casting with open sides sealed by plates, which allowed the water jackets to be carefully inspected before final assembly. The aluminum head had fitted seats for intake and exhaust valves and a unique combustion chamber design, with compact volume near the plugs and a flat space over the pistons. Staggered, transverse valve placement gave the ports unusually large cross sections. These features, plus a peaked piston design, made for well-controlled turbulence that in turn enabled the engine to run happily on fuels of remarkably low octane—essential in early postwar Europe. Valves were controlled by an overhead duplex chain-driven camshaft with automatic spring tensioning. The transmission was fully synchronized on each gear.

Daimler-Benz assigned construction of the Type 300 to its coachworks at Sindelfingen, and body styles were limited to a slim-pillar four-door sedan and a pillarless four-door convertible. Production of the latter amounted to only a fraction of the former. Like the smaller 220, the 300 looked modern yet was quintessentially German. General director Haspel had made a decision here that would have far-reaching repercussions: the new body, he decreed, must continue to incorporate the traditional, upright radiator motif that was unquestionably Mercedes-Benz. It is with us still.

The Type 300 was a tremendously impressive car, and is highly regarded today by enthusiasts and collectors alike.

Little else, if anything, its size could stay with one on a winding road, and few luxury cars rode as well. But it was the styling that was most noticed—and most clearly said "Mercedes-Benz." The American car it most closely resembled was perhaps the senior Packard Clipper of 1942-47. Both had the same sort of sweeping front fenders fading away into the front doors, a long and graceful hoodline, and a tall, distinctive radiator shell. Those Clippers were the last really tasteful and timeless Packards, and the Type 300 was the first timeless Mercedes of the postwar years.

The Type 300 went through several specification changes during its long 11-year production life. The first-series sedan was produced from late 1951 through March 1954, with regular production of the four-door convertible beginning in April 1952. The original 300s were then succeeded by the 300b, externally unchanged but sporting 10 more horsepower and larger brakes. Production totals were low: about 6200 sedans and a scant 591 convertibles in both series through the summer of 1955. The 300c, introduced that September, ran through June 1956, and featured twin compound carburetors (though advertised power output was unchanged). Altogether, D-B built some 1430 of the 300c sedans and just 51 convertibles. That might have been the end had not dealers complained when the company announced the 300's cancellation. The reason: they still had buyers. D-B obligingly reinstated the model as the 300d on a longer 124-inch wheelbase (versus the previous 120). Styling was updated by a flatter, more squared-up roofline, longer rear fenders, and a slightly wider grille. Also, the sedan lost its fixed center pillars to become a four-door hardtop. Mechanical fuel injection from the 300Sc and SL was adopted along with a higher compression

ratio that boosted output to 160 bhp (DIN). Offered from late 1957 through early 1962, the 300d saw production of nearly 3100 hardtops and a mere 65 convertibles.

The Type 220, which debuted alongside the 300 at Frankfurt, shared the same rounded postwar styling, but rode a shorter 112-inch wheelbase and used a 2195cc (133.9-cid) single-carb six with 80 bhp (DIN). This engine shared the 300's deep water jacketing, oil heat exchanger, copper-lead main bearings, and crankshaft vibration damper. At 80 × 72.8mm (3.15 × 2.83 in.) it was D-B's first oversquare engine. Body styles comprised the predictable four-door sedan, a four-passenger convertible sedan with two doors, and a more rakish two/three-seat cabriolet coupe. While the latter two remained in production through 1955, a more contemporary version of the sedan, designated 220a, appeared in March 1954. This carried a second-generation postwar body, with a boxier overall shape and only a hint of the earlier freestanding front fenders, though the upright M-B grille remained. The 220a was sold through 1956 and accounted for nearly 26,000 units. Some 16,000 of the first-series 220 sedans were built. As with the Type 300, production of the open 220s was paltry: just 2360 cars through August 1955.

Apart from the legendary 300SL treated in a separate chapter, the pinnacle of Daimler-Benz passenger cars in the early 1950s was the 300S. The "S" stood for "Super," an appropriate name, for this was something of a cross between the sporting SL and the posh long-wheelbase 300. In fact, the 300S was nothing less than the spiritual descendant of the great S- and K-series sports tourers of the prewar era. Despite new postwar clothes, it was hardly less exciting.

The 300S was actually

conceived as an interim measure after a glitch developed in the 300SL program. In 1951, Daimler-Benz had decided to re-enter sports-car racing, and chief engineer Rudolf Uhlenhaut had developed the original SL prototypes with this in mind. Then the company turned to Grand Prix instead, which required an engine for the forthcoming 2.5-liter formula, so the 300SL project was temporarily shelved. But this left a hole in the planned lineup of road cars, and D-B had decided it needed an overtly sporting model. The answer was the 300S, which relied heavily on the technology of the Type 300, presented in an altogether new and impressive format.

Although displayed in late 1951 at the Paris Salon, the 300S did not see regular production until the following July. In addition to its majestically Teutonic styling the new model offered the most power yet seen in a postwar Mercedes: 150 bhp (DIN) on 7.8:1 compression and two (later three) Solex carburetors. The four-speed transmission was fully synchronized, and both floor and column shift were available. Like the 300, suspension on the Super was fully independent: twin wishbones and coil springs up front with flexible kingpost mounting and anti-sway bar, and swing axles and coil springs at the rear. Chassis design was the rigid cruciform type with oval tubes and tubular outriggers. A 12-volt electrical system was standard and some years ahead of most American cars.

Though the superb engineering of the 300S was obvious, styling was its real allure. Proportions only hinted at in the gothic Type 300 sedans were now forcefully evident in the Super's long, sweeping lines. The front fenders jutted out ahead of the familiar Mercedes radiator, marked by the ever-present three-pointed star as a reminder of the marque's proud past. The rear

Top: 1951-54 Type 220 sedan. Right: 1954-55 Type 220 Cabriolet B. Above: 1951-52 Type 300S cabriolet. Below: 1955-56 Type 300S roadster. Immediately above: 1955-57 Type 300Sc cabriolet.

123

Top: the fixed-roof Type 300S coupe in its 1955 form. Above left: the graceful rear aspect of the Type 300Sc cabriolet. Above right: the cozy, well-appointed 300S cockpit. Dash was shared with Type 300 models.

deck was gracefully curved, and vestigial concealed running boards linked front and rear fenders. To some it seemed a heavy-handed affair that could only have been created by the Germans, but the 300S was a car that simply oozed personality and the *luxus* aura of bygone days. Likewise, it was a car only the super-rich need consider. Max Hoffman, the import-car impresario who began M-B sales in this country at his New York distributorship, sold the 300S for a cool $12,500—which would be

equivalent to the price of a new Rolls-Royce today.

The 300S was initially available in two body styles: a fixed-roof coupe with an elegantly formal air and a convertible/cabriolet with functional landau bars. The cabriolet carried its folded-up roof in a huge bustle at the rear, again very much in the German idiom. If you didn't like that, you could soon specify a third model called the "roadster," which had no landau bars and a top that disappeared completely when folded. In all the seating was strictly 2+2, though the rear cabin was somewhat more spacious than we normally expect in close-coupled four-seaters today. Rear seats could be folded down to provide extra room for cargo inside.

Interiors were finished with a level of quality that was now routine at Sindelfingen, which means it was very high by world standards. Top-grain roll-and-pleat leather upholstery was combined with veneers in the buyer's choice of burled or straight-grain walnut lacquered to a glass-like finish. Fitted luggage was available for all models and there were twin spare tire wells in the trunk. The steering wheel of the 300S (and the Type 300) featured another typically German invention: a directionals switch combined with the horn ring. To signal a turn you simply rotated the horn ring as appropriate. The 300S abandoned the little flapping semaphores of the 170/220 (and VW Beetle) in favor of proper blinking lights.

124

The rear ones were mounted high up on the body over the fenders, just below beltline level. Another unusual feature, made mandatory by the highly variable octane ratings of those years, was dashboard-controlled ignition timing.

"One of the reasons I've always enjoyed my 300S is its mix of old world coachwork and appearance together with such an impressive list of contemporary mechanical components," says M-B *aficionado* John R. Olson. "There's power capable of two miles a minute and terrific acceleration, plus extreme safety through the rigid frame and cross members, the backbone chassis, independent rear suspension, headrests, effortless steering, and ventilated, bi-metal vacuum-assisted brakes— perhaps the highest development of the drum brake ever made anywhere. There are items you expect in a modern car, such as backup lights, nonglare mirrors, a signal-seeking radio, windshield washers, reclining seats—plus many that you don't, like matched luggage and driver-controlled chassis lubrication. A few other cars offered some of these features in the early 1950s, but where else could they *all* be found?" Styling is a subjective matter, of course, but perhaps the most representative comment came from *Road & Track* magazine: "Where the Mercedes-Benz 300S has been seen since its first appearance...it has caused a quiet riot of enthusiasm with its low, sleek lines and its attitude of 'going' even when standing still..." In *R&T's* opinion, the German car was "one of the finest road vehicles in the world today."

The "beautiful people" were quick to recognize the 300S as a worthy successor to the classic Mercedes sports-touring models, particularly the glorious 540K. The 300S was considerably smaller and lighter, however, with only half the displacement and no supercharger. Yet comparisons are intriguing:

	540K	300S
weight	5735 lbs.	3880 lbs.
bhp	180	150
lbs:bhp	31.9:1	25.8:1
top speed	100 mph	110 mph
0-60 mph	12 secs.	14 secs.

Except in all-out acceleration the 300S packed higher performance. Without its supercharger (and many of them are today) the 540K was a slug. The greatest factor here, of course, was the power-to-weight ratio, but the advantages of the 300S didn't end with top-end performance. It also handled better, was more responsive to the helm, and was far more comfortable to ride in. Cornering at 100 mph is a piece of cake for the 300S, but not something intelligent drivers care to attempt with a 540K. In appearance, the 300S certainly didn't match the arrogant, rakish profile of its forbear, but in every other respect it was indisputably a better car. The Super reaffirmed Daimler-Benz as a builder of top-flight luxury sports cars in the grand manner.

The 3.0-liter ohc six used in both the Type 300 and 300S was upgraded through the years from its original 115 bhp (DIN) to 260 bhp for the last version of the 300SL—all without a displacement increase. A step along this path was made in 1955, when the 300S became the 300Sc by virtue of higher compression (8.55:1, up from 7.8:1) and direct-block Bosch mechanical fuel injection. These changes bumped power to 175bhp (DIN), good for a top speed of 112 mph, with 0-60 mph coming up in 12-13 seconds. Aside from styling, the 300Sc was very close in specification to the 300SL, the most significant difference being that the engine had to be shoehorned into the SL and mounted on a slant in order to clear the ultra-low hoodline. Incidentally, this injection system was typical of Daimler-Benz thoroughness. It was what we now call a multi-point or port type, with individual injectors squirting directly into the cylinders, rather than the manifold or single-point type used for most all other applications until recently. The main advantage of the port type is its virtual absence of throttle lag and consequently better response. The injection pump governor had automatic temperature and altitude adjustment to ensure maximum operating efficiency under all geographic and climatic conditions. The 300Sc also introduced "Hydrovac" power brakes, with race-tested ventilated brake drums and all-weather, four-inch-wide shoes, another advance on the excellent brakes of the 300S.

The 300Sc's relationship to the 300SL was much closer than that of the 300SL to the 190SL. Obviously, body panels and most chassis pieces differed between the 300SL and Sc but, even so, the similarities were striking. Rear suspension on the post-1957 300SL roadsters was nearly identical to that of the Sc. Though the SL offered four different axle ratios while the Sc stayed mainly with one, driveshafts and transmissions employed interchangeable components (the same applied to the Type 300, too). And, as mentioned, the 3.0-liter six was the same except for tuning. Several features of the SL were actually first introduced on the S/Sc, and some hardware items are common to all the 300 models (the dry-sump recirculating oil system, for example). All this reflects the sensible, prudent engineering policy of D-B management. But when you realize how far Uhlenhaut was allowed to go with the racing 300SLR and how little he had to do to create the roadgoing SL from the 300Sc, you can't escape the conclusion that the main specifications of the 300Sc were already pretty impressive.

"In my personal experience in gymkhanas," said owner Olson,

Above: Screen star Errol Flynn was one of the "beautiful people" who flocked to the 300S. Here he is with his cabriolet, circa 1953.

"I've surprised many an SL owner (and myself) with my 300Sc. Its sharper turning radius gains substantial low-speed maneuverability over the 300SL, and the greater power gains seconds over the 190SL and [the later] 280SL models." The torque output of the 3.0-liter ohc six as used in the Sc approached that of many larger Detroit eights, and actually exceeded its numerical cubic-inch displacement (188 lbs/ft vs. 182.7 cid). Considering that Jaguar's XK-series 3.8 dohc six in the E-Type offered 260 lbs/ft of torque from 265 cid—but only after 15 years of development—this says a good deal for the efficiency of the 300Sc engine.

Daimler-Benz left the 300Sc pretty much alone for 1956-57. The car had already been blessed with very refined styling, and there was simply no need to change that. Some experimental body styles were tried, including a handful of coupes with fully wrapped backlights, and some models had different louver treatments on the sides of the engine cover. But the styling was not conducive to annual fiddling, and Mercedes buyers didn't want it. What they did want, eventually, was an all new car; like it or not, by 1957 the 300S was becoming dated.

Of course, high sales volume was never an objective with the Supers any more than it was with the Type 300 or 300SL.

The 300S/Sc simply carried on for D-B's usual lengthy styling cycle, built carefully and without hurry, and was then phased out. It was not immediately replaced by a more modern sports-luxury Mercedes. This may have been due to the recession of 1958, which reduced the demand for cars in this lofty price bracket. (In America, Ford made a similar decision with its Continental Mark II, whose 1958 successor was a much cheaper—and cheapened—car.)

Only one 1958-model 300Sc was actually built, a sunroof coupe that's interesting in that it was equipped with a 300SL dashboard and a short floorshift. In the 1970s this car was owned by R. Kent Enigh, a former dealer who had sold 20-odd 300S models at his Indiana agency. For the entire span of the series fewer than 1000 units were built. The detailed production breakdown may interest collectors:

	300S	300Sc	Total
coupe	216	98	314
cabriolet	203	49	252
roadster	141	53	194
total	560	200	760

About half of 300S production came to the United States, and enthusiasts estimate that about two-thirds of these —some 250 cars—still exist. This is a fairly high survival figure, but entirely understandable. The 300S was not an unmemorable automobile, and its appreciation potential today cannot be understated. The $50,000 it may take to own a good example now will almost certainly prove to have been a good investment by the start of

the 21st century. Yet even that imposing sum is far less than it currently takes to own a 300SL, and the Super is more tractable for street use. The most optimistic of its fans predict the 300S will some day sell for close to 300SL prices, but it must be noted that most of these folks already own one.

Spare parts, usually a tiresome headache with collector cars, is a pleasant aspect of 300S ownership. Though dealers don't always cooperate, D-B in Untertürkheim has made yeoman efforts to maintain supplies of replacements, and even went so far as to remanufacture the model's special curved windshield. D-B has also conducted worldwide searches for rare items, and has air freighted them at its own expense. If all this sounds improbable for a car company, it is—but then this is Daimler-Benz, not General Motors.

For those of us who can only dream about owning one of these fabulous cars a word should be said about 300S literature, a satisfying substitute for the real thing. The embossed, horizontal-format sales brochures, of which there were at least three different versions, are to the typical "car folder" as a 300S itself is to a VW. Each contains three double-page color views of the three models, each spread a single sheet of paper unmarred by staples. Like the car itself, no expense was spared.

With the Type 300 and 300S, Daimler-Benz proudly reclaimed its luxury-car heritage in the postwar area. These cars were a very serious statement about what the company thought of itself—and what it would like the automotive world to think of it as well. And the world approved. Was Daimler-Benz, hardly a decade removed from almost total destruction, already producing "the best car in the world?" If not, it was getting extremely close.

MERCEDES-BENZ
IN COMPETITION 1952-79:
A NEW WINNING
TRADITION

A brace of W196 streamliners on the way to victory at the 1955 Italian Grand Prix, held at the Monza Autodrome in November.

The awesome Mercedes-Benz W196 Grand Prix car and its sports racing derivative, the 300SLR, are among those few cars that became legends in their own time. One can still see them in the mind's eye: screaming down the Mulsanne Straight at Le Mans, flashing along Italian roads lined with cheering spectators, charging uphill and down dale over the devilishly twisty Nürburgring, skimming along Sicilian precipices at speeds few earthly beings ever knew. These mighty Silver Arrows of the postwar era recall at once names like the Targa Florio, the Tourist Trophy, and the Mille Miglia. They conjure up heroic visions: an oil-covered Stirling Moss and a bedraggled Denis Jenkinson arriving first at Brescia in the 300SLR; bulky Juan Manuel Fangio winning race after race to dominate the Grand Prix seasons of 1954-55; the 300SLRs flat out on the special stage of the Mille Miglia, drivers raising their hands in mute tribute past the cemetery at Mantua, where the remains of Tazio Nuvolari rest with this epitaph: "You will travel faster still upon the highways of heaven."

The great open-road races are gone now, Grands Prix of the '80s bear little resemblance to those '50s contests, and somehow the cars now look more like billboards, splattered with sponsors' names. Daimler-Benz never sold off its W196s and SLRs, and every so often at Untertürkheim the beasts are fired up again to recall the triumphs now 30 years distant. These machines and their modern counterpart, the fascinating C111, were the state-of-the-art in competition automobiles—classics in the truest sense of the word.

In less than two years, 1954 and '55, Daimler-Benz came, saw, and conquered the postwar racing world. The reasons why it had to wait so long before reentering competition have been explained in the previous

chapter. The main reason it left again so soon is that management wanted to channel all the firm's resources into its next generation of production cars. In another sense though, D-B left because it had nothing further to accomplish: it retired the champion, the automotive Joe Louis.

The impetus for D-B's return was Alfred Neubauer, the firm's virtuoso team manager in the 1930s and the most prominent racing enthusiast in Germany. The *Fédération Internationale de l'Automobile* (FIA), the reconstituted successor to the AIACR, had laid down a new 1.5-liter supercharged/4.5-liter unsupercharged Grand Prix formula. Neubauer remembered the two 1.5-liter W165 cars that had run at Tripoli in 1939. Rudi Caracciola had spirited them into Switzerland in 1945. They fit the new formula perfectly, but the Swiss government failed to release them until 1950. The high bidder that year was the Swiss Mercedes-Benz distributor, who enthusiastically handed them back to the factory. Neubauer thought these artifacts, properly tuned, could challenge the then-dominant 1.5-liter Alfettas in Formula 1. He even convinced management to field a team of five cars plus five spare engines. But by the time he did, the Ferraris and BRMs had arrived on the scene and the old W165s simply couldn't match such modern rivals. They were retired to the Daimler-Benz Museum. A brace of 3.0-liter W154s was also tried, but with little success.

In 1952, technical director Fritz Nallinger called a meeting of all departments, including Neubauer's. From this emerged an all-new three-pronged competition program: a sports car, a 2.5-liter GP car (the FIA had created this formula for the coming 1952 season), and a sports racer. The last would become the famous 300SLR, and was based on the Grand Prix chassis. But the sports car, the

Center spread top and above: the aluminum-body 300SL prototype in 1952. Note foreshortened gullwing doors. Far upper right: D-B racing manager Alfred Neubauer clocks his charges in the rain, circa 1955. Far right: the 300SL coupe ready for the 1952 Carrera Panamericana. Near right: Neubauer and John Fitch before the start of the '52 Carrera.

soon-to-be 300SL, was the first order of business. Nallinger and engineer Rudolf Uhlenhaut admitted the concept was borrowed from Jaguar's Le Mans winning 1951 XK120C: a special body hiding a highly tuned version of an off-the-shelf engine. In Jaguar's case it was the famous dohc XK-series six; for Daimler-Benz it was the sohc

six from the Type 300/300S. And the engine would be accompanied by every other 300 component deemed feasible for racing use: rear axle, transmission, front and rear suspension. All of course would be heavily revised for the competition 300SL, which was given the factory designation W194. It may be well to note at this point that the SL nomenclature referred to *sehr leicht*—very light or lightweight—thus maintaining a link with the glorious SSKL of the '30s.

Where the new car differed from the 300/300S was in chassis design. The engineers had wanted the ultimate—a genuine multi-tubular space frame—and they got it, albeit with certain necessary compromises. Space-frame construction is ideal for racing cars, being light and tremendously strong. But racing cars do not ordinarily have to be engineered for such practical considerations as easy entry/exit, and D-B intended that the 300SL would eventually be a production model. In order to provide adequate beam strength, the space frame had to be extended relatively high between the wheels. This dictated the door design—large panels hinged at the top and lifting straight up—though the tall frame rails created a high, wide sill that occupants had to scramble over when getting in or out. Thus was born the now-beloved Gullwing, but of necessity rather than preference. The space frame itself was made up of 25 x lmm, 25x2, and 18xlmm chrome molybdenum tubes. Engine, transmission and rear axle support was provided by three large oval cross members. The whole complex was finished in glossy black, and it was a shame, wrote Gullwing fancier Lynn Yakel, that "most of this beautiful array of tubing is hidden from view."

The competition 300SLs fielded during the 1952 season employed three different gullwing styles. The first cars, which finished 1-2 in that year's Mexican Road Race, had tiny doors ending at the beltline just under the side windows (you had to be a real contortionist to squeeze through these). The later cars for Le Mans had deeper doors, while the sports racers had open bodywork with the doors hinged conventionally at the front.

The 300SL's arrival marked the racing renaissance of the three-pointed star. Its debut at the 1952 Mille Miglia was a slight disappointment as Rudi Caracciola and Karl Kling finished fourth and second, respectively. But after that, Mercedes swept to victory: 1-2-3 at Bern and 1 and 3 at Le Mans (where they outlasted both the Jaguars and the Talbot-Lagos). Then came the toughest of them all, the car-killing *Carrera Panamericana*, 1993 miles of dusty open road between Tuxtla Guitterez and Ciudad Juarez, Mexico. The 1952 contest was the third running of the *Carrera* and the first with different classes. This assured a "stock" victory for big American cars, in this case Lincolns, though the sports cars were far faster. Ferrari fielded a huge entry with drivers like Luigi Chinetti and Phil Hill, but the 300SLs piloted by Kling and Hermann Lang finished 1-2. Indeed, the team might have captured the top three places had not John Fitch's car been disqualified for having someone other than himself and his co-driver work on it. Neubauer's strategy had been to wear down the Ferraris, hoping they would break or that the drivers would tire. (The big red cars did take 3-5-6; a Lancia came in fourth).

With these victories in the bag, Daimler-Benz decided not to field a 300SL team for 1953. Instead, the company would enter the Grand Prix arena for 1954-55, and an even more competitive 300SLR would be developed for the 1955 European sports car series.

D-B's new GP contender was given the W196 chassis designation and, like the 300SL, employed a tubular space frame. Two different bodies were created to suit the different aerodynamic requirements of short- and long-distance events. For high-speed tracks there was a full-envelope body with central cockpit, driver headrest fairing, and overall lines reminiscent of the SL's. This car is usually referred to as the Streamliner. Tighter courses, where handling was more important than all-out speed, would be run with an open-wheel *monoposto* looking more like a conventional Formula 1 racer. Wheelbases varied, but the engine was the same regardless of body. Conforming to the new formula, it was a 2.5-liter (152-cid) straight eight. This mated to a rear-mounted five-speed transaxle, and there were low-pivot swing-axle rear suspension and wishbone front suspension. The power unit was unusual in its construction, a combination of sheet steel and castings, and in its "desmodromic" valvegear which opened and closed the valves by cams. As Graham Robson wrote, "it was an immensely complex racing engine which no less-well-equipped concern could ever have tackled...Reliability was astonishingly high." Initially, output was 257 bhp (DIN), but by 1955 it had reached 290 bhp at 8500 rpm.

The Daimler-Benz attack on GP in the mid-'50s was a reenactment of the company's onslaught in the mid-to-late 1930s, and it was soon apparent that these newest Silver Arrows were every bit as competitive as their prewar counterparts. Well before the effort had crystallized, team manager Neubauer told David Scott-Moncrieff: "I don't know when we shall come back to Grand Prix racing. And if I did, I should not tell you. But there is one thing of which you can be

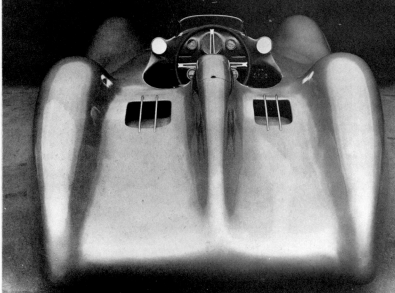

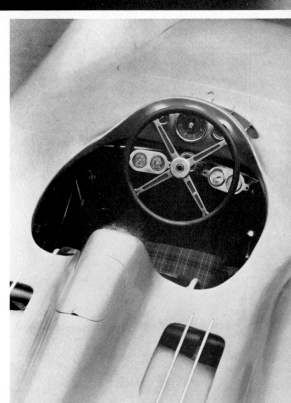

A detailed study of the long-chassis W196 streamliner of 1954. This version was used mainly for high-speed long-distance events, where aerodynamics were more important.

absolutely certain: there will be no half measures. We shall not race again until we have cars that can and will win.''

Neubauer faced an uphill battle, a late start in 1954. By the time his W196s were ready for the *Grande èpreuve* circuits, Juan Manuel Fangio, driving for Maserati, had already won two events: Argentina and Belgium. Neubauer realized that D-B must have Fangio. Not only was he the best driver of the day, he already had those two wins to

his credit for the World Driver's Championship. Wrote Karl Ludvigsen: ''The only overall recognition that would remain in the record books of the role of Daimler-Benz in those years would be as the maker of the mount of the Champion.'' (The Manufacturers Championship was not created until 1958.) With this in mind, Neubauer signed Fangio. He also gave backup drivers Kling and Hans Hermann a definite assignment: to remain well up in each race, in case Fangio faltered, and to be prepared to turn over their cars to him if he had mechanical trouble. (In those days it was not necessary for the winning driver to finish in the same car he started.) As it happened, the flying Argentine would never need a replacement.

The envelope-body silver streamliners duly arrived at Rheims for round three, the French Grand Prix. Recalling prewar days, the front row of the grid was all Mercedes, occupied by Fangio and Kling. Screaming down the straights side by side, blasting through the corners nose to tail, these two cars were soon so far ahead of the field that Fangio began taking corners wide, allowing the slightly slower Kling to close up for tandem runs past the grandstands. Herrmann dropped out with mechanical trouble, but his teammates flashed across the finish line only 1.5 seconds apart. Fangio averaged 115 mph, and broke every mark in the Rheims record book.

The British Grand Prix that followed was a disappointment. Though Fangio took pole position after unofficially breaking the Silverstone lap record in practice, it rained hard halfway through the race, and the streamliners were not nearly as formidable in the wet. D-B had planned to run the open-wheel cars on the slow airport course, but they weren't ready in time. The streamliners enjoyed no advantage, as there were no long straights on the 2.93-mile circuit. Another rapid Argentine, Froilan Gonzalez, won for Ferrari. For the European GP at the Nürburgring, the mountainous "home" track of Daimler-Benz, a victory was mandatory. Streamlining was also less

Exposed W196 Monoposto shows complex multi-tubular chassis. Bottom left: open-wheel cars had this blunt face. Bottom right: long-tail bodywork was also used occasionally.

Top and center left: the start of the 1954 French GP; Kling took second in number 20. Center right and above: Fangio in the monoposto at 1954 GPs of Europe and Switzerland. Left (l to r): Uhlenhaut, Fangio, Taruffi, Moss, Kling, and Neubauer at the British GP, July 1955.

important here, but the *monoposto* was ready at last. Fangio enjoyed a gratifying win, but more spectacular was Karl Kling's great drive from far back of the pack, recording the fastest lap in the process. The Swiss GP was a 66-lap Fangio solo, which was expected. Juan also won at Monza in September, but only because Stirling Moss' Maserati suffered a ruptured oil tank with just 10 laps to go and a comfortable 22-second lead. Kling had to retire, the third straight time he'd failed to finish. There was only one GP left, at Barcelona, and this too proved disappointing. The new Lancia D50s were obviously faster, though none of them finished; instead, Mike Hawthorn ran a superb race with his Ferrari. The best Fangio could do was third, plagued by a quirky engine and heating problems caused by discarded newspapers blowing across the track from the stands and adhering to his fine-mesh grille.

Fangio was unquestionably the World Champion for 1954, but the season had been far from a complete success for D-B. The team had won four of the eight events, but the Italian win had come only by chance and without Fangio the only D-B win would have been at Rheims. More work was needed on tires, suspension, and cooling. The team also needed another Fangio. Neubauer found one: Stirling Moss. Though Moss considered the W196 a handful, he was amazed by its straightline performance, and was attracted by the chance to drive a really competitive machine. During the winter the Untertürkheim wizards thoroughly reworked the chassis for improved roadholding, modified the desmodromic valve gear, and made other engine changes that included a new intake manifold. Horsepower was now up to 290.

The 1955 season started in the usual fashion, with Fangio pleasing the crowd at Buenos Aires in an easy win against the Lancias and Ferraris. Herrmann, Kling, and Moss shared the fourth-place car two laps behind. The tight Monte Carlo circuit was the next venue, and such courses were no place for the Mercedes. Herrmann was injured in a practice shunt, and his substitute, Andre Simon, retired early in the race. Fangio also dropped out, due to transmission trouble. Moss finished ninth, 19 laps behind winner Trintignant. More changes were made to improve reliability and at Belgium in June, the Fangio/Moss duo led the field from start to finish. Following the disastrous accident at Le Mans that same month, where Pierre Levegh's Mercedes flew burning into the grandstand, the factory announced it would not participate in any race that did not have adequate safety provisions. There was little need for decisions, however, because four GP events were cancelled in the wake of the tragedy. As three of these—the French, Swiss and German—had seen D-B victories the year before, the aftermath of Le Mans, on balance, worked against D-B's 1955 Grand Prix effort.

No matter. Of the three remaining events, D-B simply won them all. At Zandvoort in Holland, Fangio and Moss romped home nose to tail, though Kling and Piero Taruffi (now substituting for the injured Herrmann) failed to finish. The team sent five cars to Aintree for the British GP. Fangio and Moss got short-chassis models, Kling and Taruffi the medium-chassis versions. Here the team scored its greatest victory, finishing 1-2-3-4. Altering the normal plan, Moss was allowed to sweep home in his native GP for his first Formula 1 win. Short-wheelbase cars were sent to the refurbished Monza circuit in September, but the more aerodynamic streamliner was found to be faster on this now-quicker track. The one long-wheelbase car on hand was given to Fangio, while another was ordered for Moss. The factory delivered it in 24 hours! Unfortunately, Stirling was plagued with transmission trouble—but Fangio ran a beautiful race, averaging nearly 20 mph higher than he had in winning the 1954 event.

Its point proven beyond a doubt, Daimler-Benz withdrew from Grand Prix racing after the 1955 season. This decision was made before its pull-out from sports car racing, but everyone expected it: there just weren't any more prizes to win. In two years, 42 Mercedes-Benz racers had been entered in 13 GPs; 27 had finished, nine of them first.

Against the Formula 1 backdrop, winning the 1955 World's Sports Car Championship was an incredible performance for Daimler-Benz. Here was a company that hadn't raced since 1940 returning to dominate the top two series in international competition in the space of just 18 months. In sports car events, D-B's chief weapon was Stirling Moss in the memorable 300SLR.

The SLR employed most of the basic engineering developed for the W196 GP cars. Because it was a "sports car," however, it carried different bodywork with a two-seat cockpit. It was also marked by ostensible "road equipment," like a cut-down racing windshield, headlamps, and doors. In 1955 this car won every major race it entered: the Swedish Grand Prix, the Nürburgring, the Targa Florio, the Tourist Trophy—and the brutal Mille Miglia. Moss' win in the last event was the first by a British driver and the first by a non-Italian since Caracciola, a German, had triumphed in 1931.

Moss asked Denis Jenkinson to navigate for him in the Mille, because he considered the British writer and motorcycle racer cool-headed and intelligent. "Jenks" had to be: nearly a thousand miles of racing over

Top left: Fangio on his way to win the 1955 Buenos Aires GP. Upper left center: Stirling Moss captured his home '55 GP at Aintree, England in the W196 monoposto. Upper right center: Fangio leads Moss at that year's Dutch Grand Prix, and came home to win in that order. Bottom right: Fangio scored yet another win at the 1955 Belgian event. Top right and above left and right: the brutish 300SLR simply overwhelmed competitors in 1955 European sports car events. A huge flap acted as an air brake on cars with single-seat bodywork, though the two-place versions were more commonly used. Chassis engineering was basically the same as the W196 Formula 1 cars, but capacity was 3.0 liters.

open roads up and down the Italian Peninsula, never repeating any section, is a daunting prospect. It was Jenkinson's job to plot the course in advance, read the map, and advise Moss before every curve or hill on which way the road went afterward. A mistake would be disastrous: unless Moss could set up the car exactly for what lay ahead, precious seconds would be lost—and possibly even two lives. The "map" was a strip of paper 17 feet long, carefully rolled up in an oilskin. It had been laid out during several practice runs in which Moss had smashed twice (one a collision with an army truck full of live ammunition). Hand signals were devised because the wind and engine noise would make cockpit conversation impossible. Moss developed so much confidence in his co-pilot, wrote Ken Purdy, that he could "accept Jenkinson's signal that the road went straight after a blind brow ahead; he could hold his foot flat on the floor, go over the crest at 170 mph, let the car fly for 50 yards, and press on."

Entered in the over-2000cc "unlimited" class, the 300SLRs rumbled down the famous ramp at Brescia several hours after the early, low-displacement starters. Soon they were overhauling the smaller cars and careening past the competition. Near Vicenza, Moss arrived at a tight left-hander on the tail of a Ferrari. He took the turn visibly faster than anyone else—including Fangio—then slipped by the Ferrari before the next bend. The Italian crowd was momentarily stunned. Finding their voices, they shouted "Veloce!" Moss was soon leading his class, with Taruffi running over 30 seconds behind in a Ferrari, followed by a squadron of Ferraris and Mercedes that included Herrmann, Kling, and Fangio. Moss made only two fuel stops, changing wheels at the second one in Rome. Though he could not know it, Taruffi had dropped out with low oil pressure. But Stirling could only pour on the coals. "It was nine-tenths and ten-tenths motoring," wrote Ken Purdy, "absolutely flat out, nothing left. Jenkinson told of their passing low-flying aeroplanes; of Moss going down a steep hill flat out in third gear,

Below left: the battered Moss SLR at the '55 Mille Miglia. Below right: Neubauer embraces a grimy Jenkinson, Moss after '55 MM win.

shifting to fourth and standing on the accelerator . . . Jenkinson was burned by the hot gearbox; the G-forces in the turns made him vomit; he lost his glasses overboard in the slipstream; but in 10 hours, 7 minutes and 48 seconds of the fastest over-the-road motoring anyone has done since the motorcar was invented, he made not one mistake and missed giving only one signal, when a full tank sloshed a pint of petrol down his back."

Because the Mille Miglia was discontinued after the high-casualty 1957 event, the Moss-Jenkinson drive still stands as the absolute sports car performance on the open road. But in the wonder of their feat it should not be forgotten that Mercedes owned five of the first 10 places. Fangio had finished second in his 300SLR, only half an hour behind Moss—and driving alone! John Fitch won the GT class and finished fifth overall—also solo—in his 300SL. The German cars also took seventh and 10th.

The 300SLR's victory in the 1955 Mille Miglia is so spectacular that it tends to eclipse the car's equally brilliant performances in other races. At that year's Tourist Trophy, run on the narrow, twisting Dundrod circuit in Northern Ireland, Moss resorted to regular use of first gear. With short overall

gearing that limited top speed to "only" 158 mph, he won at an average of 88.32 mph. In Sicily's crippling open road race, the Targa Florio, the SLR's granitic durability was tested when Moss drove right down an embankment and ended up on a rock with the wheels spinning at maximum rpm. "Its frame was bent and its engine took almost three gallons of water when it reached the pits," recalled Karl Ludvigsen. "Yet [teammate] Peter Collins almost at once started lapping at blistering speed, eventually having his own run-in with a parapet. He and Moss, in his final turn at the wheel, brought the very used-looking Mercedes-Benz back up to first place." Said Collins: "Despite Stirling's efforts and my own to write the machine off, by going over precipices and through walls and shunting other cars, still somehow the car managed to last through this race."

The Mille, the 'Ring, the Targa Florio, the TT: these were the places where the 300SLR convincingly proved its mettle. Neubauer and his team had worked hard, and they played to win. Yet, despite many claims to the contrary, they were not determined to win at all costs, to go on even when their teammates and the innocent died. Eight hours after the fatal accident at Le Mans (the noble

Levegh was last seen alive with his arm in the air, warning teammate Fangio of the danger), a telegram was delivered to Neubauer at the pits. In the hours since, Moss/Fangio and Kling/Simon had secured first and third place, respectively, the former leading the number-two Ferrari by two minutes. The telegram was from Fritz Nallinger in Untertürkheim: "The pride of designers and drivers must bow to the grief suffered by countless French families in this appalling disaster." The pit crew hung out an appropriate signal. The two silver SLRs, running without fault, slowed, pitted, and were then wheeled away. It was an eloquent gesture of respect. Daimler-Benz would not compete at Le Mans again.

In fact, it is widely thought that the firm has not competed in *any* international events since 1955, but this is not strictly true. Granted, the racing team was broken up, and Neubauer retired to manage the company museum (he died in 1980 at age 89). But Kling and, later, Baron von Korff did some rallying and sedan racing. For example, Mercedes finished 1-2-3 in the memorable Monte Carlo Rally of 1960, the year Walter Schock

Below left: Moss takes the winner's flag in the '55 Tourist Trophy. Below right: Andrew Cowan's 280E in the '77 London-Sydney Marathon.

took the European Touring Car Championship for the *second* time (the first was 1956). Mercedes continued to hold this title in 1962-63, and was a strong contender in 1964. The company assisted many rallyists in the late '70s, and with good results: Andrew Cowan's 280E won the 1977 running of the London-to-Sydney Marathon, and a team of 280Es and 450SLCs dominated the *Vuelta a la America del Sud*, an exhausting 18,000-mile enduro. Though modest factory help is usually no match for the all-out efforts of Ford and other companies, Daimler-Benz has continued to provide rally support in the 1980s. So, in a way, the competitive urge is still strong in Untertürkheim.

As proof, one only need consider the C111. When it first appeared in the summer of 1969, this futuristic mid-engine coupe immediately touched off worldwide speculation that Daimler-Benz was preparing to go racing again. Of course the company never seriously contemplated such a move, but the C111's mere existence tantalized enthusiasts, who could easily envision what D-B could do with the car if only it would. At the very least the C111 looked quite feasible for production, an even more exciting thought. There it was: an unusual but "producible"

shape, crouched low over jumbo tires, and marked by a radically curved windshield and a mean-looking snout bearing the proud three-pointed star. It even had gullwing doors. Here, presumably, was the reincarnation of the vaunted 300SL.

Like its illustrious predecessor, the C111 was designed around technology developed from D-B's racing experience, but that's where the engineering similarities ended. While the SL had been developed as a roadgoing sports car, the C111 was intended mainly as an engineering test bed, a dramatic showcase for D-B's latest thinking. For this reason, company officials refused to speculate about competition or production prospects for the car. Still, there was the almost irresistible notion that the C111, or something very much like it, was just around the corner. "It would be unlike D-B to waste it," commented *Road & Track* magazine in 1969. But, as far as showroom sales were concerned, they did exactly that.

In its original form, the C111 employed a pressed-steel platform chassis of tremendous strength, bonded to a steel monocoque body with fiberglass panels. The front suspension consisted of unequal-length A-arms, coil springs, telescopic shocks and an anti-roll bar. At

Above left: Rudolf Uhlenhaut with D-B's original three-rotor Wankel engine in 1969. Top and center right: the three-rotor C111 in its fully finalized "Mark I" guise, 1969. Above: the turbodiesel C111/III in its super-aerodynamic 1978 form.

the rear were double lower lateral arms, single upper arms, trailing arms, coil springs, tube shocks, and another anti-sway bar. Four-wheel ventilated disc brakes (sans power assist), recirculating-ball steering, and a five-speed manual transmission

were featured. The coupe stood 44.3 inches high, its 2425 pounds carried on a 103.2-inch wheelbase. All very interesting, but the most intriguing thing about it was the engine, a three-rotor Wankel.

Daimler-Benz had begun developing its Wankel along NSU principles in the early '60s. Though it used three instead of two rotors, its design was not otherwise significantly different from NSU's. Total displacement was 1800cc (110 cid), nominally equivalent to 3.6 liters (220 cid) in a conventional reciprocating engine. In layout it was light,

compact, and ultra-clean— simpler, *R&T* said, "than what we've come to expect from Mercedes, with just three plug wires emerging from a distributor cap that looks as if it originally belonged to a 12-cylinder engine and a mechanical fuel-injection pump with only three tubes coming from it." The D-B Wankel produced 280 DIN horsepower (320 SAE) at 7000 rpm and 216 lbs/ft of torque (250 SAE) at 5000/6500 rpm. Following current trends in racing car design, the engine was mounted amidships, restricting luggage

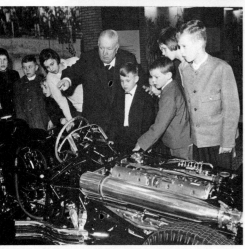

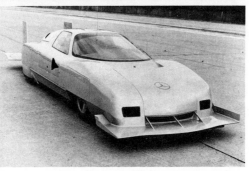

Top: the C111/III at Nardo, 1976. Above: the super-slick C111/IV of 1979. Left: Neubauer and friends with the W196 at the D-B Museum.

emissions standards and the rotary engine's comparatively high fuel thirst. (The latter had also put the kabosh on General Motors' Wankel project.) All hopes that moneyed customers would eventually be able to buy one of these *wunder* cars were quashed by the end of 1970.

The C111 would not disappear forever, though. It came back in 1976 as the C111/III, still with the basic body configuration seen at Geneva but now powered by D-B's production five-cylinder diesel engine boosted by a turbocharger. Packing 190 bhp (DIN), this car established endurance speed records up to 5000 miles in its class and up to 10,000 miles for all classes, lapping the Nardo proving grounds in Italy at upwards of 150 mph. It surfaced again two years later with a 3.0-liter turbodiesel five as used in the production 300SD and with modified low-drag bodywork. In this guise it set nine world records over a distance of 2344 miles, averaging 195.398 mph—and 14.7 miles per gallon. In 1979 the even slicker C111/IV appeared, boasting massive horizontal air dams at each end plus twin vertical rear stabilizer fins. Powered by a 500-bhp turbo V-8, this car set the world's closed-course speed record with a lap of 250.97 mph.

What we can and should conclude from such exploits is that Daimler-Benz has never really retired from competition, at least not in the sense that an executive retires from a job. Rather, the company has simply redirected its renowned engineering talent toward more relevant goals. With regard to out-and-out racing, D-B remains semi-retired at most. It is still able to produce impressive cars that could just as easily win races as demonstrate some new aerodynamic principle or body material. The C111 illustrates that, at Daimler-Benz, racing did not improve the breed. The breed improved the racing.

space and creating visibility problems. But the press couldn't figure out whether the C111 was a racer or a production prototype since it had a handbrake and all the other usual accoutrements of a road car. Top speed was an astonishing 165 mph.

The rumor then went around that D-B was definitely thinking about offering this latter-day Gullwing to buyers, and would make a final decision based on reaction to a "Mark 2" version displayed at the 1970 Geneva Motor Show. There was more glass area, a longer snout,

scooped-out bodysides, and a yet more powerful Wankel. This engine used four rotors, and developed 350 bhp (DIN) at 7500 rpm from a displacement equivalent to 4.8 liters (293 cid) in a piston engine. Factory sources state this car could reach close to 300 km/h or about 185 mph. The Geneva crowd certainly liked what they saw, but a production model never materialized. Although it strains credibility to think of such a car as feasible in today's speed-limited America, Daimler-Benz was probably influenced more by U.S.

THE SL SPORTS CARS 1954~63: MASTERY IN MOTION

Below: the alluring 300SL Gullwing coupe in its most famous—and startling—pose. Opposite page: a late Gullwing prototype from 1954. Inset door windows were eliminated on production models.

While Daimler-Benz was moving forward with its carefully orchestrated assault on Formula 1 in 1954, the production 300SL was moving forward toward reality. The early SL racing prototype, as we have seen, turned in outstanding performances in 1952. In its very first race, that year's Mille Miglia, it finished only 4½ minutes behind the winning Ferrari. Later, the cars placed 1-2-3 at Bern, 1-2-3-4 at the Nürburgring, 1-2 at Le Mans, and 1-2 in the Carrera Panamericana. The racing 300 SLs would be retired after this one season, but they would not be forgotten by those who had seen them in full cry.

The 300SL production prototype was displayed at the New York Automobile Show in February 1954, rekindling race fans' memories. It was not until a year later that the production version became genuinely available—and then only to those with the wherewithal to afford one. As might be expected with a road car based on a racing design, the production 300SL was eminently more civilized, but it also had more power as well as more luxury, something very uncommon in such transitions. Yet nothing was lost, as witness John Fitch's GT class win and fifth-place overall finish in the 1955 Mille Miglia, mentioned in the previous chapter.

In general appearance the production Gullwing and the racing 300SLR were quite similar. But because two of the nine SLRs constructed had coupe bodywork, some of the differences should be listed here. Though tubular-truss chassis construction and the 3.0-liter engine displacement were shared, the cars were quite different under the skin. The SLR's straight eight with desmodromic valvegear was canted in the engine bay some 30 degrees off the vertical axis to the right. Power takeoff was at the center of the engine to a ZF five-speed gearbox/differential unit. The massive brakes were mounted inboard at both ends, and 16-inch wire wheels were fitted. The body was constructed of lightweight Elektron, a magnesium alloy, and the car's total dry weight was a svelte 1830 pounds. The well-upholstered coupes notwithstanding, none of the SLRs were sold to the public. By contrast, the production SL was powered by an inline six inclined at an angle of 50 degrees to the left of vertical. Power was taken to a four-speed all-synchro gearbox through a Fichtel & Sachs Type H18 ST9 single-dry-plate brass-faced clutch with a spring pressure of 765kg. The brakes were initially Alfin drums measuring 10¼ x 3½ inches, with twin leading shoes at the front and leading and trailing shoes at the rear. Through chassis number 5500353, a Bendix Treadl-Vac booster was fitted (initially with a 5¼-inch vacuum cylinder, later a 6.0-inch). Later SLs had an Ate (Alfred Treves) T50 booster, as indeed did most M-B 190/220 passenger cars of the late '50s (a T50/12 unit was later introduced, but not on the Gullwing). This unit provided a boost of approximately twice brake pedal pressure, and some SL owners today feel brake effort is excessive for hauling down safely from very high speeds. Production bodies were constructed of both aluminum and steel, of which more shortly.

The 300 powerplant is thoroughly described in the following chapter. Suffice it to say here that it was a sturdy, if heavy, cast-iron six with Bosch mechanical fuel injection and a massive forged-steel crankshaft supported by seven main bearings. Dry-sump lubrication was employed, and a remote oil tank was located in the left fender. Coupled with a more-than-adequate oil cooler adjacent to the water radiator, this system permitted sustained engine speeds of up to 6000 rpm. One persistent problem that besets SL owners is not how to cool the oil, but rather how to keep it hot. Running with 10-12 quarts, rather than the maximum of 16, and blocking or by-passing the enormous oil

cooler are common solutions.

Gearbox ratios on the first 40 production SLs were 3.14, 1.85, 1.31 and 1.00:1. The lower three ratios were subsequently shortened to 3.34, 1.97, 1.39. Cars through 1955 chassis number 5500087 had a long bent shift lever emanating from the transmission tunnel; after this, a remote-control linkage was adopted. Final drive was through a double-jointed open driveline to the rigidly mounted differential, retained by rubber at three points. The SL differential varied from that in the 300-series sedans in having a cast-aluminum housing and a ZF self-locking unit instead of the conventional spiders. Standard final drive ratio was 3.64:1 on

cars shipped to the U.S., but 4.11, 3.89, 3.42, and 3.25 gearsets were optionally available. Speedometer calibrations were tailored to suit—not the speedo drive gear, as on domestic cars. With the 3.25:1 gearset the instrument read up to 180 mph, the others to 160 mph.

The 300SL's suspension used coil springs all around and tubular shock absorbers. Competition springs were optional on steel-bodied cars, standard on the aluminum ones. They didn't exactly provide a boulevard ride, but did wonders for handling. Part of the improvement no doubt stemmed from a lower center of gravity, as the car rode about an inch lower. Even the standard spring rates (290/256 lbs/in. front/rear) were considerably harder than those on the later 300SL roadster (142/142).

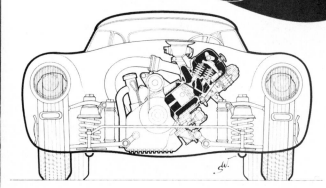

Right and below right: factory drawings highlight 300SL's slanted engine, complex chassis. Below left: another view of the late prototype.

Of course the most striking aspect of the 300SL Gullwing, at first glance anyway, is its appearance. The smooth, flowing lines are difficult to fault, timeless to the point that the car is often confused with new models by some folks. On opening the doors, it becomes clear that the styling is elegant as well as functional. What few fittings, adornments, knobs and the like are there are typical D-B both in design and execution. The longitudinal hood bulges (later imitated on the 1956 Corvette), the anodized aluminum belt trim moldings, the upward-opening doors—they're all there for a reason, be it to clear the engine, cover a seam in the body, or provide access to a complicated chassis. The 300SL was a fully integrated design, a claim few cars could ever make.

Records vary on Gullwing production numbers, and for several reasons. The factory's original figure was 1485. Later this was revised to 1402, still later to 1400: 146 in 1954, 867 in 1955, 311 in 1956 and 76 in 1957. It is not clear whether Daimler-Benz tracked production by chassis, body or engine serial number, so it's possible the count varies depending on which of these is cited. To complicate matters further, one or more of the early 1952 models were sold, and at least one—perhaps more—is known to have been fitted with production bodywork. There is, however, accurate data

on the number of aluminum bodies: 29 in all, the first of 1955 serial production. However, not all were not mounted on 1955 chassis, and there may be some aluminum-body '56s. Whatever the precise totals, aluminum or steel, the number built was far too small, and the demand is greater today than when production ceased over a quarter-century ago. A genuine, original, low-mileage Gullwing routinely commands six-figure prices on today's collector market.

The weight difference between the aluminum- and steel-bodied cars is not as great as you might think. Hood, doors, decklid, rocker panels, belly pans, and interior sheetmetal were made of aluminum on both. The lightweight version saved a few pounds through the use of Plexiglas in areas other than the windshield, but this was probably offset by the Rudge center-lock wheels invariably fitted to the aluminum cars, which added some 25 pounds each compared to the bolt-on variety. Actual weights are difficult to obtain but, according to factory sources, the standard steel car weighed 2557 pounds dry; adding tools, fuel, water, oil, spare tire and battery gave 2855 pounds at the curb. This is still reasonable by today's standards, and an indication of the 300SL's performance potential in view of its 200 + horsepower.

Early Gullwings were shod with either Englebert, Dunlop

Extra Super Sport or Continental Super-Record tires of 6.50 × 15 size. Fender wall clearance was minimal, and finding modern tires that will fit this "antique" automobile is a problem. Carried over from the 1952 racing version was a full belly pan plus a large fuel tank, although the production car carried "just" 34.5 versus the racer's 45 gallons. However, the roadgoing SL carried just one spare tire instead of two, so luggage space was vastly improved, and all manner of soft goods could be stuffed in and around the spare.

Aside from its burly good looks, the 300SL's most striking feature was its unorthodox chassis design—and, of course, it was this tubular framework that had necessitated the gullwing doors. The space frame was complex, and the methods by which the engineers incorporated the doors without compromising structural integrity were ingenious. But what really mattered is that it all worked in a practical and even remarkable way.

On the road, the 300SL was much more than the sum of its parts. The first car tested in Britain carried the 3.64:1 U.S.-standard final drive, and the remarks published in *The*

Below: a 300SL family portrait. L to r: 1954 SLR coupe, the production '55, a '53 prototype, and the original racing Gullwing of 1952. Road car differed surprisingly little from the racers.

Autocar magazine's report remind us just how well the then-new 300SL performed. To begin with, the editors noted, the car was tractable, even in dense city traffic. "But there is no doubt that its true place is outside built-up areas, where it can be allowed to come into its own. After it has trickled along in third and top gears, the time eventually arrives when the driver is able to see opportunity in front of him, and second gear can be selected, so that the car really comes to life... The effect is electrifying. [Occupants] receive at first a mild pressing back into the seat, and then, as the power comes in between 3500 and 4000 rpm, they feel as though they are being rocketed through space. Up to 70 mph is available in second gear, and then can come a quick movement into third. The rev counter needle drops back for a second or two, and again at 4000 rpm the effect of being urged forward by some irresistable force is felt. There is a somewhat harsh note from the engine, but little exhaust and wind noise; in fact, with the rev counter needle on the red mark at 6000 rpm, it is possible to converse in normal tones." The magazine recorded the 0-60 mph sprint in 8.8 seconds and 0-100 mph in 21 seconds flat. As for cruising speed, that was limited mainly by the English landscape. On an *Autobahn* it was certainly upwards of 120 mph.

The 300SL ride, again quoting the road test, was "by no means harsh," and the steering cat-quick with but two turns lock-to-lock. "Oversteer is apparent, and unless one is travelling comparatively slowly it is essential to drive the car round a corner. Any inclination to ease the throttle and the rear

continued on page 161

Top: 300SL was the first Mercedes to break with the traditional face. Center: a peek inside the Gullwing cockpit. Bottom: roadster replaced fabled coupe in 1957.

Introduced in 1955, the 300Sc was a more powerful 175-bhp version of the original Type 300S. Shown: the 1957 cabriolet.

An interesting comparison here of the Types 300S and 300Sc. The car on the opposite page is a 1953-55 Type 300S, while the one above is a post-1955 300Sc, distinguished largely by its extra chrome hood trim. Both versions are shown in the sleeker roadster configuration that did away with the landau bars and bulky top-down appearance of the normal cabriolet. Interiors were elegantly crafted and had a full complement of luxury features. The instrument panel layout was similar to that of the large 300 sedans from which the Super models were derived.

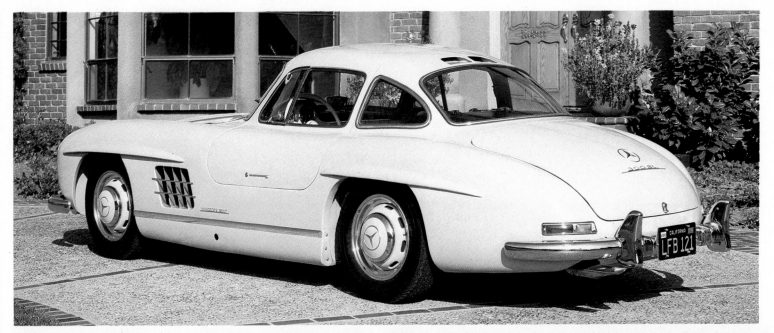

Vying for enthusiast affections with the prewar SS/SSK and 500/540K, the production 300SL Gullwing coupe was publicly announced in 1954 but did not become generally available until the following year. The car pictured here is an early American-market 1955 model. The roadgoing Gullwing used the same sort of complex, multi-tubular space frame as its racing forerunner, but had fuel injection instead of carburetors and, consequently, more horsepower—215 bhp (DIN) at 5800 rpm. Though distinctive, the gullwing doors necessitated by the chassis design made entry/exit a chore and were not suited for tight parking spots. Still, they have undeniable sex appeal.

Less distinctive than the Gullwing but no less a thoroughbred is the 300SL roadster, which replaced the fabled coupe in 1957. Besides conventional front-hinged doors, the roadster also boasted an extra 10 horsepower thanks to an increase in compression ratio, its fuel-injected six rated at 225 bhp DIN at 5900 rpm. Almost as avidly sought after as the Gullwing, the roadster saw only 1858 copies before it was phased out in 1962, one reason asking prices are high now.

Above and far left: the 300SL roadster. Near left: the 300SL Gullwing coupe. These models inaugurated the Daimler-Benz practice of using a full-width grille on its sports cars instead of the traditional upright Mercedes radiator. The roadsters shown here carry European specification headlamps (compare with the car on the previous two pages). All 300SLs used D-B's low-pivot swing-axle rear suspension and 3.0-liter fuel-injected ohc six-cylinder engine. The roadster was somewhat heavier than the Gullwing, mainly due to the structural modifications made to the tubular space-frame chassis to accommodate the front-hinged doors.

Opposite page: the all-conquering Mercedes-Benz W196 Grand Prix racer of 1954-55 with the streamliner open body used on longer, higher-speed circuits. Tubular space-frame construction was employed. The 2.5-liter straight eight produced 257-290 bhp.

Above: the W196 in its open-wheel monoposto form as first seen at the Nurburgring in the 1954 European Grand Prix. Below: only two of these prototype racing 300SLR coupes were built in 1952. They should not be confused with the 1955 SLR sports racers.

Opposite page: among the rarest postwar Mercedes-Benz models, this is a 1962 example of the 300d convertible sedan. Only 65 of these cars were built from mid-1958 to early 1962, and then only to special order. Compared to earlier models, the 300d featured mildly revised body styling and fuel injection instead of carburetors for its 3.0-liter ohc six. This page: a late example of the interim Type 300b sedan illustrates this series' rather Gothic styling. With the 300d in 1957, the pillared sedan was replaced by a four-door hardtop model.

Long overshadowed by the 300SL, the four-cylinder 190SL is nevertheless a fine car in its own right. Three examples are presented here, two with the detachable hardtop that was offered as a factory option. Launched about a year behind its big brother, the 190SL was based on the W121 chassis of the 180/190 sedans, and used a tuned version of the 190 engine delivering 105 bhp (DIN) at 5700 rpm. Though not very fast off the mark, the 190SL could reach up to 110 mph. Close to 26,000 of these cars were built before the model's phase-out in 1962 in preparation for the "pagoda-roof" 230SL. Today, the 190SL is an increasingly sought-after collectible automobile.

The cabriolet version of the Type 220S, introduced in 1956 as the successor to the 1954-56 Type 220a. A four-door sedan and two-door coupe were also offered.

continued from page 144

of the car will tend to swing round. The downhill left- and uphill right-hand bends on a daily route were taken very fast and with complete confidence... On wet roads the car slides slightly, but with judicious handling there is no tail breakaway. It is a car that teaches its lessons sharply and thus demands respect."

Much has been written about the true top end of these marvelous machines and, while some of it may not have been exactly accurate, there was almost nothing else in those years that could match the 300SL. The cars have been seen many times at the Bonneville Salt Flats in Utah, but not all the records survive. The E Grand Touring class mark a few years ago stood at 153.711 mph, held by Don Ricardo of Pasadena with a highly modified aluminum-body example. Other runs were Scace in 1955 (136.397), Schmidt in 1957 (150.647), Worthington in 1962 (144.263) and Stallings the same year (142.800 in two classes). In 1966, Gordon Worthington returned to clock 148.917 mph. Lynn Yakel of the Gullwing Group club has driven over 144 mph on two occasions, using both the 3.64 and 3.25 gearsets in one-way timed runs. His most memorable experience in his 300SL occurred just outside Wendover, Nevada, in 1965: "While 'warming up the oil' and indicating something over 150 mph, we were passed—by Gordon Worthington, who apparently had the oil quite properly heated in his SL. My own car's a little older now, but I suspect it will still do it."

Notwithstanding its romance and permanent allure, the Gullwing was not a stunning success on the sales floors. The people with that kind of money to spend—$11,000, enough to buy a decent house in the mid-'50s—tended to demand more creature comforts, especially in the matter of entry/exit. While the unusual roof-hinged doors set collectors' pulses racing today, they were hardly a sales plus back then. It was impossible to open a Gullwing door if you parked close to a wall or in a crowded garage. The doors let water in when opened and, some said, even when closed. And with that wide lower ledge to negotiate, entering or leaving a Gullwing was not something that appealed to many people over 40.

Accordingly, Daimler-Benz phased out the distinctive Gullwing coupe in favor of a 300SL roadster with conventional front-hinged, outward opening doors. Introduced in early 1957, it also incorporated a number of other changes.

The main structural alteration was in the tubular frame, which was compromised by being lowered for the new conventional doors. An optional hardtop was offered as a supplement to the folding fabric top, but neither configuration was as slippery as the Gullwing body, and about 10 mph was shaved off the top speed of comparably geared models. But the roadster handled better, and when it came to amenities it was a marked improvement.

A key suspension modification was adoption of the low-pivot swing axle originally designed for the W196 Grand Prix car. (This was later applied to the 190SL roadster and 190 sedans, but not immediately to the 300SL.) The arrangement also featured a compensating spring that created higher roll stiffness for the same spring rate; thus, the springs were made appreciably softer, as mentioned above. It made a tremendous difference. Where the Gullwing had been squirrely, except in the most skilled hands, the roadster glided over all kinds of surfaces. It had, said *Sports Cars Illustrated* magazine, "a lightness of control that amounts to delicacy... [a] huge improvement over the gull-winged coupe." *SCI's* car had the 3.89 final drive, and pickup was predictably quick: 0-60 mph in 7.8 seconds, 0-100 mph in 19.2. However, the shorter axle ratio held top speed down to the area of 124 mph. (Three years later, *Road & Track* magazine tested one of the last roadsters built. It had the same ratio, but ran generally faster, scoring 7.6 seconds, 20.5 seconds and 130 mph, respectively.)

Arguments will likely go on forever about the merits of the Gullwing versus the roadster. "Purists" tend to favor the former, "drivers" (at least those who have to deal with American roads) support the latter. But the fact is that both 300SL models were splendid cars—no-holds-barred assaults on the ordinary. They were as fine a pair of sports cars as were ever lovingly pushed off the line at Coventry or Maranello—and better than most of their Untertürkheim compatriots. To borrow an ad slogan from Stuttgart's other automaker, nothing else even came close.

That said, we now turn to the 190SL—but without the diffidence usually accorded this car. The 190SL's main problem from the historical standpoint is that it sold alongside the 300SL and was largely overshadowed by its big brother. Comparisons were—and still are—inevitably drawn because both models seated two and, one supposes, carried similar styling including grille design centered around a huge chrome-plated tri-star. Had it been built by anybody else, the 190SL would be regarded today as a classic in its own right. Still, collectors are more sophisticated now, and rapidly increasing values within the hobby suggest that the merits of the 190SL are now more widely appreciated.

First indications that the 190SL was in development leaked in 1952. The first photos appeared in January 1954, and the car itself was finally shown

Top left: roadster's restyled dash featured vertical-reading minor gauges. Top right and above: 300SL Roadster featured more power and new low-pivot rear suspension.

in prototype form at the New York Automobile Show later that year. The prototype used a "tentative" instrument arrangement, carried a hood air scoop (later eliminated), and 300SL-style "eyebrows" on the front fenders only (they were added at the rear in production).

Considerable technical details remained to be worked out, and the first deliveries were delayed some 15 months. But Max Hoffman, the New York distributor for Mercedes-Benz and widely acknowledged as the instigator of the 190SL, was in a hurry to display it. Later he helped sell an encouraging percentage of the 26,000 examples built.

The 190SL was the first Mercedes with an overhead cam four-cylinder engine, and its cylinder bore was, in fact, shared with the Type 300 ohc six.

Unlike the 300SL, the engine stood upright. Induction was by dual Solex carburetors and a conspicuous "ram" that filtered incoming air. Daimler-Benz used this design in many engines, and was researching adjustable-length air rams for the 300SLR when it terminated its official racing program. The object of changing ram length was to extend peak torque over a wider rev range. The 190SL featured welded body/chassis construction, with engine, transmission, and front axle combined in a removable front

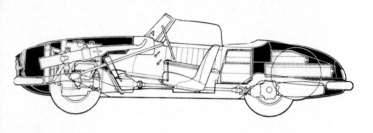

Top and above left: the 190SL, here with the optional lift-off hardtop in place. Above: cross-section view highlights 190SL's roomy two-seat cockpit and ample trunk space. Left: the prototype 190SL as seen at New York in 1954.

subframe. Suspension was independent all round. The production delays enabled D-B to adapt its low-pivot swing-axle rear end to the 190SL (it was also adopted for the 300Sc in late 1955). The floorpan was not unique but was shared with the 190 sedan introduced in 1956. (Both the 190SL and 190 sedans had the same factory chassis type designation, W121. The engine, code M121, was also the same, except that the sedans had a single carb instead of the SL's two.) This was the concept of Hoffman and others: broad use of existing componentry, the tried-and-true method of making dull sedans into interesting sporty cars that's been used at one time or another by just about every automaker.

But the 190SL was not simply another sedan-based sports car. It was exquisitely built and finished, and its engine was remarkably flexible, an eager, free-revving affair, if hardly in the same league with the 300 six. The 190SL would do 0-60 mph in about 13.5 seconds, the standing quarter-mile in 18.9, and its top speed was a shade over 100 mph. Performance, as *Road & Track* noted, was "a function of intelligent use of the gearbox. Driven vigorously through the gears it gets out and moves...we used 6000 rpm as an absolute rev limit, though the unit will go higher. Again, driven properly through the gears, it is difficult to tell that this is a four... On the highway an 80 mph cruising speed is extremely comfortable and well within the car's capabilities."

MERCEDES-BENZ ENGINEERING: THE LEGACY OF THE 300SL

Opposite page, top: the imposing face of the post-1967 standard-wheelbase (126-inch) Type 600. Bottom: the U.S.-market version of the elegant 1969 Type 280SE cabriolet. This page, top: the V-8 powered 280SE 3.5 cabriolet from 1970-71. Center: a one-year-only model in the U.S. was the 1971 300SEL 3.5, also powered by D-B's small-capacity V-8. Lower left: the contemporary 280SE six-cylinder sedan was little different externally compared to the 3.5 V-8 model. Lower right: an early American-market "New Generation" sedan from 1968-69 in the 220/220D/230 series.

Opposite page, top: a stunning laboratory on wheels, the mid-engine, Wankel-powered C111 experimental changed twice in its first few years. Shown here is the "Mark II" 4-rotor car with revised bodywork seen in 1970-71. Bottom: the C111 in its original 3-rotor 1969-70 form. This page, top and center: the two-seat "pagoda roof" Mercedes sports car of the '60s evolved through two displacement increases from the original 230SL to the 1968-70 280SL shown here. Below: the neat 250C coupe of 1970-72.

Left and below: a 1971 American-market example of the standard-wheelbase (126-inch) Type 600 Grosser. Despite a near 20-year production life, fewer than 3000 Grand Mercedes of all types were built. Above: one of the most popular Mercedes of recent years in the U.S., the 450SEL of 1973-80 was termed the best sedan in the world. Right: the current Mercedes sports car, launched as the 350SL in 1971.

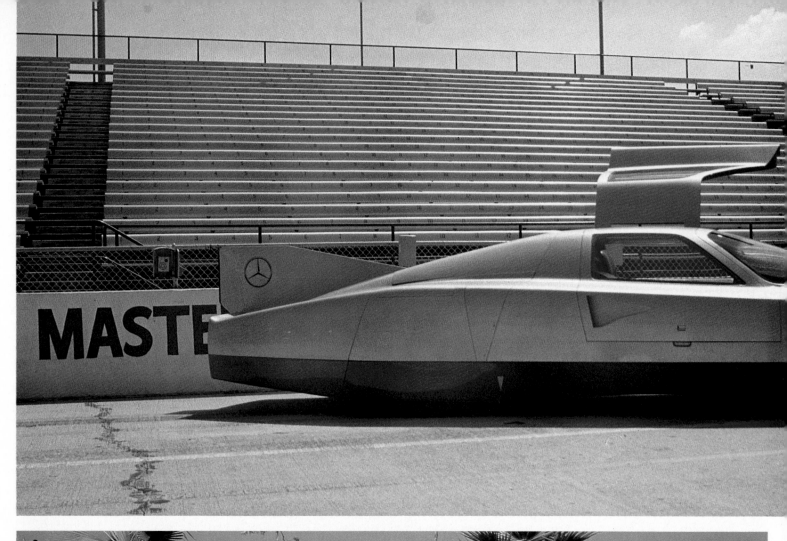

Above left and right: third in the C111 series of experimentals was this sleek aerodynamic version powered by a 230-bhp version of the Daimler-Benz five-cylinder turbodiesel engine. Overall length on this car was 212 inches, and weight was 3140 pounds. It set nine world speed records in April 1978 at the Nardo circuit in Italy. Lower left: the American-market 450SLC of 1979, a four-seat stretched coupe based on the 450SL chassis. Below: the U.S. 300TD from 1980, the first factory-built Mercedes wagon.

This page: for 1981, the successful W116 S-class models were replaced by the more aerodynamic W126 design, the current senior Mercedes. Shown is the editors' 300SD Turbodiesel test car. A gas-engine 380SEL model on a longer wheelbase was also offered in the U.S. that year. Opposite page: for 1982, the S-class lineup was expanded with the four-place SEC coupe, successor to the SLC. For the American market it was offered only with the all-aluminum 3.8-liter V-8 introduced with the W126 series.

Top and above: the 1982 300D Turbodiesel sedan in U.S.-market form. All the W123 Mercedes sold here, except the normally aspirated 240D, used the turbocharged 3.0-liter diesel five beginning this year, though the six-cylinder gasoline engine continued in the smaller D-B cars for European customers. Opposite page and upper and lower right this page: the editors' test 1983 380SL.

Newest member of the Mercedes-Benz family is the aerodynamically designed W201 sedan. It is also the smallest Mercedes since the early 1950s. Shown here are the American-market versions, the diesel-engine 190D 2.2 and the gasoline-powered 190E 2.3. Both are four-cylinder cars. Standard equipment is generous.

New to America for 1984, the 5.0-liter version of the all-aluminum Mercedes V-8. Top: the 500SEC. Above: the 500SEL.

continued from page 192

continued apace, however, and soon the engineers at Gaggenau were reporting more favorable results. Efforts now focused on two areas: smoother running behavior and a lighter structure. Much of this work can be credited to young Julius Witzky, who had joined the company in 1928 and worked almost exclusively on high-speed diesel engine design from 1932 on. (Witzky would go on to the U.S. after the war to join Packard, where he would be responsible for six-cylinder and V-12 marine diesels built for the U.S. Navy.)

Back at Untertürkheim, Max Sailer was getting impatient, and delegated young Fritz Nallinger to look into the diesel car project and make recommendations. Nallinger went to Gaggenau and came back in only two days—with a plan. The production car diesel would be a 2.6-liter (159-cid) four with the same 90x100mm (3.54 × 3.94-in.) cylinder dimensions as the aborted 3.8-liter six. As installed in the Type 230 chassis, it delivered 45 bhp at 3000 rpm and, after further refinements, was judged suitable for production. The 260D was born.

Each of the 260D cylinders had a displacement of 636cc (39 cid)—about 50 percent larger than the cylinders in the typical D-B spark-ignition engine of the day but one-third the size of the truck engine cylinders. Prudently perhaps, it was closer to a truck diesel than a gasoline car engine in basic architecture. A gear-driven camshaft was placed low in the side of the block. Long but sturdy pushrods operated rocker arms above the cylinder head, and the overhead valves were mounted vertically and in line, offset to the ported side of the head. Compression ratio was 20.5:1. Located opposite the valves was a wide-bore "shooting hole" leading to the pre-chamber. The whole injector assembly and

pre-chamber were disposed at a 45-degree angle to the cylinder axis, in line with the hole. Glow plugs were inserted at an angle from below into the pre-chambers. The block and head were iron castings, and the bores ran without liners, as in the gasoline engines. The rocker cover was an aluminum casting, extended to include part of the intake manifold. Pistons were made of Nelson-Bohnalite alloy, with a shallow cavity in the crown area facing the shooting hole. Skirts were slotted, and an Invar steel insert was placed above the wrist pin to equalize thermal expansion. At the bottom end was a hefty forged-steel crankshaft with five main bearings, secured by four-bolt caps. Connecting rods were wide H-section steel forgings.

Since the 260D was intended mainly for taxi service it was geared for agile sprinting in city traffic, so its top speed was only about 60 mph. Under typical conditions it averaged 26 mpg, making it about 25 percent thriftier with fuel than the gas-engine 55 bhp six-cylinder 230. Along with the rest of Daimler-Benz production, the 260D fell victim to the Nazi war machine in 1941, but the company judged its experience with the car favorably. The 260D had established not only the feasibility of diesel power for automobiles but also its acceptance in certain types of service. And it had given ample evidence of the diesel's fuel saving potential. Proof of its reliability came within its first year or two on the market, but the most convincing evidence did not emerge until long after the war, when many 260Ds were still giving excellent service after 10 or more years on the road.

In 1945, Daimler-Benz began picking up the pieces of its war-shattered operations, but the 260D was not among them. Its engine tooling no longer existed, and there was no thought of reviving the chassis it shared

with the Type 230. As noted previously, it was the smallest prewar model, the 170V, that was selected to begin postwar production. But there was still a definite desire to have a diesel car in the lineup, so it was decided to convert that model's spark-ignition four to compression ignition. This way there would be diesel and gasoline versions of the same car, thus continuing the policy begun with the 260D. (This practice would be followed with every new D-B platform introduced in the postwar era right up to the present.) Also, spinning off diesels from existing spark-ignition powerplants rather than using scaled-down truck diesels or purpose-designed engines made economic sense from a manufacturing standpoint in that many components and much tooling could be shared. And D-B's gasoline engines were hardly lacking the structural strength necessary to withstand the higher stresses associated with diesel operation.

The new 170D model was not announced until 1949, but much of it was already familiar from the 170V. Its four-cylinder engine retained side valves and the 73.5 × 100mm (2.89 × 3.94-in.) bore and stroke dimensions of the gasoline power unit. Block and head were cast iron, but the cylinder head was redesigned for the diesel, with vertical overhead valves and a rocker arm shaft. The camshaft was located as before, and space was provided in the side of the block for pushrods to operate the rocker arms. Because of this arrangement, symmetry in the block structure was lost, and the amputation of some water-jacket capacity had to be compensated for in other available areas. Cylinder dimensions were not altered despite the lower specific power output of the diesel configuration compared to spark-ignition engines of equal capacity. From its 1732cc (105.6 cid) the 170D had a maximum of

38 bhp at 3200 rpm.

Much had been learned about pre-chambers since the 260D, and D-B's considerable truck engine experience came in handy for the new small car diesel. A revised pre-chamber was adopted for the 170D engine, its shape closer to spherical than the conical profile used in the 260D. It proved to give more efficient combustion. The injector nozzle was no longer inclined at 45 degrees but stood at about half that angle, with the shooting hole lined up accordingly. Compression ratio was dropped to 19:1.

This new little diesel did a good job in the 170D, but the car's accelerative powers with a normal payload were not much better than those of a big diesel truck. Thus, in planning a diesel version of the new and heavier 170S introduced in 1949, it was deemed advisable to increase displacement—though the actual enlargement was amazingly modest. The 170DS duly appeared in 1952 with a 75mm (2.95-in.) bore, which only raised displacement to 1767cc (107.8 cid) and maximum output to 40 bhp at 3200 rpm. This engine, designated OM636, would be

carried over briefly in the new W120 chassis of the replacement 180D, introduced in 1953.

Besides the drawbacks of the side-valve four, there were several factors that led to a new generation of D-B car diesels in the '50s. Up to this time, D-B had used pumps having fixed injection timing (relative to crankshaft position). In association with Bosch, the company had succeeded in developing a centrifugal timing-advance mechanism that varied the start of injection in accordance with crankshaft speed. This was introduced on the production 180D at mid-year 1955, and resulted in a little more power, now 43 bhp (DIN) at 3500 rpm. The big benefit was in fuel consumption, for the waste caused by premature injection at low rpm had been eliminated. Also, D-B was now profitable enough to begin turning away from small, low-priced sedans and take its entire line upmarket. The diesel engines required for these plusher, costlier models would thus have to be more powerful, but preferably not much heavier. Finally, buyers in the higher price classes tend to be more

This page, clockwise from top left: 1936 Type 260D standard sedan, 1939 Type 260D six-seat limousine, 1955 Type 170S-D sedan, 1949 Type 170D. Opposite page, top: the OM636 diesel four, 1953. Bottom: 1953-56 180D.

critical of noise and vibration. For the diesel to retain its appeal, it had to become more refined.

There was also a manufacturing angle. There had been something of a revolution in the engineering of the company's spark-ignition powerplants with the 1951 introduction of the overhead-cam 220 and 300 sixes. And four-cylinder derivatives had quickly followed. This meant a tremendous investment in production machinery and equipment. Suddenly, the diesel was out of step with both design principles then in force and the firm's overall engine manufacturing setup. Such a state of affairs could not last long: it was illogical and only added to rising production costs. Clearly the passenger-car diesel had to be brought into line with the gasoline engines.

And it was. A brand-new diesel four arrived in September 1958 for the new 190D model

(confusingly, it was also used in the older 180D from 1961 on, thus creating the 180Dc). This was not an extension of the OM 636 unit the 170/180 series, but was derived from the new spark-ignition M121 engine in the 190 and 190SL. Identified as OM 621, it represented a radical departure from usual diesel practice in its short-stroke design, usually chosen for high-rpm capability. By contrast, most diesels are essentially slow-running engines, where a relatively long stroke is beneficial to good low-end torque. But this characteristic was ignored: D-B had other priorities.

Another big difference in the OM621 was its chain-driven overhead camshaft. Naturally this was dictated by the design of the gas engines. Valve operation was accomplished by the same means, namely finger-type cam followers. Dual coil

springs took care of closing the valves. Compression ratio went up to 21:1, mainly to assure quicker cold starts. The injection system was revised in collaboration with Bosch and yielded an important gain in the rpm range as well as output, now 55bhp (DIN) at 4000 rpm.

Compared with the 180D, the new 190D was superior in every way. Its top speed was 78 mph versus 72 and its 0-50 mph acceleration time was shortened from the 22.5 seconds of its predecessor to a more acceptable 18 seconds. And despite greater weight (2510 versus 2470 pounds) the 190D offered a definite edge in fuel economy: about 5 percent overall. The engine's maximum rpm had been raised to 4350 rpm, the limit being preset by the injection pump governor.

In fact, the speed at which D-B's diesels developed maximum power was climbing

steadily—from 3300 rpm in 1950 to 4200 rpm in 1960. More advanced injection equipment played a part in this, of course, but so too did years of patient, detailed study of such things as piston contours and clearances and piston ring and cylinder wall surface materials. Come to that, the concept of the diesel passenger car could not have succeeded in the market had it not been for careful design, quality construction, and a no-nonsense attitude about correcting defects.

It is no exaggeration to say that in the years from 1950 to 1960, Daimler-Benz singlehandedly laid the foundations for today's diesel-car market. But it took time: the half-millionth Mercedes-Benz diesel didn't come off the line until April 8, 1965. Things went faster after that, and D-B passed the one-million mark in diesel passenger car production on September 7, 1971.

The OM621 had a fairly long production life, the end not coming until January 1968. The 190D and its 200D sibling (1966-68) were dropped for the replacement 200D and the upmarket 220D companion model, both built on the same "New Generation" W115 platform. Both were four-cylinder models powered by differently sized versions of the new OM615 engine.

The essential features of this design were its pre-chamber shape, now nearly spherical, and an injector nozzle and shooting hole angle of about 20 degrees. A chain-driven overhead camshaft was retained, as well as finger-follower valve operation and the 21.1 compression ratio. The cast iron, linerless cylinder block extended to the crankshaft centerline as per tradition, and the timing chain case was now integrated with the crankcase. Intake ducts and exhaust pipes remained on the engine's starboard side as installed, with the injection pump and oil pump drive on the left. At a time when Peugeot was switching to distributor-type injection pumps, D-B remained totally faithful to the camshaft-and-plunger type. The sump nestled under the forward part of the crankcase for easier engine installation, and an aluminum clutch housing was bolted to the rear of the block, enclosing the flywheel.

Most automakers, including Daimler-Benz, usually vary bore and keep stroke constant to produce different displacements of a basic engine design. That way only one crankshaft is needed. But for the OM615, D-B did it the other way round, thereby standardizing piston and ring size. An 87mm (3.43-in.) bore was chosen for both the 2.0-liter and 2.2-liter versions. The smaller unit had a stroke of 83.6mm (3.29 in.), the large one 92.4mm (3.64 in.). Respective displacements were thus 1988cc (121 cid) and 2197cc (134 cid). Maximum output for the 200D unit was 55 bhp (DIN) at 4200 rpm. Interestingly, the longer-stroke 220D also ran to 4200 rpm, delivering a maximum of 60 bhp (DIN). The figures seem low, but the cars had tolerably good performance in spite of their highish curb weights (3022 and 3043 pounds). Acceleration times from standstill to 100km/h (62 mph) were 31 seconds for the 200D and 28.1 seconds for the 220D. Top speeds were 81.5 mph and 84 mph, respectively, and average fuel economy worked out at 28.3 mpg and 26.1 mpg.

The OM615 family expanded in September 1973 with the addition of the 240D, basically the 2.2-liter engine bored out to 91mm (3.58 in.), which raised the displacement to 2404cc (146.6 cid). Maximum output was 65 bhp at 4200 rpm, and in the same bodyshell it delivered predictably more urge. The time for 0-100 km/h acceleration dropped to 24.6 seconds, and top speed went up to 88 mph. Average fuel economy suffered, but not much: 24.8 mpg overall.

The next step came in September 1974 with the arrival of the 300D sedan. Its engine, designated OM617, could be described as a 240D unit with an extra cylinder tacked on. Yes, it was an inline five. Capacity was 3005cc (184 cid), and rated maximum power was 80 bhp (DIN) at 4000 rpm. Why five cylinders and not six? For one thing, a six with the cylinder spacing of the OM615 would have been too long for installation in the W115 "New Generation" cars. Also, the 300D engine weighed 515 pounds, only 68 pounds more than the 240D OM615. A six built with the same materials would have tipped the scales at 600 pounds or more. Of course the new engine had to have a very special crankshaft due to the inherently greater roughness of a diesel and the odd 1-2-4-5-3 firing order that required spacing the crankpins 72 degrees apart. Nonetheless, the OM617 turned out to be a very smooth-running engine, quite comparable with a six in that respect.

Initially the 300D was geared at 3.46:1 (compared with a 3.69:1 final drive in the 240D). This raised top speed to 92 mph, and the car could go from standstill to 100 km/h in under 20 seconds. Average fuel economy was 22.5 mpg—hardly bad for a mid-size sedan boasting the expected Mercedes amenities.

The energy crisis of 1973-74 greatly stimulated buyer interest in diesel passenger cars, not just in the U.S. but in Japan and many European countries as well. The diesel's greater mileage potential and the generally lower price of diesel fuel became increasingly powerful arguments as the '70s wore on, due mainly to soaring gasoline prices—fueled in many places by runaway inflation. And, as inflation continued to push car prices ever higher, many buyers liked the idea of the diesel's greater overall sturdiness compared to gasoline engines, especially as a growing number

of people could no longer afford to change cars as often as they used to. Even with all this, though, the market no longer seemed willing to put up with the diesel's performance penalties. In fact, this may have been a factor in the demise of the lowly 200D in 1978.

Daimler-Benz responded. Again reaching into its bag of truck diesel technology, it introduced a turbocharged version of the OM617 five-cylinder unit. It was initially offered only in the U.S. for the 1978 model year in a new variant of the W116 S-class sedan, the 300SD. The development program included a series of speed record attempts by a C111 experimental equipped with a pre-production version of the new powerplant. A Garrett turbocharger squeezed intake air to a pressure of about 2 bar or 29 psi. As in most turbo installations, compression ratio was dropped, to 17:1. An intercooler was fitted to reduce the charge-air temperature for greater efficiency. A new oil cooling system for the pistons was developed, the crankshaft was gas-nitrided, and valve heads were thickened, all for better reliability given the higher internal stress levels. The prototype turbodiesel delivered 190-200 bhp in the 4200-4700 rpm band. The specially equipped C111 set speed records for distances from 100km to 1000 miles and for durations from one to 12 hours at speeds up to 199.87 mph.

After this impressive demonstration, the engine was torn down for analysis. The verdict was favorable, so D-B management ordered the engineering staff to prepare a production version. Turbocharger boost pressure was lowered to 11 psi (0.75 bar), and compression ratio was raised to 21.5:1. This was enough to get a maximum output of 115 bhp (DIN) at 4200 rpm. After two years' further development it was putting out 125 bhp at

4350 rpm. For the 1981 model year the turbodiesel five was extended to the T-series station wagon based on the smaller W123 platform to produce the 300TD Turbodiesel model. The following season it became available in the W123 coupe and sedan as well, these being designated 300CD/300D Turbodiesel.

Bringing the Daimler-Benz diesel story up to date is a brand-new four-cylinder oil-burner, introduced with the advanced W201 190-series sedans in 1983. Considering how infrequently D-B brings out new powerplants, especially diesels, this OM601 engine is a significant development. It is, in fact, the first of a new breed, and is closely akin to D-B's 2.0/2.3-liter M102 four-cylinder gasoline engine, introduced to the European market in 1980.

Some traditional engineering features are still present in the OM601, such as the Benz-type pre-chamber, carefully evolved from the first diesel truck engine of 60 years ago. Also retained is chain drive for the overhead camshaft; the day of the cogged belt has yet to dawn at Untertürkheim. Yet there are breaks with the past. Valve operation has been revised, with direct-acting bucket tappets taking over for D-B's beloved finger followers. Also, the cylinder head is of the crossflow type, something unique in diesels but a feature of dubious value. Most likely this was chosen to provide extra underhood space, and moving the exhaust manifold to the right of the W201 engine bay has made it possible to accommodate all engine accessories on the left. The injection pump is still an inline unit—D-B still doesn't believe a distributor-type pump can provide adequate pressure control—driven by the timing chain. All other accessories are driven by a single flat V-belt operating in one plane. The older diesels have a number of belt

drives at different angles and levels, each one needing to be checked frequently for wear and tension. This new setup is maintenance-free. Another new idea is a fuel pre-heating system. At low ambient temperatures, fuel is routed through a heat exchanger via a thermostat to prevent unwanted fuel "waxing" and to promote correct viscosity.

Compared with the OM615, this new engine has a lot less beef in its basic structure, which means smaller water jackets but less weight. Less coolant speeds warmup, however, and there is ample protection against overheating in the effective radiator and 6-liter (6.3-quart) sump. Coolant capacity is cut to just under 3 liters (3.2 quarts). Ready for installation, the OM 601 weighs about 110 pounds (about 23 percent) less than the 2.0-liter OM615. To ensure easier cold starting, compression ratio has been raised a point, to 22:1.

The new diesel also runs to higher rpm than the old ones, which helps to explain its gain in output. There are two versions of the OM601. The European unit has bore and stroke dimensions of 87×84mm (3.43×3.31 in.) for swept volume of 1.9 liters. Rated power output is 72 bhp (DIN) at 4600 rpm, which compares with 60 bhp at 4400 rpm for the 2.0-liter OM 615. For the American market, stroke is increased to 92.4mm (3.64 in.), bringing capacity up to 2197cc (134 cid), though rated power remains the same. However, the U.S. engine puts out slightly more rated torque, 96 lbs/ft versus 90.5 lbs/ft, both at 2800 rpm. This compares to the 83 lbs/ft at 2400 rpm of the old 2.0-liter four.

One final distinguishing point of D-B's newest diesel is that it shares block castings with the M102 gasoline engines. This means that all four powerplants, gasoline and diesel, can be machined on the same line. Up to now, Daimler-Benz has always had separate diesel

engine machining lines, and this change was undoubtedly made in the interest of keeping production costs as low as possible.

What does it all do for the finished car? D-B claims the U.S. 190D 2.2 with five-speed manual gearbox will hit 60 mph from rest in 17.1 seconds and top out at an even 100 mph; with the available four-speed automatic the figures are 17.7 seconds and 93 mph (both with 3.42:1 final drive). Projected EPA city fuel economy works out to 35.8 mpg with manual and, a bit surprisingly, 36.5 mpg with automatic. In everyday driving, the compression-ignition 190 runs very smoothly for a large-displacement diesel-four, and is very quiet in the bargain thanks to a virtually encapsulated engine compartment. Unfortunately, off-the-line acceleration is in short supply, though overtaking ability is strong enough provided you keep the engine working in the 3000-3500 rpm range.

With the OM601, Daimler-Benz again stakes its claim to being the world leader in diesel-engine passenger cars and their technology. As for future technology it seems clear that direct injection must supplant the pre-chamber some day soon. D-B made just such a change on its truck diesels some years ago, but the resulting extra noise and roughness may have precluded direct injection from being applied to the automotive engines. Also, electronic injection seems certain to take over from the well-established mechanical system. And turbocharging will spread, too: in fact, there may come a day very soon when you can't buy a Mercedes-Benz diesel without it.

One thing we do know: Daimler-Benz will be in the forefront of diesel development, as it has been from the very first. The proud people behind the three-pointed star wouldn't have it any other way.

MERCEDES-BENZ IN THE 1970s: NOTHING BUT THE BEST

Discreet trunklid badges identify the W116 S-class variants offered in the U.S. for 1976. 450s were V-8s, the 280S a twincam carbureted six.

What Daimler-Benz called its "New Generation" cars, the sedans and coupes introduced in the mid- and late '60s, have long been a familiar sight all over the world. In some of the more affluent parts of this country, for example, they seem to be as ubiquitous as Chevettes and Escorts are everywhere else, and the sensible diesel versions are almost a part of the landscape in university communities. Such popularity isn't hard to understand: these were cars built to stand the test of time in more ways than one. The basic design was attractive, modern if a bit sober, and durable in the sense of not being slavishly trendy. All of which is expected of D-B. Yet even the least expensive models had not an ounce less engineering integrity or attention to craftsmanship compared to their predecessors. Clearly, D-B was still following the motto that had graced the wall of Gottlieb Daimler's workshop in Cannstatt some 80 years before: *Das Beste oder nichts*—nothing but the best.

Because of the plethora of Mercedes-Benz models in these years and the sometimes

Below: a sampling of the W109 S-class range from the '60s and early 1970s. Clockwise from top right: the 1967 Type 280S (to European

confusing nomenclature, let's sort out these cars before going any further. The easiest method is by chassis type. The 230SL sports car of 1963 represented the first phase of what would amount to nothing less than a top-to-bottom product overhaul at Daimler-Benz, and by 1968 all models except the limited-production Type 600 *Grosser* would be affected. The second phase involved a new line of upper-range six-cylinder sedans, the S-series or S-class, to replace the W111/W112 design that dated from the 220b/220Sb/220SEb of 1959. Designated W108, this new unit body/chassis platform rode a 108.3-inch wheelbase; a slightly longer 112.2-inch-wheelbase version, W109, was fielded for a successor to the previous 300SEL. Styling on all these cars was directly inspired by the large Mercedes coupes and cabriolets launched in 1961, and retained most elements of what was by now viewed as the "Mercedes look." The old tailfins were eliminated in favor of a lower hood, flat rear deck, and deeper beltline, all of which made the new models look sleeker despite their still four-

specification, 1968-69 U.S. Type 280S/SE, the American 280/300SEL for 1968-69, and the U.S.-spec Type 250S, 1968.

square shape. Naturally the famous Mercedes radiator and star mascot were retained, but the grille was now somewhat shorter and wider to suit the new lines. Introduced at the Frankfurt Automobile Show in late 1965, the first versions of the new style were a carbureted 250S and fuel-injected 250SE. The 300SE and the long-chassis 300SEL were added a year later.

D-B then updated its junior models in much the same way. Confusingly, this platform had the same 108.3-inch wheelbase as the S-series but carried a different type designation, W114/115. General appearance was much the same too, although this newer design featured slimmer C-pillars, a revised rear window shape, and an even more shallow rendition of the traditional grille. Trim and equipment varied only slightly between the many models which, in time-honored D-B fashion, were named according to engine. Here there was more confusion, for you could get a 250 sedan with the 2.5-liter six from the "senior" 250S, and there was a six-cylinder 230 as well. The base models were the four-cylinder 200 and 220 gasoline and diesel sedans. All the W114/115 cars were introduced in late 1967, again at Frankfurt,

and are the ones usually referred to as the "New Generation," though you could be forgiven for thinking the W108/109 models deserved that nickname, too. To preserve sanity all round, we'll observe this practice from here on, referring to the earlier design as the S-class, which of course it was.

It used to be conventional wisdom that you couldn't distinguish between the various Mercedes models except by reading the trunklids. In many cases this was true—and still is— which created a potential sales problem. After 1967, a plebian 200D didn't look that much different from, say, a 250SE—and, except for greater overhang on the S-class cars, there wasn't that much difference in size, either. Some may question whether potential S-class buyers weren't put off by this, but it turns out that snob appeal wasn't much of a factor in the sales of either model group. The fact was that, by the late '60s, owning a Mercedes— any Mercedes—had become an end in itself. This had been Packard's experience before World War II. It wasn't until that firm downgraded and cheapened its products after the war that its great prestige reputation suffered. And Daimler-Benz never did anything like that.

Compared to the S-class, the New Generation body design was "more compact in overall dimensions but contains very nearly the same volume in the interior." At least that's what company publicists said. It was certainly better-looking than the last of the aging, finny sedans it replaced—lower and wider but no longer. Interiors in both junior and senior cars of this period emphasized occupant safety, and exceeded U.S. standards in many areas. Examples included a deformable steering wheel, collapsible steering column, knobs and switches covered with soft rubber, an instrument panel

designed to collapse on impact in a collision, and thickly padded sunvisors.

With the new S-class, Daimler-Benz made a subtle but revolutionary change in its rear suspension design, and this was naturally carried forward on the New Generation models. The old swing-axle rear geometry, though constantly improved over the years, cried for a replacement by the mid-'60s, especially in cars without air suspension, which continued to display some bizarre rear camber changes under certain conditions. The solution was termed *Diagonal-Pendelachse* (diagonal swing axle), which was a misnomer. Actually it was a straightforward semi-trailing arm arrangement, quite similar to the design pioneered by BMW. The separate halfshafts with universal joints were attached to an ordinary differential. An optional hydraulic system used oil under high pressure to adjust special struts that replaced conventional shock absorbers, thus providing automatic self-leveling at the rear regardless of passenger and cargo weight. Up front was new A-arm geometry with an enormous steel crossmember. Extreme care was paid to suspension insulation to minimize the effects of road shocks on handling as well as occupant comfort. Four-wheel disc brakes with an improved servo were now standard, and a new gearbox was developed with ratios tailored to match the engine in each model. The four-speed automatic with first-gear starting was standard on the 3.0-liter S-class cars, and was optional elsewhere.

Although engine specifications didn't seem to change, the factory had spent time and money improving its powerplants, seeking more torque and greater flexibility rather than just top-end power and higher cruising speeds. The four-cylinder M115 gasoline engine in the 220, for example,

had newly fitted Stromberg carbs for the U.S. market. The six-cylinder 230 and 250 were powered by the M180 and M114 engines, respectively, and these also received detail running improvements.

The S-class lineup was revised in 1968 with a range of four new models, the 280S and 280SE sedans and the 280SE coupe and convertible (the latter replacing the previous 300SE and 250SE two-doors). Power was supplied by the new 2778cc (169.5-cid) M130 engine with 140 bhp in carbureted form, 160 bhp with injection, and more torque. The design of this smooth, flexible power unit was basically unchanged from that of the M189 six but improved in detail. This powerplant was also installed in the 300SEL from 1968 on, at which time the standard-chassis 300SE sedan was dropped.

Though the mammoth Type 600 continued as the ultimate Mercedes, it was somewhere off in the troposphere compared to everything else, so the 300SEL was effectively the top of the "real world" lineup. It headed a range of cars that had been carefully planned and sorted to fill a full spectrum of needs from all-purpose economy to total luxury. Critics pointed out that, improvements aside, there really wasn't anything very new about the engines. Some wondered why. They had only to wait another year.

Rumors of a new V-8 model had been circulating off and on since mid-1967, and when it appeared in early 1968 its trunklid badge read 300SEL 6.3. The engine was, of course, the hefty 250-bhp overhead-cam power unit from the 600, lifted intact and wedged under the

Opposite page: D-B's junior series in 1968-76 was the W114/115 "New Generation" of sedans and coupes. Clockwise from top left: the "face" of the European Type 250 from 1968, the sensible control board of the U.S. Type 220 (shared by all models), and the 1968 U.S. Type 220D sedan.

S-class hood. Engine displacements were now getting out of whack with D-B's usual model nomenclature. It's surprising they didn't christen this one 630SEL, though perhaps that would have stolen some of the 600's thunder. In any case, this was a spectacular sports sedan. D-B's new four-speed automatic was standard, and the final drive was altered from 3.23:1 in the 600 to a mere 2.85:1. This very tall ratio was all the 6.3 needed to gallop from 0 to 60 mph in 6.5 seconds flat and to run on to over 135 mph flat out. By any measure this was the quickest sedan in Daimler-Benz history, yet it handled beautifully. Although the V-8 added some 400 pounds to curb weight, most of it up front, the six-cylinder

300SEL had been so well balanced in the first place that excessive nose-heaviness was not a problem with the V-8 aboard, and front/rear weight distribution in the 6.3 was a moderate 55/45 percent.

The 300SEL 6.3 listed at $14,000 at the time of its U.S. debut, and had surpassed $16,000 by 1972, its last year on the market. This was a staggering amount for a six-passenger sedan in those years. But then this was no ordinary car. In addition to exciting performance and sports car handling, it was simply loaded with all the right equipment: 600-type air suspension, air conditioning, leather upholstery, radio, power steering, power windows. *Road & Track* magazine called this unassuming

yet impressive flyer "the greatest sedan in the world . . . truly the executive road racer. [It] does more different things well than any other single car." Incidentally, the factory fuel consumption figure was 15.2 miles per gallon—not at all bad for this kind of performance. It's hard to imagine a full-scale sedan able to outrun and outhandle an E-Type Jaguar, but the 6.3 could and would. Anytime.

Of similar configuration but not directly related to the 6.3-liter engine were the M116 3.5-liter and M117 4.5-liter V-8s. They arrived in 1970 and '71, respectively. They had been designed to fill a wide gap in the displacement range, and were being perfected when the S-class was announced—which explains

Above left and opposite page right: the 300SEL 6.3 had 250-bhp V-8 from the Type 600, and was a true muscle car. Center spread: the handsome "New Generation" 250C coupe, 1970. Left: the 1970 Type 250 sedan.

why that series' original engine lineup looked so underwhelming. The gap, of course, was between the 2.8/3.0 sixes and the big 6.3-liter V-8. Installed successively on the 280SE/SEL (including the two-doors) and 300SE/SEL models, these engines proved to be tremendous performers. The 3.5 developed 200 bhp (DIN); the 4.5 had 225 (215 SAE in the U.S.)—enough to give all these cars a top speed of well over 120 mph.

Writer Allan Girdler pointed out some key differences between the new V-8s for *Road & Track* readers. His description is a telling commentary on the trials and tribulations of selling cars in the U.S. in the early '70s: "Mercedes started with the 3.5

V-8 introduced last year [1970] for the 280SEL...Because of the timing of the 350SL's introduction, Mercedes wished to have the car qualify for sale under the 1972 [emissions] rules. What was required, in general, was a retarded spark advance and fuel mixtures leaned almost to the critical point. And the compression ratio had to be reduced, mostly to lower the oxides of nitrogen (NO_x). Thus modified, the 3.5 engine had no power left. So, Mercedes retained the basic engine, with sohc, Bosch fuel injection, transistor ignition, et al. The 92mm bore applies to both 3.5 and 4.5 engines. But the U.S. version has a taller cylinder block, new crankshaft and longer

stroke, up from 65.8mm to 84.7mm. This adds one full liter of displacement. The 4.5 cylinder heads have enlarged combustion chambers, for a low compression ratio of 8:1.

"After all that, we break even. The 3.5 V-8 produces 230 bhp by SAE rating method and 200 bhp by DIN measurement. The U.S. 4.5 does exactly the same at lower engine speed. We know therefore, that it takes another full liter of displacement to make up for emissions-based spark curves and fuel curves and a drop of 1.5 points of c.r....The immediate penalty is surprisingly small. The cost of making different blocks and cranks isn't too high and the planning for them was already taken care of since the possibility of enlarging the engine was taken into account when the V-8 was designed... The cost comes later, when the car is being operated. The 4.5 requires 10% more fuel than the 3.5 to do a given amount of work. The fuel isn't being used as efficiently, so more fuel is needed. It's as simple, and as depressing, as that."

Next on the agenda was a new six. The M189/M130 unit had reached its displacement limit

and was fairly long in the tooth by this time (remember, its origin was in the 1951 Type 300 engine). American emission laws had to be met, yet a new six had to deliver better fuel economy than the old unit or the new V-8s. The answer was the clean-sheet M110 engine, a twincam unit of 2746cc (167.6 cid). Though it was almost the same size as the outgoing six, it had room in the block for enlargement and, thanks to the dohc head, considerably more power. Introduced to Europe in 1971, it was initially offered in the New Generation bodyshell as the 280 and 280E. Designed to burn its fuel/air mixture more completely, the M110 scored a 10-percent reduction in carbon monoxide emissions and a 15 percent decline in hydrocarbons compared to its predecessor. Equipped with a dual downdraft Solex carburetor, the M110 produced 160 bhp (DIN) and 166.4 lbs/ft of torque; the 280E, with electronic fuel injection, had 185 bhp (DIN), 176 lbs/ft torque, and furnished up to 124 mph (against 118) with no penalty in fuel consumption, which worked out to about 19 mpg. This engine also found its way into the handsome New Generation coupe body style that had been introduced as the 250C in 1970, thus creating the 280C/CE. It was later offered in the W116 S-class series as the 280S/SE/SEL, although these

carried no further engine modifications and delivered the same performance as the lighter New Generation models.

Most of the design and engineering innovations we've mentioned up to this point were aimed squarely at the United States. Unlike many of its expensive—and some not so expensive—European rivals, Daimler-Benz was determined to maintain its place in the American market—and to capture even more of it. In 1971, D-B was selling upwards of 30,000 units a year in the U.S. (the figure has since risen significantly), and a growing proportion of these were the higher priced offerings. This was of crucial importance to the folks in Untertürkheim, and thus planning for future models began looking directly upmarket.

One of the first results arrived in late 1970 as a replacement for the 280SL and represented a complete change in character for the M-B sports car. This was the new 350SL, powered by the 3.5-liter V-8 and mounted on a new 96.9-inch-wheelbase platform dubbed R107. A year later, the derivative 4.5-liter 450SL was debuted, mainly for the U.S. Daimler-Benz now had a sports car the like of which had rarely been seen by any manufacturer, including D-B itself. Compared to its 230/250/280SL predecessors, the new R107 was longer both

overall and in wheelbase. This provided room for both "occasional" seating in the rear and the installation of air conditioning up front, which was standard for American-market models. It was also wider to accommodate federally mandated door guard beams and, at the same time, to allow the use of wider tires. The latter was almost a necessity, because the R107 lacked the previous SL's aluminum body panels and, with its added bulk, emerged over 300 pounds heavier. The American 450SL, with standard automatic transmission, power steering, and both hard and soft tops, weighed in at close to 3800 pounds. This was far from "Super Light," but the V-8s gave both SLs adequate performance. In the U.S. 450SL the 0-60 mph dash took about 9 seconds, and top speed was around 125 mph.

Though the pagoda-style hardtop of the previous SL series was retained—and even mimicked by a slight concavity in the trunklid—the R107 body was brand new, with a mild wedge shape that forecast the W116 S-class sedans to come. In contrast to the earlier two-seaters, which looked nimble and delicate, the new sportsters looked heavy and, on the road, somewhat clumsy (one magazine described the styling as "Americanized" and "Anti-agile"). The European versions

Following past practice, D-B bowed its new 3.5 V-8 in the existing S-class toward the end of its model run. Clockwise from top: 1969 Type 280SE 3.5 coupe and 1970-71 cabrio (Europe), the U.S. 300SEL 3.5 of 1971, and the European 300SEL 3.5 from 1969.

had up-to-date "styled-to-fit" headlamps, with the lenses smoothly blended into the wraparound turn signal/side marker lamps. American regulations dictated relatively

"stone age" lighting via four circular sealed beams, mounted in odd, clear plastic surrounds. Thus, the new SL received fairly mixed reviews by the American press on first sight.

Once inside, however, most Yanks approved. The instrument panel, again prefiguring the forthcoming S-class, was completely redesigned, with a substantial pad sweeping from the right into a deep oval hood in front of the driver. This

enclosed an array of all-business circular instruments. The thickish "A" pillars had special troughs designed to catch and channel away rain to keep the side windows clear. Another step toward good foul-weather visibility was the ribbed taillamp design, which D-B said stayed cleaner than flat lenses. Inertia reels had been fitted, making the effective three-point seatbelts really easy to use. There would come a day when every automaker would have seatbelts like these.

Unfortunately for performance fans, Daimler-Benz chose not to offer the new SL with manual transmission in the U.S., and the acceleration of our automatic-equipped versions was leisurely compared to that of the European manual cars. *Road & Track* magazine's initial assessment was pointed: "The ultimate in a 2-seat luxury car. Its great weight, luxury equipment and mandatory automatic transmission keep it from being a sports car or an entertainment machine, but if one desires merely to drive fast in supreme comfort and avoid the clumsiness of a big sedan, there is no better choice than the 350SL [4.5]." On the whole, damning with faint praise.

As a part of its overall model strategy, Daimler-Benz used the R107 as the foundation for something a bit different, the 350/450SLC. Essentially the two-seat car stretched 14.2 inches, all of it in wheelbase, the SLC offered a more useable rear seat area at the expense of 150 extra pounds and lots more dollars. Although the SL had appeared first, the SLC had been developed alongside it, but as a fixed-roof coupe only. Considering the SLC's extra passenger and cargo capacity, the 3600-pound unladen weight of the base European version (3800 pounds in U.S. trim) doesn't seem that out of the ordinary. Many observers had felt that the SL was overweight, at least in part, because it had to carry some of the extra beef necessary in the SLC. There was considerable interchangeability of course: the entire front end ahead of the cowl, the doors, exterior hardware, and much interior componentry were the same on both models. The main difference, aside from its obvious greater length, was the SLC's curious vertical slats on the fixed aft sections of its rear side windows. Apparently this was a styling device used for a sportier, more close-coupled look. (Had the windows been one-piece they would not have rolled down all the way; better to mask off the rear segment and let the front half roll down.) With this much interchangeability, the SLC was quite economical for D-B to build. Yet it sold for a profitable $14,000 plus—and the dealer markup was glorious.

Unlike the SL, emission regulations prevented a 3.5-liter SLC from reaching U.S. shores by the time the model was launched. Thus, the detoxed and detuned, 195-bhp (DIN)/230-bhp (SAE net) 4.5-liter unit was the only one offered. Later, engine output suffered—to 190 bhp (SAE net) and, in 1975, 180 for California.

So what *was* this car anyway? A truncated sedan? A product planner's creation, neither sports car nor sedan? Actually neither, though both were suggested when it first appeared. No, the SLC was to be the "personal Mercedes," a sort of teutonic Thunderbird—not the blowsy

Below left and right: effects of U.S. bumper and lighting standards are evident in this comparison of 1974 New Generation models (the U.S. 240D is at left). Bottom: the U.S. 280C coupe for 1975, powered by the M110 twincam six.

Ford product of the early '70s but the close-coupled four-seater of the early to mid-'60s. As such, the SLC was heavy on gadgetry but, being a Mercedes, the gadgets were useful and not merely gimmicks. Air conditioning, automatic, power steering, all-disc power brakes, Becker Europa AM/FM stereo, electric antenna, pricey Michelin radial tires, leather upholstery, electric window lifts, heated rear window, and fog lights were all there to help ease your sticker shock. Once you'd finished marveling at these you'd notice the central locking system for both doors and the fuel filler flap, the vacuum-restrained seatbacks (locked with the engine running and doors closed, but the rear passengers had a pushbutton override), a timer for the rear window heater, and a removable glovebox map light. One touch of opulence was probably overkill but should be mentioned: door panels ducted to the comprehensive all-weather climate control system, the air flow serving to keep the side windows demisted. It was shared with the SL, and would show up on subsequent Mercedes models, too.

The SLC wasn't all superficial people-cosseting, though: it was also a very purposefully designed automobile, made to be driven fast by serious drivers. Cockpit ergonomics were close to perfect: comfortable, easy-to-grip steering wheel; a full cluster of white-on-black instruments, easily readable at a glance; marvelously adjustable bucket seats; and an air conditioning/heating system capable of handling any climate from a Brazilian rain forest to the Alaskan tundra. As always, the very best materials were used everywhere, assembled with consummate care. And as with so many modern Mercedes the SLC felt reassuringly solid and "all of a piece", whether standing still or racing down a twisty two-lane. The ride just "gets more impressive as the

road gets worse," said one road test. The handling, thanks partly to D-B's communicative variable-ratio power steering, was predictable, true and nearly dead neutral.

We can't leave the SLC without mentioning a notable trip we made in one to New England during February of 1978. At that time of year the region's normally good secondary roads suffer from the well-known phenomenon of "frost heaves," caused by the wide variations in late-winter temperatures. Every other vehicle we saw, up to and including competent-looking Jeep Wagoneers and Cadillac Sevilles, treated these teeth-chattering, brain-jarring washboards with respect, braking to a near crawl and then proceeding at maybe 15 or 20 mph. So did we, until one particularly bad section took us by surprise. The 450SLC simply carried on at its 60-mph gait, with nothing more than a faint rubbery rumble somewhere far beneath the floor to suggest anything out of the ordinary. "That comes of having a *suspension* under you," they said back at Mercedes-Benz North America—as if every other car on the road lacks springs and shocks and gets along merely on axles and a frame. But compared to the SLC, perhaps they do. After all, our experience was only typical Mercedes behavior.

We should not forget that there was a 280SL in the '70s. This one was introduced for the 1975 model year along with a 280SLC companion as "energy crisis" specials following the fuel shortages of 1973-74. They were essentially identical with the V-8 cars except for the 2.8-liter dohc six borrowed from the 280 sedans. Both cost about $1000-2000 less than the 350/450 models, but they also weighed less, so their performance was not far off the V-8 mark. Unhappily, neither came to the U.S., though these reborn six-

cylinder sports cars sold at the rate of 1500-2000 per year in Europe and elsewhere.

The R107 SL/SLC was the start of another Daimler-Benz product renewal cycle, just as the 230SL had been a decade before. This one would carry the firm through the '70s and into the '80s but, as always, would not be rushed. The next step would be the W116 series: bigger, swoopier, more aerodynamic, more "important" looking than the W108/109 S-class. Characteristically it would carry the traditional radiator motif (albeit in a more streamlined form) that has distinguished most every Daimler-Benz model since the company was formed in 1926.

By the advent of the W116 in 1972, Daimler-Benz was building about 300,000 passenger cars and 160,000 commercial vehicles per year, hardly small potatoes even by world standards. It is difficult to imagine that a company capable of cars like the 300SEL 6.3 or the Type 600 *Grosser* was also ably churning out large numbers of rather more mundane sedans—albeit well-built ones—not to mention workaday trucks and buses. Of course, the cars the W116s replaced were not particularly obsolete. They had simply run as long as needed, roughly five years. Now, something better was ready after the usual long and thorough gestation period that marks every new model from Untertürkheim.

Introduced at the Paris Automobile Salon in 1972, the W116 body/chassis platform was the basis for the new range of upper-echelon models. The first were the carbureted 280S and fuel-injected 280SE, both powered by the then recently introduced M110 twincam six, and the injected 350SE with the M116 V-8. This trio was available with any of four transmissions: three- or four-speed torque-converter automatic or four- or five-speed manual. At Geneva in March

1973, the 450SE and 450SEL, powered by the M117 V-8 from the 450SL, joined the stable, and these eclipsed the others by a country mile.

There were two wheelbases for the new S-class, the standard 112.1 inches and 116.7 inches for the long sedans. The 450SE/SEL were the only W116s initially offered in the U.S., arriving in 1973 fully equipped: air conditioning, power brakes, power steering, power windows, AM/FM stereo radio, three-speed automatic and, of course, the 4.5-liter V-8 engine, rated at 190 bhp in SAE net measure. Styling was sleek for Mercedes, specifications somewhat exotic for sedans, even premium ones. Prices on the East Coast were initially pegged at about $13,000 and $14,500, respectively, which included just about everything except, on the SE, leather seats (a $350 extra). Those prices sound fairly routine today, but 10 years ago these were among the most expensive production sedans in the world. Nevertheless, the new S-class was destined to be extremely popular. M-B of North America planned to sell some 15,000 of these cars in their first year on the market. Two years before, this would have represented half of D-B's total U.S. sales; now it was only about a third.

The W116s were moderately larger than their predecessors: a bit over two inches longer and lower, fractionally wider; wheelbases were longer by some four inches. They were also more heavily padded inside, particularly the roof pillars, side window sills and headliner, but there was a bit more passenger room. They were somewhat heavy cars, approaching two tons at the curb, which put them at a performance disadvantage

vis-a-vis the Jaguar XJ12 (the only comparable import, though it cost $3000 less and was entirely different in character). But they were hardly slow: the U.S. 450SE could cruise at 120 mph with 10 mph in reserve, and the traditional 0-60 mph sprint took about 10 seconds.

A great deal of American tax money was being spent in the early '70s on the government's Experimental Safety Vehicle program, which produced an odd assortment of prototypes, some impractially bulky, all amazingly ugly. Washington might well have invested some of that money for studying the S-class Mercedes. Naturally, the interior had been devised with a sharp eye on "passive" safety—protecting occupants when a

crash was unavoidable—but these cars also demonstrated the importance of "active" safety—a car's ability to *avoid* a crash—with high levels of handling, roadholding, and braking performance, all in a package that was the very definition of class. The W116 structure was the latest development of D-B's patented "rigid passenger cell/deformable extremity" construction. It was designed so that the front and rear ends absorbed the forces of an impact while the passenger cell remained undistorted and intact. Inside that cell, the dashboard was decorated with a discreet strip of fine wood veneer (available in three choices) but was mainly a huge, energy-absorbing pad. The newly styled

Above right: the U.S. 450SLC coupe of 1979. It used the two-seat SL platform with a 14-inch wheelbase stretch. Right: the 450SL on the banked D-B test track in Stuttgart.

This page, top: 1975 ESF 24 safety vehicle was a modified W116 S-class sedan built to underscore the road cars' crashworthiness. Above: the U.S. 450SEL for '75. Opposite page: on the Stuttgart skidpad in 1976.

round instruments were recessed, SL/SLC-style, and shrouded by a deep hood to minimize stray reflections. The steering wheel hub was also amply padded—a passive restraint all by itself. Seating was high on firm, fully adjustable bucket seats. Inertia-reel three-point seatbelts were provided in front (and in the rear on European models). The knowledgeable Ron Wakefield, who has spent many years in Germany observing the native industry, said that while Daimler-Benz "consider their experimental safety vehicles mainly a public relations effort to impress the U.S. Government, their W116 [is] a really substantive attack on the

problem of automotive safety... I consider the W116 the best combination of active (accident avoiding) and passive (protection in a crash) safety yet devised for a production car."

So the 450SE and SEL had gobs of performance, were built with a jeweler's precision, and were as safe as modern production cars could be. Were they anything else? Yes. On the road, these big sedans acted more like small, sporty coupes—surprisingly agile, always composed. The ride was firm by Detroit standards, but that's only because D-B engineers feel a car's suspension should be calibrated to keep the driver informed of what is going on at the tires, not mask it. Beyond that there was hardly room for criticism. The effort required by the variable-ratio power steering was, again, high by U.S. yardsticks, but it was always exactly right for any speed, and the steering marvelously communicative. The all-disc brakes were capable of hauling

the car down from 80 mph in 260 feet with a pedal pressure of 25 pounds. "For 10/10 driving, a 911 Porsche or a Maserati Bora will corner faster," said *Road & Track* magazine, "but in exchange for their ultimate cornering ability one must accept nervous, twitchy behavior at speed on all but the smoothest of surfaces...As a roadgoing sedan [the 450] has no equal. [It] requires a rethink of usual driving habits. That dip at the end of the block where all mortal cars bottom? Forget it. That chatter-bump curve where most rear ends break loose? It's gone. That bump you always slow down and brace yourself for? It never happens...The truth will out, so here it is: The Mercedes 450SE is the best sedan in the world." And, notwithstanding the latest W126 models, there are a good many people who still agree with that assessment. Summarized Graham Robson: "Everything known about safety engineering, and the 70 accumulated years of passenger-car experience by Daimler and Benz, went into these S-class sedans. They were so quiet and refined, so roadworthy, so fast and—as experience proved—so very reliable that it was clearly going to be difficult to make dramatic improvements when the time came to replace them."

As if to emphasize the point, the wizards at Untertürkheim conjured up a successor to the "Best Car in the World," the 300SEL 6.3, which had been discontinued in 1972. This was the fabulous, cost-be-damned 450SEL 6.9, a staggering car that sold for some $50,000 by 1979. It had been introduced to Europe in 1975, but it took another two years to reach wealthy U.S. buyers. The reason was that D-B management felt it would be inappropriate to offer such a fast and thirsty car in America so soon after the energy crisis. Ironically, another fuel crunch hit the U.S. only about a year after this super sedan went on sale, but that wasn't the principal cause of its demise after the 1979 model year. Rather, it was CAFE, the federal government's new corporate average fuel economy mandates that effectively made the 6.9 a liability in North America.

In all, 7380 6.9s were built, but only 1816 of the U.S. versions were sold. Too bad, for this was truly an elite car. And a millionaire could always argue rationally that the 6.9 actually represented a savings. When it arrived, the price of a Rolls-Royce Camargue was pushing past $100,000; for that amount you could buy a 6.9 for conquering your favorite country lanes and have more than enough left over to buy a 240D for shopping trips.

As usual, there was little to distinguish the 6.9 from the "ordinary" 450SEL, although the factory installed a nice set of alloy wheels that made it stand out a little. It came equipped with everything imaginable except orthopedic front seats ($43), reinforced front seat springs ($30) and electrically heated seats ($456 all round). Velour upholstery was a no-cost alternative to the standard leather. The engine—by that time one of the largest production powerplants available anywhere—was developed from the 6.3-liter V-8 that had originated with the 600, but featured hydraulically actuated valves, Bosch K-Jetronic fuel injection, and dry-sump lubrication. A bore increase to 107mm (4.22 in.) brought displacement up to precisely 6834cc (417 cid), good for 250 very healthy horses in emissions-certified, SAE net-rated trim.

The 6.9 suspension was basically the same as on other W116s, but employed hydropneumatic springing *a la* Citroën, with oil/nitrogen struts instead of air bags as on the 300SEL 6.3. But the effect was the same: automatic self-leveling compensation for cargo load, plus an even smoother ride—absorbent at low speed, firmer as speed rose. To prevent unwanted squat and dive, a Watt linkage was used at the rear plus stiffer sway bars front and rear. The hydropneumatic suspension didn't react rapidly to braking/acceleration forces, and *Road & Track* noted that the 6.9 was definitely slower through their slalom test than the 280SE and 450SE.

R&T also offered some interesting performance comparisons of the 6.9 and its immortal predecessor (see chart). The 6.3 was obviously quicker through the gears, though the 6.9 would pull away at higher speeds. "But mechanically, the 6.3's engine sounds harsh compared to the K-Jetronic-equipped 6.9," said the editors. "The new engine is a current, state-of-the-art powerplant, just as the 6.3 was in its day." They found the interior of the 6.9 colder and more clinical, but excused this once on the road: "That's when the sophistication of the new car and the relative crudeness of the old car become apparent."

If the W116 series was the "best sedan in the world," then the 450SEL 6.9 was surely the best of the best. And considering all it could do and all it offered, it's almost amazing Daimler-Benz could sell this *wunderwagen* at "only" $50 Grand. To say that the 6.9 is a platinum-guaranteed collectible is almost superfluous.

The 450SEL 6.9 stands as perhaps the ultimate expression of the "nothing but the best" ideal that so separates Daimler-Benz from just about every other automaker on earth. It was the latterday equivalent of the glorious SS/SSK and 500/540K of a bygone era. All were magnificent automobiles, the brightest and the best that could be conceived, intended only for only a fortunate few and with no apologies for it. Unfortunately, cars like this were doomed to extinction in the auto industry of the '70s where component interchangeability, production volume, sales projections, profit margins, and other "bottom line" considerations had come to be more important than the pursuit of excellence for its own sake.

Of course, Daimler-Benz would continue to produce finely crafted, eminently roadable cars into the next decade, and these are the subject of the chapter that follows. But there will never again be anything like the 6.9. Never.

	300SEL6.3	450SEL 6.9
0-30 mph	2.9 secs	3.3 secs
0-60 mph	6.9 secs	8.2 secs
0-100 mph	18.4 secs	21.1 secs
¼ mile time	15.1 secs	16.4 secs
¼ mile speed	90.0 mph	90.0 mph
top speed	131 mph	137 mph
fuel mileage, avg.	12.8 mpg	13.0 mpg

MERCEDES-BENZ IN THE 1980s: THE LEGEND CONTINUES

The European W201 poses in the D-B wind tunnel for a standard smoke test.

The Arab oil embargo of 1973-74 cast grave doubts over the world's future oil supplies, and threw the politics of energy into sharp focus. It had perhaps the most serious repercussions in the United States, but it was no less thoughtfully viewed at Daimler-Benz. For some time, D-B had conducted research into both alternate engines and fuels and, of course, had long been the leading exponent of diesel power. Thus, it was no surprise when the 240D 3.0 appeared. Called 300D in the U.S., this new version of the smaller W114/115 sedan was powered by a rather astonishing but completely logical engine: a five cylinder inline diesel.

Now diesel fives had been around for quite awhile, but always in commercial vehicles where they made a lot of sense. Here, the idea was to upgrade an existing four-cylinder engine family without a whole new set of parts. Refining a five-cylinder extension of the 0M616 engine to the point where it was suitable for passenger-car use involved a tremendous amount of engineering work, but it was a typical Daimler-Benz project, carefully worked out and with all the angles fully considered. Why not, for example, a diesel six? The main reason was that the New Generation bodyshell had been designed to handle engines only up to a certain physical size, and a 3.0-liter six-cylinder version of the existing diesel—the minimum a larger diesel would need to be—simply wouldn't fit.

The 300D was remarkably lively. An early example driven by noted Belgian critic Paul Frére touched 75 mph in third gear, and certainly reached or exceeded the factory's claimed top speed of 92 mph (it showed 110 on the speedometer). Frére found it "refreshing to drive a diesel in which you could see the three-pointed star rise over the horizon and feel something happen when you put your foot down...There is no doubt that this is easily the fastest diesel on the market."

But not for long. In 1978, D-B engineers bolted a Garrett AiResearch turbocharger onto the OM617 engine of the 300D, although "bolted" doesn't really describe the work that went into it. The result was a new variation of the S-class, the 300SD. The blown diesel was initially rated at 110 bhp (SAE net) at 4200 rpm and 168 lbs/ft of torque peaking at a usefully low 2400 rpm. With this newly fortified powerplant, the 300SD was the new holder of the "world's fastest diesel car" title.

The rationale behind this model is interesting, and crucial to Mercedes-Benz developments in the '80s. Having made the decision to import primarily its top-line cars to the United States, Daimler-Benz now faced the federal government's CAFE (corporate average fuel economy) standards, which took effect with the '78 model year. In essence, CAFE mandated that the average fuel economy for all cars sold here by a given manufacturer, domestic and foreign, had to be at least 18 mpg. The legislation also called for the target to rise in steps, reaching 27.5 mpg by the 1984 model year. Meeting CAFE was tough, especially for makes with a high proportion of heavy luxury models. Not meeting it was tougher: a penalty of $5 per car sold for each 0.1 mpg a company fell short of the target. CAFE had a dramatic impact industry-wide, and luxury-car nameplates predictably were hit hardest. Rolls-Royce, for example, sold only about 2000 cars annually in the U.S. at the time, and simply decided to pay the fine, passing it along to the customer. The theory was that if you're going to spend $90,000 for a Roller, another $500 won't make much difference. But in 1978 there was also talk of a gas guzzler tax of as high as $4000 per car, and while that may not have much bothered the builders

of the Silver Shadow, it certainly worried Daimler-Benz. A new small Mercedes, the W201, was then being developed to improve the fleet average. In the meantime, M-B North America had little choice but to import a high proportion of diesel models, which by now were far and away the most popular Mercedes in the U.S.

The 300SD combined diesel economy with gasoline-engine performance, and it worked beautifully. Though based on the 112.8-inch-wheelbase W116 chassis, it had a few differences in its construction, mainly to hold its government certification weight to below 4000 pounds. These included hood, deck, and trunk partition made of aluminum instead of steel, plus a smaller fuel tank. It was a typically Teutonic solution to a knotty problem. Here at last was a diesel that didn't need to be rowed along with the gearlever or shot down slopes flat-out in order to build up enough speed to crest the next rise at 50 or 60 mph. Remarkably, the 300SD proved thriftier than the normally aspirated 300D, with most examples averaging about 25 mpg.

Introduction of the 300SD gave rise to speculation in some quarters that Daimler-Benz had now sold its soul not only to diesels but also to turbocharging. But it wasn't true. The 300SD was an ideal solution to a peculiar set of conditions in the American market, but turbochargers were not grafted right away onto the firm's existing gasoline engines, nor did new diesel engines appear. The 300SD was initially built only for the American market, mainly because in Europe a diesel car was viewed as basic or "commercial" transportation. Also, in some nations the price difference between gasoline and diesel fuel was (and still is) not as great as it was here. In the U.S., the 300SD was just another luxurious, pricey Mercedes, and as such sold well. Recently, U.S. gas prices have stabilized owing to a worldwide oil glut, and this has cut severely into diesel car sales. This situation is likely to be only temporary, however, and it's interesting to note that the turbodiesel engine is now available in Europe.

A year before it launched the 300SD, D-B took another step forward by introducing a newly designed junior series, the W123, to replace the New Generation cars that had been around since 1968. Most W123s for Europe arrived in early 1976; U.S. deliveries began with the 1977 model year.

This new body/chassis platform was slightly larger than the W114/115 in most dimensions. Sedans were mounted on a 110-inch wheelbase, about an inch longer than before, while the companion C-model coupes returned on a shortened 106.7-inch chassis. Styling was only a mild evolution of the New Generation look, though recognizably smoother and bearing fewer sharp creases and corners. Compared to the W116, the W123 was less "wedgy," which disappointed some observers, but was similar in certain details, such as the ribbed taillights, prominently wide bodyside moldings, and a lower, wider Mercedes grille. And the new design benefited from everything D-B had learned since the New Generation had been drawn up. Its structure was stronger and boasted considerably more interior space. There was also a new front suspension with lower A-arms, upper lateral links, and anti-roll bar, and minor improvements to steering and brakes were instituted along S-class lines.

In line with established Daimler-Benz policy, the W123 series spanned a broad array of models, from the four-cylinder 200 and 200D through five-cylinder diesels to gasoline sixes. As usual, American buyers were

offered only a fraction of the European offerings: the four-cylinder 240D, the five-cylinder 300D and 300CD and the twin cam 280E and 280CE. These cars are with us yet, though the gasoline models were withdrawn from the American market after 1981 in deference to CAFE. For the 1982 model year, the 300D/CD acquired the turbocharged diesel from the 300SD. This marked the first time since it resumed car exports after the war that Mercedes-Benz did not have a six-cylinder model in the U.S. range. The 240D remained basically unchanged for '82 except for exhaust gas recirculation. At about $23,000, it remained the least expensive way to put a Mercedes in your garage. Diesels accounted for 80 percent of U.S. sales in 1982-83, by which time gasoline engines were restricted to the S-class and SL cars at the upper end of the spectrum.

What no one knew at the time of its appearance was that the W123 had been designed with a third body style in mind, the first-ever Daimler-Benz station wagon. For many years, several independent coachbuilders on both sides of the Atlantic had been carrying out such conversions on various M-B sedans—and making a hefty profit in the bargain. Daimler-Benz has never looked favorably on such unauthorized "tampering," especially when it comes to warranty work or

Above: the initial W116 version of the 300SD turbodiesel sedan bowed as a U.S. exclusive for model year 1978.

owner complaints related to non-factory modifications. Accordingly, the firm displayed a wagon of its own, in prototype form, at the 1977 Frankfurt Automobile Show. It was designated T-series which, according to your sources, denoted either "transporter" or *turnier* (wagon). Built on the 110.0-inch sedan wheelbase, it was basically similar to the W123 four-doors in most respects. There were fractional differences in width, track and height, but the structure ahead of the B-pillars was the same for both. Unique to the wagon were a reinforced floorpan, differently styled rear doors, its rear roof area and liftgate, and a revised rear suspension that made use of automatic self-levelling via hydropneumatic struts, similar to those employed on the 450SEL 6.9. Wagon production was assigned to the brand-new D-B facility then opening in Bremen, which would eventually turn out about 30,000 of them a year.

Except for the 2.0-liter fours, which were considered too underpowered for the heavier wagons and their greater cargo carrying capacity, the T-wagons were available in Europe with the full range of W123 drivetrains. Although the twincam 280TE would have been just the thing for hauling cargo while "hauling" down the road,

U.S. and Canadian customers were offered only the five-cylinder diesel-engine 300TD beginning in March 1979. For the 1981 model year, the wagon was treated to the 300SD turbodiesel powerplant to become, perhaps confusingly, the 300TD-T.

In its normally aspirated form the 300TD had only leisurely performance at best, a function of trying to move close to two tons curb weight with but 77 bhp (SAE net). The turbo engine improved matters dramatically, packing 120 bhp (SAE net) at 4350 rpm and a yeoman 170 lbs/ft torque at 2400 rpm, making this one of the few diesels that wasn't handicapped by its compression-ignition engine. Besides all the usual Mercedes virtues, the wagon offers close to 40 cubic feet of cargo space, plus thoughtful features like a roll-up net to keep cargo or small animals at bay. In all, it is probably the ultimate station wagon, especially for those who don't want to sacrifice roadability for utility. M-B North America cheerfully sells every one the Germans can ship over though the price has risen from an initial $24,000 to a cool $35,000 or so at this writing.

The first Mercedes developed in what has been termed the "post-energy crisis" era arrived for the 1981 model year. Putting the new W126 S-class in perspective, *Road & Track* magazine's Joe Rusz noted: "'Übung macht den Meister' is

what the Germans say. Translation: Practice makes the master...Mercedes designers and engineers had seven years of *Übung* creating the newest 4-doors. This means that before the 1973 energy crisis D-B was thinking lighter weight and fuel efficiency. But they had a unique problem: the German car buyer who demands that an S-class Mercedes should look, feel, and drive like a Mercedes. The car must be luxurious, roomy, and above all, fast. Germany is a country without a national speed limit. How could Daimler-Benz maintain that reputation, yet build a car suited to the changing times? By reducing car

weight and drag, which then enabled the factory to decrease engine displacement of its two V-8s, and by minimizing power loss in the transmission. What finally evolved is...the best S-class sedan M-B has built."

The W126 retained the basic suspension layout of the W116, but was new almost everywhere else. Styling, created by chief designer Bruno Sacco, was still recognizably Mercedes-Benz but discernibly sleeker and smoother. Notable features included a slightly raked front end, still

New junior W123 series arrived in the U.S. for '77. Above: that year's dohc 280E. Below: the 1981 300TD wagon. Bottom: 1978 240D.

dominated by the traditional M-B radiator motif; wrapped wind/rain gutters on the A-pillars; a "faster," more smoothly faired backlight; a modest Kamm kickup on the decklid; fully hidden wipers (a first for D-B); and very sparing use of chrome trim. As before there were standard- and long-wheelbase four-door sedans, though wheelbases were now about three inches longer at 115.6 and a massive 121.1 inches, respectively. The new models were also a bit longer overall than their predecessors and measured a significant two inches narrower for reduced frontal area, yet boasted a wider track. Proportions were altered with a stubbier rear deck and longer hood, and the profile was definitely wedgy. With all this, the new S-class not only belied its size but also proved quite aerodynamically efficient. In fact, the coefficient of drag (Cd) was reduced by some 14 percent. With a 0.36 Cd (compared to 0.41 for the W116), the W126 emerged as one of the most slippery cars of any type made anywhere.

Clearly Daimler-Benz was not about to "downsize" its most prestigious offerings just for the sake of fuel economy, so weight reduction through the use of

lightweight materials and simplified componentry was a key goal of the engineering effort. The W126 thus employed high-strength/low-alloy steel, aluminum, and plastics extensively, and ended up 400-600 pounds lighter than previous S-class models despite its slightly greater size.

D-B saved more weight with a new V-8 engine featuring low-pressure die-cast block construction of silicon/aluminum alloy. There were three versions of the new power unit, two for Europe, one for the U.S. The last was a 3839cc (234-cid) engine, with bore and stroke of 88×78.9mm (3.46×3.11 in.), rated at 155 bhp (SAE net) at 4750 rpm and 196 lbs/ft torque at 2750 rpm.

This unit powered the American 380SEL, and also took over for the 4.5-liter V-8 in the SL roadster and SLC coupe to create the 380SL and 380SLC. A second 3.8 V-8 with slightly different dimensions (92×71.8mm/3.62×2.83 in.) and 3818cc (233 cid) was offered for the European 380SE and SEL, along with a 5.0-liter companion

with 96.5×85.0mm (3.79×3.35-in.) bore and stroke for the corresponding 500SE/SEL sedans. The W126 was also available overseas as a 280S/SE/SEL powered by the M110 twincam six in either carbureted or fuel-injected form and, in the U.S., as the 300SD, mechanically unchanged for the most part from its W116 predecessor.

Though brand-new on the outside, the W126 was pure Mercedes inside. There were fractional reductions in overall interior width and front headroom compared to the W116, but rear seaters enjoyed a generous 3.3-inch gain in head clearance plus extra knee space through the use of hollowed-out front seatbacks. A novel touch was an adjustable upper mount for the front seatbelts to suit occupants of different heights. Another logical innovation was power seat controls mounted high up on the door panels instead of on the seat for easier viewing and operation. They were shaped like the seat itself; you simply pushed the control corresponding to the part of the seat you wished to adjust. SEL buyers could also order a power *rear* seat, with an electrically operated sliding cushion that simultaneously altered angle of the hinged backrest that moved with it. Of course the requisite Mercedes features were much in evidence: large-diameter steering wheel with big crash-pad hub, the deeply hooded cluster of eminently readable instruments, the stout multi-function steering column stalk, and the unusual but intelligent "wiggle worm" gate for the console-mounted automatic transmission selector. A bit of Detroit-think, but much appreciated, was D-B's new and effective automatic climate control system. This was standardized for all American-market Mercedes beginning with the 1982 model year.

In Europe, the big 5.0-liter S-class sedans were, in Paul Frére's opinion, more than a match for the vaunted 450SEL 6.9 except in high-speed comfort, where he rated the latter's hydropneumatic suspension system in a class by itself (a similar setup was optional on European SELs, however). Frère reported low-speed harshness "noticeably reduced," with no loss in the exquisite handling of the previous S-class, and the car was pronounced extremely quiet compared with the 6.9. In performance, he pointed out that less weight (by 620 pounds), less drag, and D-B's new four-speed torque-converter automatic (lighter and more mechanically efficient) more than compensated for the 5.0-liter engine's slightly reduced power and torque. His test 500SE leaped from 0 to 60 mph in 7.1 seconds and recorded a top speed of 140 mph—faster off the line and only 8 mph slower flat-out than the European 6.9 he tested back in 1976. And fuel consumption proved up to factory claims, a solid 15 percent better.

Was the 5.0-liter W126 now the "best car in the world" like the 6.3 and 6.9 before it? That depends on your sensibilities. If

you're content merely to glide along in cushioned luxury, insulated from the world around you, a Rolls-Royce will provide a better ride and less noise. For that matter, so will a Jaguar XJ. But if you really aim to *drive* instead of just steer, the best car is still made in Germany.

With the new sedans firmly established, D-B chose the Frankfurt Automobile Show of 1981 to premiere its replacement for the SLC. Built on a shortened 112.2-inch-wheelbase version of the W126 chassis, the new 380/500SEC was roomier, arguably more stylish, and even more refined. Like the SLC, this new body was a true pillarless hardtop, and featured another D-B innovation. To eliminate the usual difficulty in two-doors of front seat passengers having to reach far back to grab the seatbelts, the SEC was equipped with a *gurtbringer*, literally a "belt giver." This electrically operated arm extends forward from the rear quarter panels, presenting the belts to front seaters when the ignition is turned on. When it's switched off, the arms quietly retract, thus ending the usual annoying seatbelt clutter that afflicts so many cars. If an occupant refuses to buckle up within a few seconds, the arm returns to its home to prepare for the worst.

Though styled along the same lines as the W126 sedans, the SECs gain individuality through use of the more shallow, SL-style

grille, which is partly responsible for their even lower, 0.35 drag coefficient. Most body panels are unique to the coupes, and the hood and trunklid are made of aluminum to save weight, as on the sedans. All 380SECs regardless of where they're sold carry the American 3.8-liter V-8 with its more compact combustion chamber, and employ slightly higher compression. This resulted in a five percent gain in torque over the European 3.8 at the expense of 13 horsepower. The 5.0-liter SEC engine was unchanged except for a compression increase, and has the same torque/horsepower tradeoff. Final drive gearing on both was numerically lowered in the interest of fuel economy, but this had only a slightly detrimental effect on performance.

For the 1984 model year the long-rumored "baby" Mercedes, the all-new W201 190E and 190D, arrived in the U.S. It was an important development. These smaller, lower-priced sedans, offered with a choice of four-cylinder gasoline or diesel engines, were intended to take over for the mid-size 300D as the volume sellers in the American lineup. They were also designed to open up an entirely new buyer group for Mercedes-Benz North America, the sort of people who might have considered only Audis and BMWs before. Significantly, the W201s' superior mileage ratings boosted the firm's overall fleet-

average fuel economy tally. And because compliance with CAFE is figured on a "sales-weighted" basis, MBNA could now afford to sacrifice a bit of mileage in its other model offerings for the sake of better performance.

Accordingly, the U.S. lineup was considerably realigned for '84. At the bottom, the normally aspirated four-cylinder 240D in the W123 series, previously the least expensive offering, was withdrawn to make room for the new 190s. At the top, the 380SEL and 380SEC were supplanted by 5.0-liter equivalents. This was good for MBNA in that it effectively ended the "gray market" in European 500SELs and SECs that had grown up here, which created all sorts of problems in after-sales service and parts. Oddly, a federal version of the 500SL was not brought over, perhaps because the R107 design was due for replacement soon. However, there was a new 380SE sedan built on the standard W126 wheelbase previously limited to the 300SD, which returned much as before. The turbodiesel W123 trio, the 300D/CD/TD, also returned little changed, except that the previously optional sliding steel

sunroof was made a no-cost option. Unusually, prices throughout the lineup were held at about 1983 levels. The popular 300D listed at $31,940 East coast P.O.E; the 380SL sold at $43,820.

In its newly tuned U.S. form, the 5.0-liter V-8 (4973cc/303.5 cid) was rated at 184 bhp (SAE net) at 4500 rpm, compared to 155 bhp at 4750 for the 3.8 . Maximum torque was a muscular 247 lbs/ft peaking at only 2000 rpm, quite a bit more than the smaller engine's 196 lbs/ft at 2750 rpm. Interestingly, the 500SEL was a scant 90 pounds heavier than the former 380SEL, and the new 500SEC was actually 10 pounds lighter at the curb than the 380SEC. Though MBNA has not quoted performance figures for the new models at this writing, both acceleration and top-end speed should be quite close to that of the equivalent European cars. As MBNA put it, the 500s "represent what we feel to be the current best level of achievement in high-technology, limited-production motoring." And splendid achievements they are.

An equally splendid achievement is the newest

Daimler-Benz product, the W201. Marketed in the U.S. as the 190D and 190E, these are the smallest Mercedes since the old 180/190 series of the early '50s. Yet they give away nothing to their larger brothers in craftsmanship, engineering sophistication, or that ever-satisfying feel that is distinctly Mercedes. That D-B engineers were able to imbue the 190s with the character of the larger Mercedes is perhaps the most impressive aspect of the W201. It also says a lot about the firm's engineering skill.

Planning for the "baby" Mercedes began in early 1976. At that time, U.S. fuel economy legislation was pending and probable, and a smaller, lighter car was seen by management as the most straightforward way to meet the new standards we now call CAFE. Yet the company couldn't hope to produce a third model line profitably unless it could be sold in sufficiently high volume. This was projected to be a minimum of 100,000 units annually for the North American market alone; an equal or greater number would have to sold in Europe and other prime export areas. The clincher was series of market surveys that

showed considerable "enthusiasm for . . . a smaller, sportier Mercedes that would be attractive to a younger group of first-time buyers . . . as well as to some present Mercedes customers."

Development goals for the W201 were ambitious: lower fuel consumption than any existing model, ride and handling and active and passive safety equivalent to S-class levels, high comfort, ease of service and repair, high durability, and a high ratio of usable interior room to exterior size. There was also one very thorny problem: the new car had to be smaller and less expensive than existing models so as not to steal too many sales from them, yet it couldn't be so much smaller as to compromise room and comfort or so inexpensive as to compromise the Mercedes-Benz reputation for quality.

The result is a car based on the styling and engineering principles established with the W126 but comparable in size with a U.S. compact. The W201 rides a 104.9-inch wheelbase, some five inches shorter than the W123 sedan's and nearly a foot shorter than the standard W126 length. At 175 inches overall, the W201 is shorter by about 14 inches and a whopping 25 inches, respectively. Overall width is 66.1 inches, some 4-5 inches slimmer than on its stablemates. Curb weight differences are striking: the W201 tips the scales at around 2650 pounds, compared to 3500 for the U.S. 300D and some 3700 pounds for the standard W126 sedans. As with the S-class, the W201 makes extensive use of HSLA steel (16 percent of its raw body weight), aluminum, and polycarbonate plastics. Unit body/chassis construction also helps keep weight down.

The W201 chassis is, perhaps, conventional by current standards but finely honed in typical D-B fashion. Though front-wheel drive was considered for the 190 early on, it was decided to stay with rear drive for reasons of handling and comfort as well as the greater flexibility afforded by this traditional layout for fitting different engines and transmissions. As explained in a previous chapter, the 190 is available with a choice of gasoline and diesel powerplants, both newly designed overhead-cam fours, designated M102 and OM601 respectively. These engines were actually introduced in Europe as running changes for the W123-based 200 and 200D some three years before the W201s appeared, so D-B chose the 190 designation for the new models to avoid confusion. Larger-displacement versions of both powerplants are specified for the American market, so model designations here are 190D 2.2 for the diesel car and 190E 2.3 for its fuel-injected gasoline companion. A carbureted 2.0-liter model is also available in Europe.

It is in suspension design that the W201 differs most markedly from past Mercedes. At the front is a Ford-like modified MacPherson-strut setup, with coil springs mounted separately from the struts, ahead and inboard of the shocks. This contrasts with the familiar unequal-length A-arm geometry D-B has used for some time and that remains a fixture of the

larger Mercedes. At the rear, Daimler-Benz has forsaken its typical diagonal pivot axles (semi-trailing arms) for a new five-link arrangement. This is described as a "light and compact rear axle assembly...mounted to the floor/frame by four large rubber thrust bearings. The five links, which essentially function as precisely placed split double wishbones with a tie rod, are properly termed spring link, pulling strut, pushing strut, camber strut, and track rod. They connect the axle carrier and the wheel carrier. The coil springs and gas-pressurized shock absorbers are located between the spring link and the frame/floor, with the shocks packaged quite closely to the wheel carriers outboard of the springs." D-B claims many advantages for this new irs, including excellent straightline tracking, good lateral stability and anti-squat/anti-dive control, minimal rear-wheel steering effect in trailing-throttle cornering, better distribution of road shocks into the main structure (because of the mounting arrangement), and easier service and adjustment.

As you'd expect, the 190 comes with disc brakes at each wheel (the front ones have floating calipers), and power assist is standard for both brakes and the variable-ratio recirculating-ball steering. Negative offset steering geometry is employed to minimize the effects of either front wheel losing traction, as in cornering on slippery roads or in the event of a blowout. Transmission choices comprise standard five-speed overdrive manual gearbox or optional four-speed non-overdrive automatic. Final drive ratio with either is 3.42:1 on the U.S. 190D and 3.23:1 on the 190E. Tires are

reasonably but not generously sized 175/70 steel-belted radials mounted on 14-inch 5J rims.

In appearance, the W201 is clearly from the W126 mold, but is not as extreme as it might be. It simply represents Bruno Sacco's latest thinking about aerodynamics within the framework of D-B design philosophy. As the company says: "What this boils down to is that the 190 looks like a Mercedes-Benz, starting with the familiar grille." The 190's styling resulted from an "evolutionary design process, with clear relationship to previous models," yet maintains the desired "relationship in design to other Mercedes models in production at the same time. The corollary of these tenets is that proven features are retained and improved if possible. Novelty isn't pursued for it own sake." Despite the inherently greater difficulty of achieving the aerodynamic efficiency of a long car in a shorter one, D-B actually managed to improve on the W126 with its new small car. The European 190 comes in with an impressive 0.33 Cd. The U.S. models aren't quite as good— 0.35—mainly because they carry an extra door mirror and can't use flush-fitting headlamps. Nevertheless, these are fine results considering D-B wasn't after aerodynamics at all costs, and they're not far off the

current 0.30 benchmark established by the second-generation Audi 5000, a much larger and longer car.

Of course, the proof of any automobile—even a Mercedes—is on the road, and here the 190 fully lives up to the standard of excellence implied by the three-pointed star it bears. Perhaps the most striking thing is how much it feels like any of the current larger Mercedes despite its much reduced size and weight. There's the same masterful power steering with proper weighting and excellent feel, the same firm yet absorbent ride over the worst roads you can find, the same feel of quality and precision about the controls, the same understated class in cabin appointments, the same meticulous craftsmanship everywhere you look. At first this impression seems a bit incongruous in a car about the size of a Chevy Citation, but then the 190 is, after all, a Mercedes and that makes all the difference. And somehow the smaller dimensions lend an extra dash of sportiness that's absent from the large cars. That's confirmed in tight cornering, where the 190 is definitely more agile and responsive than you'd think in view of its solid, substantial feel in a straight line.

As nice as it is, however, the 190 does have a few faults. At this writing, CONSUMER GUIDE® magazine's auto editors haven't been able to test the five-speed models, but we're not very fond of the four-speed automatic with either engine. Both the 190D and 190E we sampled exhibited erratic part-throttle upshift behavior: slurred and lazy on some occasions, harsh and abrupt on others. Worse, the wide-ratio gearing apparently chosen for economy doesn't seem to mate well with the torque curves of these engines. The result is a transmission reluctant to kick down readily, which can leave you short of power just when you need it most. We noticed this especially with the diesel car after backing off the power momentarily to prepare for low-speed corners. Getting back on the power brought little response, and the car simply could not be hustled through very quickly. Most annoying.

As for performance, neither automatic 190 is sparkling off the line. Our 190D needed a lethargic 17.9 seconds to reach 60 mph from a standstill though this isn't far off the factory's claimed 17.7 seconds. We weren't able to make timed runs with our test 190E, but it felt nowhere near as quick as the suggested 11.4-second 0-60 mph figure. Even with manual, the factory's quoted acceleration times aren't that much better:

17.1 and 11.3 seconds for the diesel and gasoline models, respectively. In fairness, both engines rev smoothly for large-displacement fours, and both have good mid-range response with automatic. Unfortunately, neither powerplant is outstandingly quiet at higher rpm, especially the diesel, which sounds as though it's reached its limit at an indicated 60 mph. Wind noise suppression could also be better, particularly on the 190E, which otherwise cruises in relative calm at speeds that are quite illegal in this county.

On a more positive note, the brakes are superb, providing swift sure stops from high speed in commendably short distances and with excellent pedal feel and system modulation. Equally laudable is the 190's roadholding. The car tracks confidently through high-speed sweepers and tight switchbacks, aided by the fine steering, though it could be higher-geared.

Inside, the 190 offers the usual commanding Mercedes driving position, aided by exceptionally long-travel seat tracks that afford ample leg-stretching room for front seaters. Headroom is limited all around, though, and rear legroom is in short supply for adults even if the front seats are moved far forward. The seats are likely to be too hard for American tastes, especially on

long trips—a pity as this somewhat negates the fine ride. The standard automatic climate control system is more versatile than the one in the larger Mercedes, with manual control for the four-speed fan and a new provision for recirculating cabin air. But the AC has trouble coping with Midwestern summertime heat, and the fan is noisy on its upper two settings.

If we sound overly critical of the 190, perhaps it's because hard-to-please people like us tend to expect more from a Mercedes-Benz than they do from lesser cars. But while it's easy to criticize certain details, there's no doubt that taken as a whole the 190 represents a real advance—not only for Daimler-Benz but for the state of the automotive art as well. Once again, a new Mercedes stands as a model of how all cars in its class should be designed and built. And, as with its many illustrious predecessors, you can bet that other carmakers will be rushing to copy the W201. At least they'll try.

What's ahead from Daimler-Benz in the '80s? Arriving around the summer of 1984 is a redesigned successor to the current mid-range W123.

Below: Long-hood/short-deck proportions and subtle wedge shape are evident in this profile view of the American-market 190E 2.3 model.

Dimensionally, this new W124 said to have a wheelbase longer by at least an inch, and it will be two inches longer overall and about a half-inch wider. Trunk space goes up by about 10 percent, and there are fractional gains in interior dimensions as well. Significantly, the W124s are expected to weigh in some 200 pounds lighter on the average than the cars they replace. This plus more aerodynamic styling, with a drag coefficient on the order of 0.30, will make them not only thriftier but much faster. A choice of three diesel and four gasoline engines is expected to be offered in Europe, including two new sixes of 2.6 and 3.0 liters. These could very well make it to the U.S. also, though chances are we'll first see the W124 with the familiar 3.0-liter tubodiesel five so well-proven in the most recent 300 models. Sources indicate the new four-cylinder 230E will be able to top 125 mph, and the six-cylinder 300E should be good for about 10 mph more. Naturally the W124 will follow the W126/W201 in appearance, but hood/rear deck proportions are said to be different, and a vee'd trunk opening will reportedly set these cars apart from other Mercedes-Benz models.

Also due shortly, perhaps even before the W124, is a high-performance version of the 190. This exciting BMW-killer will be powered by a modified version of the M102 2.3-liter four with electronic fuel injection and—the real news—a 16-valve twincam cylinder head developed in cooperation with the renowned Cosworth Engineering firm in England. Rated power is rumored to be in the vicinity of 185 bhp (DIN), and the hot "baby" Merc will have numerous mechanical changes to handle it: 205/55VR-15 tires, uprated suspension components, special internally ventilated disc brakes, and other modifications. External identification will be provided by a deeper chin spoiler, a small trunklid spoiler,

markedly flared wheel openings, and "ground effects" rocker panel extensions, all done in body-color plastic. One interesting possibility is an electronically controlled hydraulic suspension system with ride height that progressively lowers as speed increases, thereby reducing air drag for higher top-end speed with improved fuel economy. No word on U.S. plans for this model, but its introduction is a welcome reminder that high-performance cars have not been forgotten in Untertürkheim.

Slated for introduction in D-B's centennial year is the long-overdue replacement for the current R107 SL sports car. According to European reports, it's being developed under the R129 designation, and will likely be offered in 3.0-, 4.0- and 5.0-liter versions beginning in 1986. The new SL will remain a fully open two-seat convertible—no roll bar or Targa top here—but will feature new low-drag styling along the lines of the current SEC. A detachable hardtop will continue to be offered (probably as standard equipment in the U.S.) along with the folding cloth top, which will be power-operated for the first time. Among the intriguing technical features whispered for the new SL are a computerized progressive-acting limited-slip differential and a revised four-speed automatic transmission with Toyota-style selector for "power" and "economy" shift points.

Incidentally, D-B says that electronic differential monitoring to sense and prevent incipient wheelspin "offers 90 percent of the advantages of four-wheel drive at 10 percent of the cost." Given the success of cars like the Audi Quattro, however, the temptation to field an all-wheel-drive Mercedes may prove too strong for D-B to resist. We wouldn't look for such a car before 1986, but it would make a grand limited edition to crown the centennial lineup.

Though difficult to believe, D-B is already hard at work on a successor to the current S-class, which was introduced only a short time ago. Following the company's usual model change cycle, this new W140 series should appear for 1988. Well before that—possibly as soon as 1985—D-B is expected to offer a larger-capacity version of its 5.0-liter V-8 in the existing S-class sedans and coupes. Displacement is rumored to be in the region of 5.6 liters (342 cid), output around 260 bhp. As for the next-generation S-class, it will likely embody much of the styling and technical makeup of the "Auto 2000" concept car displayed at the 1981 Frankfurt Show. Among its features that seem likely production possibilities is a variable-displacement cylinder shutoff system, which could very well be applied to the new big-bore V-8.

The Daimler-Benz "Auto 2000" prototype was a fully operational, ultra-slippery fastback designed to accept any one of three alternate engines. Besides a gas turbine and the 3.8-liter "V-8-6-4" gasoline engine, the car was also tested with an interesting 3.3-liter turbocharged V-6 diesel. This employed twin turbos, mounted aft of the engine and operating in tandem above 2000 rpm. The result was a peak 150 bhp at 4300 rpm. The company claims that staged operation of two smaller turbochargers yields better low-end response than a single turbo. Coupled with the slippery body, this engine enabled the "Auto 2000" to deliver 35 mpg—nearly 10 mpg better than a contemporary 300SD. This will be an expensive proposition if it is ever developed for production, and whether or not that happens remains an unknown. For now, we can be sure that if it does decide to go ahead with it, Daimler-Benz will settle for nothing less than the best.

Nothing but the best—a fitting way to conclude this

"Auto 2000" concept car hints at Mercedes to come. Three alternative engines were envisioned, including twin-turbo V-6 diesel (above left).

book. Daimler-Benz, like the separate Daimler and Benz companies before it, has been dedicated to that principle longer than any other automaker. Today that tradition is almost a century old, as indeed is the record of great achievements that was its inevitable consequence. Yet uncompromising excellence is as relevant now as it was when Carl Benz and Gottlieb Daimler started tinkering their first cars together. In fact, the tradition they began may be even more relevant in our turbulent, uncertain world than it was in their more tranquil, less complicated one. It's certainly no less important.

If there is a single element that looms largest in the Mercedes legend, it must be this ceaseless pursuit of perfection. As Daimler-Benz prepares to enter its second century, we can be certain that pursuit will go on and with renewed energy. And no matter how the world may change in future years, we can be equally certain that Daimler-Benz will work to ensure that "the legend continues."

THE COLLECTIBLE MERCEDES-BENZ: CONNOISSEUR'S CHOICE

If you're interested in buying an older-model Mercedes-Benz, whether for investment purposes or simply the sheer satisfaction of owning one, you couldn't have made a better choice. And the choices are numerous and tempting. Of course, it goes without saying that some cars are generally more collectible than others and that some makes and models deliver a better financial return than others. But almost any Mercedes-Benz scores on both counts. In fact, it's hard to find a real "loser"; even the diesel engine cars have a certain aura of respect because of the mystique that has grown up around the three-pointed star. Nevertheless, there are certain Mercedes that depreciate less or less quickly and those that offer greater value appreciation potential for the future.

What makes Mercedes-Benz automobiles in general so collectible? For one thing, Daimler-Benz ordinarily keeps a basic design in production for seven to 10 years. This means new models tend to hold their value longer than most other makes. Another factor is the old law of supply and demand: there have always been many more buyers than there have been new cars to go around. Again the result is comparatively higher values than for other cars of the same age and condition, even though the survival rate for older Mercedes is much higher than the average for all cars.

Rarity affects the collectibility of anything, of course, but Mercedes is an exception to this rule. For example, Ferrari enthusiasts regard the 365GT 2+2 as a "high production" V-12 model—801 units. Yet Daimler-Benz built nearly four times as many 300SL coupes

and roadsters, and these fetch similar if not higher prices on today's collector market. The 190SL saw 25,881 copies— hardly limited production even by Detroit standards—and 48,912 of the successor 230/250/280SLs were built. Again, these models bring many times their original purchase prices even when inflation is factored in. Lest you think vehicle age and buyer nostalgia are at work here, consider that a current R107 SL from any model year customarily sells for twice the price of a used Cadillac Eldorado of the same vintage and condition. Admittedly the American car was less expensive to begin with and produced in much higher volume, and it's true that the dollar gap in the price of new models has risen since the SL appeared in 1971. Even so, the Mercedes maintains its strong value lead.

One telling observation should be made at this point. Over the past 10 years sales of Mercedes-Benz cars in the U.S. have defied periodic swings in the national economy, rising steadily each year. In 1972, MBNA sold 41,556 cars; in 1982 the total was nearly 66,000, an increase of some 60 percent. Yet the number of potential Mercedes buyers has swelled at an even faster pace. As one indicator, consider that the number of millionaires in America rose 207 percent from 1962 to 1972—and by another 161 percent from 1972 to 1980. So it's obvious there are more than enough affluent people around to absorb M-B's annual

production. Of course, not everyone driving a Mercedes is a millionaire, but the fact remains that, in the U.S. at least, a Mercedes is now an even more exclusive commodity than in the past. This situation naturally spurs demand for older models and keeps their values high.

Like most automakers, Daimler-Benz produces many more sedans than coupes or convertibles, yet traditionally the latter body styles have greater collector interest and nostalgia appeal. For this reason, anyone with an eye to buying for appreciation potential should look for these less common models even though they cost more to buy and, in some cases, to restore. As with all collectible automobiles, certain desirable accessories—if they are original factory equipment for that model— increase the value of any Mercedes, even sedans. These would include such items as leather upholstery, sunroof, or higher-performance engines. If you have a choice among several cars and can afford the higher asking prices, let engine displacement be your guide. The smaller-capacity models were produced in much greater volume, and will never command the same values as the less numerous, larger-displacement cars. Among body styles, coupes and the open types are better bets than sedans as both short- *and* long-term investments, all else being equal.

One final point: a percentage appreciation is, or should be,

more important to the Mercedes investor/collector than gross dollar gain. While a $15,000 car might rise in value to $25,000 in five years, a 66.6 percent increase, a $5000 model might go to $10,000 in the same period, a 100 percent gain. If your insurance, licensing, and garage costs are about $3000 for either vehicle, the less expensive car is the better investment, though both may warrant consideration.

With these general points in mind, then, here is a review of Mercedes models we see as most desirable, both as automobiles and investment opportunities.

Pre-1945 Models

For entertainment, nostalgia, and dollar return almost any "vintage" Benz, Mercedes. or Mercedes-Benz is tough to beat. These cars are becoming more scarce with each passing year, and because of the company's far-flung reputation they are virtually "international commodities" that give the owner a degree of protection from shifting currency values. Thus, if the dollar is high relative to the deutsche mark or Yen, for example, look to buy one of these cars in Germany or Japan, where it will be comparatively less expensive than in the U.S. Conversely, an American wishing to sell can readily find overseas buyers in the event exchange rates move the other way.

This principle also applies to an extent with some of the rarer postwar models like the 300d convertible sedans. However, Americans interested in the newer, post-1967 cars are better off with the federalized versions originally sold here and selling within this country. Overseas enthusiasts are generally not interested in U.S.-market models, and owning a non-federal car presents special problems in this country when it comes to parts, service, and restoration assistance.

One drawback to the prewar Mercedes is that nostalgia for cars tends to wane as the generation that originally knew them dies off. Peerless, for example, built some great and fascinating cars, but the number of people who really care about them has dwindled severely. The implications of this for parts and restoration, not to mention values, are obvious. Mercedes-Benz is somewhat less affected by this, partly because the company is still in business, but it's something to keep in mind, especially if your potential purchase is a pre-1920s antique.

The most commonly available prewar models are the larger and more expensive offerings of the 1930s, the Types 290, 320, 400, 500, and 540. Most of the grand Model K and S/SS/SSK cars were spoken for ages ago, and the volume models of this period—the original Type 170, the later Type 170V, and the interesting *heckmotor* 130/150/170 series—have simply not survived in large numbers. The best investment from a percentage standpoint might well be the 1933-34 Type 380K. Though less numerous than its more famous bigger brothers, it has much the same allure: supercharged engine, a variety of body types with very elegant lines, and status as the first of the sports touring cars.

While a restorable car with all its parts is always the better buy for a collector, it's virtually essential with these prewar models. And it should be more

of a watchword the older your prospective purchase is. It does little good to buy a car that can't be restored because parts for it no longer exist. In short, do your homework before you buy, and make sure any car you consider is "all there." You'll save a lot of time, money, and grief in the long run.

We might mention that the Mercedes-Benz Club of America published a register of vintage cars and their owners a few years ago, a potentially invaluable resource for anyone interested in prewar Mercedes. The club welcomes M-B enthusiasts and cars of all ages. For more information write: MBCA, P.O. Box 9985, Colorado Springs, CO 80932.

1951-62 Type 300 and 1951-57 Type 300S/Sc

These regal, imposing machines were the best Daimler-Benz had to offer in the early postwar years, and have much to recommend them both as collectibles and investments. The stately Type 300 combined pre- and postwar styling elements, yet its engine was all-new and has historical significance as the progenitor of the fabulous 300SL powerplant. Other attractions include meticulous craftsmanship, elegant cabin furnishings, and limousine ride and passenger room. Low production is another plus point, especially for the very rare four-door convertible, itself an unusual body style for this

Opposite page: 1951-53 Type 300 sedan. Above: the fabled 300SL Gullwing from 1955. Both these are eminent early-postwar collectibles.

period. The short-wheelbase Super coupe and cabriolet share many of these qualities, and add superior performance (better than that of even the vaunted 540K), fine roadability, and arguably nicer, if still somewhat "Gothic," styling.

Over the next decade, values for both these series should continue rising far above the general rate of inflation. During the past 10 years or so, both have gained in value at 150-200 percent of inflation. Even the Type 300 sedans, which tend to appreciate the least quickly, have quietly exceeded owner expectations.

With all this, none of these models is particularly inexpensive today. The later fuel-injected 300Sc leads the list, with good-condition examples already running consistently above $50,000. Premium specimens routinely command twice that. It is generally true of collector cars that prices on some models "peak" and then decline, while values on others may level off or even decline temporarily following an abnormally high rate of appreciation. However, we don't see either happening in this case. The 300 and 300S models that bring $75,000-$100,000 now will likely sell for twice that in another 10 years.

1954–63 Type 300SL

What can one say about desirability of the legendary big Mercedes sports cars that hasn't already been said? A direct competition heritage, near-timeless styling, sophisticated engineering, pulse-quickening performance, civilized accommodations, even reasonable fuel economy (average 18-21 mpg)—all this and more made the 300SLs destined to be preserved and revered from the day the last one was built. If you want to buy one today you'll need to be either very well-heeled or on very good terms with an understanding loan officer.

The Gull Wing Group (GWG), the principal club for current and would-be 300SL owners, has compiled some interesting facts on distribution and survival of the cars. Of the total 1402 originally built, some 330 are known to have been destroyed over the years. Some 270 cars were originally sold outside the U.S. Of the approximately 800 cars estimated to exist in the U.S., roughly 250 are judged to be in above-average to concours condition, 250 in poor to average condition (though they are running and licensed), and 250-300 either not running, not licensed, or used only for parts. The largest number of survivors are found in California, where some 40 percent of the American-specification models were originally sold.

Rising SL values have

encouraged many owners to undertake ground-up restorations that nearly turn back the clock to the date of manufacture. Parts availability for both the Gullwing and the Roadster is well above average thanks in part to GWG members, who have reproduced selected items, and in part to the goodly number of available parts cars. In addition, a surprising number of new or new-old-stock parts are still available through Mercedes-Benz dealers, though only on a special-order basis.

The 300SL's survival prospects are probably better than for any other low-production exotic. GWG publishes a technical service manual covering every detail on both models. The club also publishes a monthly newsletter and a quarterly magazine through which owners can learn more about their cars and get in touch more easily with each other to exchange hints and information. GWG currently numbers 900 members worldwide. For more information write Business Office, Gull Wing Group International, 2229 Via Cerritos, Palos Verdes Estates, CA 90274.

Gullwing coupe values have risen over 10 times original purchase price in the 30 years since production ceased. Every few years someone announces a peak has been reached—then prices climb still higher. As mentioned, there is probably no such thing as a price peak in highly collectible cars, and a continuing upward climb is the natural result of scarcity and inflation acting in concert.

One often-heard misconception is that the Gullwing is about to be overtaken in value by the 300SL Roadster, which sold for about $10,000 back in the days when coupes commanded $15,000 in comparable (good) condition. Over the long term, however, it's unlikely the Roadster will ever catch up. When Gullwing prices rose to $30,000, the open model averaged $20,000. In 1977-82 the coupes sold for $70,000 and more, but Roadsters failed to go above $45,000 right away. A few sold at that level or above, but the average was actually closer to $32,000. In 1983 the Roadster moved up and over the $40,000 mark while the Gullwing slowed, but this was no surprise and the basic value relationship between these two models remains unchanged.

Perhaps the main reason is the essentially different character of these cars. The Roadster is generally perceived as a better driving car, primarily by dint of the low-pivot swing axle rear suspension found on most examples. Not all experts agree with that assessment, but hardly anyone denies that the Gullwing has unmistakeable flair. It continues to attract attention today. It was the Stutz Bearcat of its day and much closer to racing machinery than the Roadster. Let your taste and pocketbook be your guide.

1955–63 Type 190SL

Despite its status as the 300SL's "little sister," the 190SL has a strong American following today. The nearly 26,000 units built over nine years exceeded predictions of Daimler-Benz executives, and a great many of these cars came to the States. Today, interest in the 190SL has never been higher, a growing number are being restored, and values have approximately doubled in the last five years, generally following the percentage increases of the 300SL.

The current range of asking prices is wide: from $5000 to $20,000 (the average as of mid-1983 was $13,100). This compares to the 1955 retail price of $3980, not including accessories like the lift-off hardtop. The broad price spectrum reflects the high cost of a thorough restoration, particularly the higher-than-average rust tendency of the

unit body/chassis. Prospective 190SL owners should examine any car closely—particularly underbody, rocker panels, and lower fender areas—for signs of the dreaded tinworm. Be prepared to budget for repairs accordingly.

The 190SL appeals to a different sort of personality than the 300SL. The editor of the *SL Market Letter*, for example, rarely finds subscribers who own both models; it's either one or the other. Some view the 190SL not so much as a sports car as a sporty car—a friendly, forgiving tourer, a higher-class VW Karmann-Ghia. And that may be a large part of its appeal among today's collectors. Unlike British sports cars of the period, the 190SL had a heater that actually worked, a convertible top that could be raised or lowered in 20 seconds by one person, and such niceties as windshield washers, backup lamps, even first-gear synchromesh. Also, both the standard cloth top and optional hardtop actually keep out rain, something a few much newer convertibles we could name don't do. Though "purists" may not have understood or appreciated it, the 190SL effectively catered to a new and growing market, and Daimler-Benz would pursue it further with subsequent SLs.

If there are picks among 190SLs they might be the 1955-59 models. The later cars were heavier (by about 300 pounds), and though this didn't much affect performance (0-60 mph in 13 seconds, 103-106 mph top speed), fuel economy suffered appreciably—25+ mpg versus 18.5 mpg, according to contemporary road tests. Regardless of model year, however, we expect 190SL values to double by the early 1990s.

1960-71 W111/112 Coupe and Cabriolet

Near his retirement, Daimler-Benz chief engineer Rudolf

Uhlenhaut was quoted as saying that, in his view, the most significant factor in the company's comeback after World War II was the 2.2-liter overhead-cam six. Simply stated, this engine worked admirably in diverse driving conditions all over the world. Much the same can be said about the elegantly lined generation of two-door Mercedes it powered, cars already hailed in some quarters as "modern classics."

This coupe and cabriolet design debuted at the Frankfurt Automobile Show in late 1959 as a two-door companion to the tailfinned "b-series" 220/220S/220SE sedans, and shared their newly revised W111 chassis. All these cars were sleeker and more modern than their immediate predecessors, as Daimler-Benz shed the last remains of late-'30s/early-'40s styling. There were certain concessions to then-popular trends including modestly wrapped windshields and, on the U.S. versions, vertically stacked quad headlamps. But the coupe and cabriolet, with lower beltlines and no fins, were not at all faddish. It is this style that so captivates the growing number of collectors flocking to these models.

Though the W111 sedans were phased out in favor of the "New Generation" S-class beginning in 1965, the two-doors continued through 1971. In the interim, Daimler-Benz progressively raised engine displacement to keep pace with rising weight and, later, power losses to emissions controls. All these coupe and cabriolet variants were powered by fuel-injected engines, all of which save one were sixes. The original 220SEb was joined two years after its launch by the luxury 300SE models powered by the aluminum-block version of the M189 engine from the 300SL. In late 1965, the 220 gave way to a 250SE successor (M129). This in turn was followed in late 1967 by the M130 powerplant in a mostly unchanged 280SE, at which time the 3.0-liter cars were withdrawn. The final development appeared in late 1969 as the 280SE 3.5, powered by D-B's new overhead-cam M116 V-8 soon to be seen in the 350SL. The V-8 cars were marked by a slightly lower and wider interpretation of the familiar M-B radiator.

All these cars were low-production items, with more hand assembly and higher equipment levels than their sedan relatives. The 300SE versions are the least common (3127 of both body styles), while the 2.2-liter models are the most numerous (nearly 17,000). The V-8 cars are the second scarcest (4502 units), and this plus their better performance has made them rather pricey on today's market despite their being the newest of this series. At this writing it's difficult to project future appreciation with precision except for the early 220SE. Asking prices on these range from $1500-$2000 for a restorable coupe to $11,000-$13,000 for a prime-condition cabriolet. Still, there's little doubt all the two-doors will rise appreciably on a percentage basis, which we tag at about 30 percent over the coming five years.

As with so many unit body/chassis cars, these Mercedes warrant close inspection for signs of rust, as extensive corrosion can make restoration a potentially devastating business. If damage is extensive, steer clear. Many mechanical parts are still readily available, but some unique body panels are in short supply. As with any collector car more than 10-12 years old, your first choice should be the one in best condition. It'll cost more initially, but will save you both money and grief in the long term.

1963-71 Type 230/250/280SL

As noted earlier in this book, the "pagoda-roof" SLs were the last Mercedes two-seaters faithful to the spirit of the *sehr leicht* designation. Compared to their R107 replacement, they had a more youthful, more athletic character, yet fell midway between the earlier 190SL and 300SL in size, performance, and price. These were the first SLs available with automatic transmission, and both steering and brakes were power-assisted as standard equipment. So, the SLs of the '60s might be termed "civilized" sports cars, with ample but not breathtaking speed, enough dash and verve to keep serious drivers entertained, and all the creature comforts necessary for refined, low-effort touring.

Choosing among these models is very much a matter of "horses for courses." For example, some aficionados regard the 230SL's four-main-bearing six as more resilient and "fun" than the "stiffer" but stronger seven-main-bearing unit introduced with the 250SL. The larger-displacement engines, of course, were D-B's response to the advent of emissions regulations and "detox tuning" in the '60s, but the 250 and 280 are both a bit faster than the 230. They also need lubrication less frequently as the intervals were tripled (to 6000 miles). The 280SL has slightly softer, more "rubbery" handling than the earlier cars, but all are fine road machines. To illustrate the point, D-B reportedly brought a 3.0-liter V-12 Ferrari to the press introduction for the original 230SL, staged at the challenging Montreux circuit in France. As the story goes, chief engineer Uhlenhaut did some "hot laps" in both cars. His time in the Ferrari was 47.3 seconds. The 230SL, with only 75 percent the displacement and much less horsepower, was timed a scant .2 second slower. But then Rudi *was* a good driver . . .

These SLs are not that rare, and current values are reasonable even for collectors of more limited means. As with the

Below: a late British-market 250SL from early 1968. All the W113-series SLs are reasonably affordable and readily available now, yet show strong future value appreciation potential, especially the 230/250.

1963–81 Type 600 *Grosser*

The postwar counterpart of the massive 1930s *Grosser* is a bit like Texas: everything about it seems outsized. Here is luxury and power on a grand scale, the product of top-flight engineering and the kind of meticulous attention to detail that can be lavished on a car only when its maker refuses to be rushed. The Type 600 is the most imposing Mercedes you can own, the ultimate creation of Daimler-Benz. In fact, more money was probably invested to produce this single model, relative to production volume, than any other in history. The result was a car of immense size and sophistication with performance that defied all logic.

Like its prewar equivalent, the 600 was the preferred mode of transport among popes, potentates, and petroleum power brokers. When it comes to owning one, though, it helps to have a Texas-size bank account. Actually, the 600 is not outrageously priced in view of its low production—less than 2700 over a remarkable 18 years—and its formidable array of equipment. Keeping in mind that the last examples sold at prices comfortably exceeding 100 grand, the current $30,000-$35,000 it takes to buy one in excellent condition seems quite reasonable—and less well-maintained cars might be found for even less. Unfortunately, these figures are a bit misleading because 600s don't change hands as frequently as most other cars (the majority are still in daily service), and this makes it difficult to tell precisely what they're worth. Also keep in mind that the 600 was designed in the late 1950s, so its technology is hardly state of the art. And it's a dauntingly complex beast, filled with hydraulic and electrical gadgets that can and do pack up. The bottom line: opt for a prime-condition specimen even though it will cost more; you'll save

190SL the price range is broad—anywhere from $3500 to $17,000 or more—so it's more important than usual to weigh potential restoration costs against your purchase price. Even a tired, slightly rusted example can sell for over $10,000, especially if the owner is set on cashing in on the Mercedes cachet, and it wouldn't take much engine and/or body work to put your total investment well over $20,000. So, be selective and take your time. These cars are sufficiently plentiful that you needn't feel compelled to take the first one that comes along, and prime-condition specimens are about as numerous as really ratty ones. It's wise to look for cars beyond your local area—it's a good way to get a perspective on prices, too. Despite its much lower production (some 5200), the 250SL is not considered any more collectible than either of the other models.

As for appreciation potential, these SLs have to be considered fine investments based on their

Top: the 1965-67 Type 600 Pullman landaulet. Above: the six-door Type 600 Pullman from 1969. The Grand Mercedes is a surefire collectible, but its mechanical complexity makes it essential to check condition thoroughly before purchase. Prices are surprisingly reasonable today.

past performance. Most collector cars need about 15 years or so to reach and surpass their original purchase price, climbing above it only later when attrition makes them truly rare. But well-maintained 230 and 250SLs have doubled in value over 20 years, and the 280SL has climbed 2½ times its original sticker price in less than 15 years. Because the three versions do not seem to appreciate at equal rates, however, the earlier cars may be the better buys for those interested in maximum percentage return. Values should rise by at least 50 percent across the board in the next five years, and a 100 percent gain is probable over the coming decade.

money in restoration and maintenance, either of which can easily cost you more than the car itself. If you don't know where to look for signs of wear or failure, then bring along someone who does to check things out before you buy.

The limited turnover in Type 600s makes it difficult to project value potential. However, a rise of 30 to 60 percent over the next 10 years seems likely, and the rate could easily exceed that should attrition prove higher than expected. As an investment you can drive, the 600 doesn't much make sense. It's too large for most garages and parking spaces, ditto for easy maneuvering in city traffic (hire a chauffeur?), fuel consumption is high enough to make even J.R. Ewing turn pale, and the complex mechanicals wouldn't be out of place on the space shuttle. Still, there's no denying the appeal of this most magnificent postwar Mercedes.

1968-71 Type 300SEL 6.3/1975-79 Type 450SEL 6.9

Prestige with punch, plus the usual virtues of the senior Mercedes sedans, led many motoring critics to label these two closet supercars as the best sedans in the world. Powered by derivatives of the Type 600 V-8, both offered sizzling off-the-line go and amazing top-end performance, combined with matchless handling and roadholding and supreme long-distance comfort. In their respective eras each was almost without peer. Perhaps the closest rivals to the original 6.3 in concept and ability were the original Maserati Quattroporte and, later, Jaguar's XJ12. Cars like the 6.3 had come to be almost anti-social in the late '70s, and there was nothing comparable to it on the U.S. market. In Europe the Jaguar, a second-generation Quattroporte and, barely, the Aston Martin Lagonda were in the same

league. Nowadays, of course, we have the 500SEL, but it's not as specialized or as exciting as this pair.

As the model designations suggest, the 6.3 has less engine displacement than the 6.9—387 versus 417 cid—but no less rated horsepower, which is in the vicinity of 250 bhp on both. However, the 6.3's horses appear to be stronger, perhaps because of less stringent emissions tuning. And because the earlier car is lighter, it handily outperforms the newer one in U.S. tune; the European versions were more closely matched. Both models had a different rear suspension than their lesser siblings. The 6.3 used an air-bellows arrangement instead of springs, but these are every bit as prone to air leaks as late-'50s Detroit air suspensions were. The 6.9 employed a more sophisticated hydropneumatic system, which seems more reliable.

Which to choose? If you favor refinement and the greater comfort of a newer body over all-out speed, it's the 6.9. The 6.3 engine is generally conceded to be harsher and "guttier," and there's less back seat space in the W109 bodyshell than in the W116 platform used for the 6.9. The V-8 was a shoehorn fit in the earlier car too, so engine mechanical work is not easy. The newer S-class was designed to accommodate the big engine from the outset, so its underhood area is roomier and more orderly. Either model will be quite costly to maintain, and fuel consumption is alarmingly high.

Based on past market record, our choice for the investment-conscious collector would be the 6.9. More modern engineering, greater room and comfort, easier serviceability and, perhaps, greater mechanical reliability give it the edge in collector esteem and thus appreciation potential over the 6.3. Rarity is not a deciding factor as production is about the same:

6526 for the 6.3 (including 1840 U.S.-spec cars) versus 7380 for the 6.9 (1816 American models). Partly because of greater age, a "used" 6.3 will cost less, but its ultimate percentage value gain will probably lag behind that of its successor. We expect the 6.3 to go up by no more than 25 percent over the next five years, while the 6.9 should easily exceed that, perhaps reaching as high as 50 percent in the same period. Prices for the 6.9 are difficult to peg at present, but prime specimens should be available for about what the last cars sold for new, say $30,000 or so. Pristine 6.3s are now in the $18,000-$20,000 range, and good-condition cars run $12,000-$15,000. Whichever your choice, you're better off with a clean, low-mileage car, particularly if you intend to use it on the road regularly. And with either of these executive hot rods, it would be a crime not to.

1971-date R107 SL series

The current R107 two-seaters have the distinction of being the most numerous and the longest running SL generation yet. Since its introduction in 1971 as the 350SL, nearly 120,000 have been built with various engines and equipment specification. Never in automotive history have so many two-seaters been sold at 1½ times the price of a Cadillac. And the total continues to mount. As this body/chassis type is due to be replaced in 1985 or so, these cars seem poised to join the ranks of collectible Mercedes in the not-too-distant future.

We think the R107 series will be highly sought-after future collectibles for two reasons. First, a large percentage of their owners are not collectors but ordinary consumers, people who want utility—the finest utility they can buy—for both business and personal use combined with a dash of sport. More cars are on company leases than ever before, accruing high mileages, accidents, engine rebuilds, and general recycling to further their life. The number of original, low-mileage "show quality" specimens is not that great in the car population over five years old. Oh, some do exist, but the point is that the majority—say, 70-80 percent—are being used up beyond the point collectors consider ideal. Second, the Mercedes-Benz reputation and the wide presence of these SLs are creating strong nostalgia among owners and the general public alike. In future years, these cars will be fondly remembered by "old car" enthusiasts and for all the usual reasons: an eminent marque, the allure of a fully open body style, top-line status, full equipment, and a high reputation among automotive experts.

It isn't often nowadays you can buy a brand-new car already certified collectible, but you can with the current SL. And that's recommendation enough to think about visiting your local Mercedes-Benz dealer before these cars pass into history.

1971-81 Type 280/350/380/450/500SLC

With the end of production following the 1981 model year, these four-place coupes derived from the two-seat R107 platform have achieved "instant collectible" status. The main question now is just *how* collectible these cars will eventually become. Because the SLCs are such recent "orphans," their collector prices—as opposed to ordinary used-car values—are still in flux, and it will be some time before a true picture of their actual worth and investment potential emerges.

Even so, there's little doubt the SLCs will be sought-after in future years. Introduced with D-B's 3.5-liter V-8 at the 1971 Brussels Show, this was the replacement for the "classic" W111/112 coupe and cabriolet. Its main selling points were genuine four-passenger seating,

made possible by extending the SL wheelbase some 14 inches, combined with the roadster's more dashing body styling. Not all critics admired the SLC's aesthetics, especially the rear roof treatment, but the engineering was highly regarded. Ample suspension travel combined with the model's favorable wheelbase-to-width relationship to give superb handling control, and the SLC demanded less effort to drive fast than almost any other Mercedes of the '70s. Though rear cabin space was marginal for grownups despite the wheelbase splicing, the SLC was the closest thing yet seen from Daimler-Benz to a genuine 2 + 2 *gran turismo.*

Most American-market SLCs were equipped with the low-output 4.5-liter V-8 designed around U.S. emissions requirements. In its final year, the SLC received D-B's new all-aluminum 3.8-liter V-8 as fitted to the 1981 SEL sedan and SL roadster. The earliest U.S. models carried 350SLC nameplates but did, in fact, have the 4.5-liter engine. Initial deliveries began in February 1972, and only 333 units were brought in. Badging was changed the following year, and U.S. deliveries totalled 2318. The original list price at East Coast port of entry was $15,094; by 1980 this had risen to $42,800. By any yardstick the SLC cost a lot of money, yet the performance of the U.S. version disappointed many, especially in relation to the price. Perhaps as result, the SLC ultimately proved less popular in the States than in Europe, where buyers had a choice of four engines, five counting the 3.8 V-8. Interestingly, only a quarter of total production was built to U.S. specifications.

A small but vocal demand for more Mercedes performance created a lucrative American "grey market" in European models, particularly after release of the big 5.0-liter V-8. The SLC

was no exception, and a small number of 500SLCs (as well as 500SLs and 500SELs) were imported privately, much to the chagrin of Mercedes-Benz North America. The 500SLC actually weighed less than the shorter SL due to its aluminum-block engine and aluminum hood and decklid. A reply to the Porsche 928, this car actually had more torque than its Stuttgart rival, matched the 928 in 0-60 mph acceleration, and had about the same top speed, over 140 mph. Yet it weighed 500 pounds more and had more useable rear seat space. The 2.27:1 final drive kept engine rpm quite low even at speeds that would be cause for arrest in the U.S. Undoubtedly this was the gem of 1970s Mercedes sports models, even though it seemed woefully out of place in 55-mph America.

Collectibility of the 500SLC in the U.S. is questionable—not because the car isn't desirable but rather because of the disadvantages of owning any Euro-spec model, especially when it comes to compliance with DOT and EPA regulations. While a whole mini industry now exists to serve the owners of such cars, the cost of the necessary modifications could easily offset whatever savings you might realize by buying a car overseas, though it's an attractive prospect given the dollar's renewed strength against the deutsche mark and other European currencies. Also, some states like New York and California prohibit non-federalized models, and impose hefty fines on owners. Our advice is to check first with your state authorities if you're contemplating one of these cars, then weigh the costs of making it U.S.-legal against purchase price.

The SLCs have experienced zero depreciation so far, mainly

due to the deutsche mark's high value relative to the dollar through the last half of the '70s. Asking prices, however, are not expected to change appreciably despite the present reversal of this situation. While all these models are eminently desirable, the 1976-80 versions offer a broader, flatter torque curve and thus more relaxed performance, plus more sophisticated exhaust emissions control and thus slightly better mileage. However, some may prefer the early 1972-73 cars for their greater maximum horsepower and tidier bumpers. All these comments also hold for contemporary SLs. The final 380SLC is the scarcest of the U.S. models—only 1503 were sold—and have appeal as the last of the breed plus the practical advantage of a current-production engine.

AMG Cars, 1980s Models, Final Comments

It may seem presumptuous to think about today's Mercedes as tomorrow's collectibles, but then again maybe not. The handsome, graceful SEC coupes seem certain to increase in both value and enthusiast esteem by the early 1990s once D-B introduces the W140 successor to the current S-class. And the U.S. debut of the 5.0-liter V-8 for 1984 seems certain to render all models so equipped as much sought-after cars well into the next century. Though it's impossible to project future values or appreciation potential at this writing, it's safe to say that the desirability of 1980s Mercedes will follow the established patterns discussed above.

It's difficult to improve on the design or engineering of a Mercedes. Indeed, Daimler-Benz has held for many years that you can't—or certainly shouldn't. Each new Mercedes model is the product of years of careful study and work, according to the company line, so why should one tamper?

Nevertheless, D-B has given more or less tacit approval to the efforts of one aftermarket Mercedes specialist that carries out conversions on complete cars and also markets a full line of accessories and performance parts designed exclusively for Mercedes. This is the Stuttgart-based AMG firm, the creation of former D-B development engineer Hans-Werner Aufrecht and today known worldwide among car enthusiasts of all stripes. AMG's activities are wide-ranging, the results exciting, and many of its products—from engine tuning kits to complete cars—are developed with direct factory assistance. The firm is perhaps best known in the U.S. for its many special components that enable M-B owners to give their cars a personal touch. But in recent years there has been growing awareness of and rising demand for complete AMG-modified cars sporting color-keyed grille and body trim, rocker panel skirts, deep air dams, rear spoilers, fender flares, racing-style bucket seats, special interior equipment, fat wheels and tires, special suspension pieces, and tuned 5.0-liter V-8s boasting up to 410 horsepower.

Are the "AMG Mercedes" collectible? The answer is both yes and no. Some authorities insist that these cars have a special niche in the hobby because of their greater exclusivity and generally higher performance levels compared to the "stock" products. However, this runs counter to the long-established pattern among collectible automobiles that modifications or accessories of any kind make a car less desirable—and therefore decrease its value—unless they were available as original factory- or dealer-installed equipment for that model. In short, collectors are purists, and tend to value the untainted car over one with even the slightest non-standard alterations. If you don't believe it just visit a concours judging,

where something as minor as incorrect tire tread is considered a gross restoration fault and marked down accordingly. The AMG cars may ultimately prove exceptions. If they do, we suspect the reason will have less to do with the worth of their modifications than with the prestige of the Mercedes-Benz badge. However, there is always the problem of restoring a modified car to its original state, and this gets to be a tricky, costly, and time-consuming business the older the car is. While this won't be much of a factor with the AMG Mercedes for quite some time yet, it will eventually affect their status and values among car collectors of the distant future. The next 20 years will provide a more definitive answer.

A car doesn't have to be collectible to be interesting or rewarding to own. As we said at the outset, any Mercedes is a desirable commodity and worthy of any garage. That includes the many diesel and junior-series models not generally regarded as collectible. There's no reason to feel offended if you own one of these—or discouraged if you're thinking about buying one because of budget or other considerations. They still have the status of the three-pointed star, and benefit from the same integrity and care that goes into every Mercedes-Benz regardless of price, performance, or production volume. It's one of the reasons for the company's continuing worldwide success today and the enviable reputation of the marque. The models not singled out here—we hate to call them "lesser"—may not be as rare or interesting or have the same investment potential as the high-status collectibles. But even the most humble 200 sedan can introduce you to the pleasures of owning and driving a Mercedes-Benz. For many folks, enthusiasts and non-enthusiasts alike, that means a good deal more than mere dollars and cents. Enjoy!

PRODUCTION AND SPECIFICATIONS FOR POSTWAR MODELS

model	chassis	production from	to	body styles*	engine type	cc	bhp DIN	weight (lbs)	wheelbase (in.)	top speed	production sedan	other
170V	136 I-V	6/46	5/50	1	ohv 4	1697	38	2550	112	65		
170Va	136 I-V	5/50	5/52	1	ohv 4	1767	45	2575	112	72	49,367	
170Vb	136 I-V	5/52	9/53	1	ohv 4	1767	45	2607	112	75		
170S	136 IV	5/49	3/52	1,3,4	ohv 4	1767	52	2685	112	75	31,197	2,433
170Sb	191	1/52	8/53	1,3,4	ohv 4	1767	52	2750	112	75	8094	
170S-V	136 VIII	7/53	2/55	1	ohv 4	1767	45	2685	112	70	3122	
170D	136 I-VI	5/49	5/50	1	ohv D4	1697	38	2750	112	62		
170Da	136 I-VI	5/50	4/52	1	ohv D4	1767	40	2750	112	65	33,823	
170Db	136 I-VI	4/52	10/53	1	ohv D4	1767	40	2750	112	65		
170DS	191	1/52	8/53	1	ohv D4	1767	40	2805	112	65	12,985	
170S-D	136 VIII	7/53	9/55	1	ohv D4	1767	40	2860	112	65	14,887	
220	187	7/51	5/54	1,3,4,5	ohc 6	2195	80	2970	112	90	16,154	2360
220a	180 I	3/54	4/56	1,3,4,5	ohc 6	2195	85	2860	106,111	95	25,937	
300	186 II-III	11/51	3/54	12	ohc 6	2996	115	3916	120	100	6214	591
300b	186 II-III	3/54	8/55	12	ohc 6	2996	125	3916	120	100		
300c	186 IV	9/55	6/56	12	ohc 6	2996	125	4002	120	100	1432	51
300d	189	11/57	3/62	12	ohc 6	2996	160	4290	124	105	3077	65
300S	188 I	7/52	8/55	3,5,6	ohc 6	2996	150	3880	114.2	110	216	344
300Sc	188 II	12/55	4/58	3,5,6	ohc 6	2996	175	3924	114.2	112	98	102
180	120 I	7/53	6/57	1	ohv 4	1767	52	2596	104.3	78.4	52,186	
180a	120 II	6/57	7/59	1	ohv 4	1897	65	2662	104.3	84.0	27,353	
180b	120 III	7/59	8/61	1	ohv 4	1897	68	2662	104.3	85.0	29,415	
180c	120 IV	6/61	10/62	1	ohv 4	1897	68	2662	104.3	85.0	9,280	
180D	120 I	2/54	7/59	1	ohv D4	1767	40/43	2684	104.3	70.0	116,485	
180Db	120 II	7/59	8/61	1	ohv D4	1767	43	2684	104.3	70.0	24,676	
180Dc	120 III	6/61	10/62	1	ohv D4	1988	48	2684	104.3	75.0	11,822	
300SL	198 I	8/54	5/57	5	ohc 6	2996	215	2885	94.5	145-165	1400	
300SL	198 II	8/57	2/63	6	ohc 6	2996	215	2950	94.5	135-155		1858
190SL	121 II	5/55	2/63	6	ohc 4	1897	105	2552	94.5	110		25,881
190	121 I	3/56	8/59	1	ohc 4	1897	75	2728	104.3	86.0	61,345	
190b	121 III	6/59	8/61	1	ohc 4	1897	80	2728	104.3	89.0	28,463	
190D	121 I	8/58	7/59	1	ohc D4	1897	50	2750	104.3	78.0	20,629	
190Db	121 III	6/59	9/61	1	ohc D4	1897	50	2750	104.3	78.0	61,309	
219	105	3/56	7/59	1	ohc 6	2195	85/90	2838	108.3	92.0	27,845	
220S	180 II	6/56	10/59	1,4,7	ohc 6	2195	100/106	2970 +	106.3/111	100.0	55,279	3429[1]
220SE	128	10/58	11/60	1,4,7	ohc 6	2195	115	3014 +	106.3/111	100.0	1974	1942[1]

[1]Includes hardtops and convertibles

* 1 = 4 door sedan
2 = 4 door conv. sedan
3 = cabriolet 'A' (conv. cpe., 2 pass.)
4 = cabriolet 'B' (conv. cpe., 5 pass.)
5 = coupe
6 = roadster
7 = hardtop cpe., 2 door
8 = long sedan
9 = limousine
10 = wagon

model	chassis	production from	to	body styles*	engine type	cc	bhp DIN	weight (lbs)	wheelbase (in.)	top speed	production sedan	other
190c	110	4/61	8/65	1	ohc 4	1897	80	2816	106.3	93.0	130,554	
190Dc	110	6/61	8/65	1	ohv D4	1988	55	2904	106.3	81.0	225,645	
200	110	7/65	2/68	1	ohc 4	1988	95	2805	106.3	98.0	70,207	
200D	110	7/65	2/68	1	ohv D4	1988	55	2915	106.3	81.0	161,618	
220b	111/1	8/59	8/65	1	ohc 6	2195	95	2904	108.3	99.5	69,691	
230	110	7/65	2/68	1	ohc 6	2281	105	2871	106.3	104	40,258	
230S	111/1A	7/65	1/68	1	ohc 6	2281	120	2970	108.3	109	41,107	
220Sb	111/2	8/59	7/65	1	ohc 6	2195	110	2959	108.3	103	161,119	
220SEb	111/3	8/59	10/65	1,4,7	ohc 6	2195	120	3200	108.3	107	66,086	18,842
300SE	112/3	4/61	12/67	1,4,7	ohc 6	2996	160-170	3650	108.3	112-125	5,202	3127[1]
300SEL	112/3	12/62	8/65	8	ohc 6	2996	160-170	3600	112.2	110-120	1546	
230SL	113	7/63	1/67	6	ohc 6	2306	150	2900	94.5	124		19,381
250SL	113A	12/66	1/68	6	ohc 6	2496	150	2900	94.5	124		5196
280SL	113E28	1/68	3/71	6	ohc 6	2778	170-180	3000	94.5	121-127		23,885
600	100	8/63	5/81	8	ohc V-8	6332	250	5400	126.0	115	2190	
600	100	8/63	6/81	9	ohc V-8	6332	250	5800	153.5	110	487	
200	115 V20	1/68	12/76	1	ohc 4	1988	95	2805	108.3	100	288,785	
200D	115 D20	1/68	12/76	1	ohv D4	1988	55	2970	108.3	81	339,927	
220	115 V22	2/68	3/75	1	ohc 4	2197	105	2890	108.3	100	128,739	
220D	115 D22	1/68	12/76	1	ohv D4	2197	60	2997	108.3	84	420,273	
230	114 V23	1/68	3/75	1	ohc 6	2292	120	2911	108.3	102	216,877	
230/4	115 V23	8/73	12/76	1	ohc 4	2277	100-110	3100	108.3	100-106	87,765	
230/6	114 V23	8/73	11/76	1,8	ohc 6	2292	120	3003	108.3	109	84,590	
240D	115 D24	8/73	12/76	1	ohv D4	2376	65	3058	108.3	85.7	131,319	
250	114 V25	12/67	5/72	1	ohc 6	2496	130	3014	108.3	112	78,303	
250	114 V28	7/70	75	1	ohc 6	2778	140	3179	108.3	118	36,061	
250C	114 V25	10/68	5/72	7	ohc 6	2496	130	3069	108.3	112		8824
250C	114 V28	7/69	12/75	7	ohc 6	2778	140	3075	108.3	115		11,678
250CE	114 E25	10/68	5/72	7	ohc 6	2496	150	3080	108.3	120		21,787
250S	108 II	9/65	3/69	1	ohc 6	2496	130	3168	108.3	110-113	74,677	
250SE	108 III/ 111 III	9/65	1/68	1,4,7	ohc 6	2496	150	3450	108.3	120	55,181	6213
280	114 V28	10/71	10/76	1	dohc 6	2746	160	3200	108.3	115	44,537	
280E	114 E28	1/71	10/76	1	dohc 6	2746	185	3200	108.3	124	22,836	
280C	114 V28	12/71	8/76	7	dohc 6	2746	130-160	3200	108.3	108-118		13,151
280CE	114 E28	4/71	7/76	7	dohc 6	2746	185	3200	108.3	124	11,518	
280S	108 V28	11/67	9/72	1	ohc 6	2778	140	3212	108.3	112-115	93,666	
280SE	108 E28/ 111 E28	1/68	4/71	1,4,7	ohc 6	2778	160	3400	108.3	115-118	91,051	5132
280SEL	108 E28	1/68	4/71	8	ohc 6	2778	160	3305	112.2	115-118	8250	
280SE 3.5	111 E35/1	8/69	7/71	4,7	ohc V8	3499	200	3600	108.3	127		4502
280SE 3.5	108 E35	7/70	9/72	1	ohc V8	3499	200	3800	108.3	124	11,309	
280SEL 3.5	108 E35	6/70	8/72	8	ohc V8	3499	200	3875	112.2	124	951	

[1]Includes hardtops and convertibles

* 1 = 4 door sedan
2 = 4 door conv. sedan
3 = cabriolet 'A' (conv. cpe., 2 pass.)
4 = cabriolet 'B' (conv. cpe., 5 pass.)
5 = coupe

6 = roadster
7 = hardtop cpe., 2 door
8 = long sedan
9 = limousine
10 = wagon

model	chassis	production from	to	body styles*	engine type	cc	bhp DIN	weight (lbs)	wheelbase (in.)	top speed	production sedan	other
280SE 4.5	108 E45	4/71	9/72	1	ohc V8	4520	190-225	3825	108.3	118-127	13,527	
280SEL 4.5	108 E45	5/71	11/72	8	ohc V8	4520	190-225	3850	112.2	118-127	8173	
300SE	108 IV/ 112/3	8/65	12/67	1,4,7	ohc 6	2996	170	3600	108.3	115-124	2737	3127
300SEL	109 III	9/65	12/67	8	ohc 6	2996	170	3650	112.2	115-124	2369	
300SEL	109 E28	12/67	1/70	8	ohc 6	2778	160	3575	112.2	118	2519	
300SEL 3.5	109 E35/1	5/71	9/72	8	ohc V8	3499	200	3675	112.2	127	9483	
300SEL 4.5	109 E45	5/71	10/72	8	ohc V8	4520	190-225	4075	112.2	118-127	2553	
300SEL 6.3	109 E63	12/67	9/72	8	ohc V8	6332	250	3828	112.2	137	6528	
280SL	107 E28	5/74	date	6	dohc 6	2746	185	3300	96.9	125		18,822
280SLC	107 E28	5/74	10/81	5	dohc 6	2746	185	3425	110.8	125		10,178
350SL	107 E35	11/70	3/80	6	ohc V8	3499	200	3500	96.9	120-130		15,304
350SLC	107 E36	6/71	3/80	5	ohc V8	3499	200	3600	110.8	120-130		13,925
450SL	107 E45	3/71	11/81	6	ohc V8	4520	190-225	3650	96.9	125-135		66,298
450SLC	107 E45	2/72	10/81	5	ohc V8	4520	190-225	3750	110.8	125-135		30,972
450SLC 5.0	107 E50	8/77	12/79	5	ohc V8	4973	240	3390	110.8	140		1,470
500SLC	107 E50	12/80	10/81	5	ohc V8	4973	240	3400	110.8	140		1,299
240D 3.0/ 300D	115 D30	5/74	11/76	1	ohc D5T	2971	80	3150	108.3	92	53,690	
200D	123 D20	7/75	date	1	ohc D4	1988	80	3025	110.0	82	348,058	
220D	123 D22	7/75	3/80	1	ohc D4	2197	60	3036	110.0	84	56,736	
240D	123 D24	7/75	date	1	ohc D4	2404	62-67[2]	3000	110.0	86	384,073	
240TD	123 D24	2/78	date	10	ohc D4	2404	62-67[2]	3344	110.0	89		26,231
300D	123 D30	7/75	date	1	ohc D5	2998	80	3180	110.0	93	299,538	
300TD	123 D30	8/77	date	10	ohc D5	2998	80	3480	110.0	92		28,859
300CD	123 D30	5/77	3/81	7	ohc D5	2998	80	3495	106.7	89		7502
300D-T	123 D30	4/81	date	1	ohc D5	2998	120[2]	3476	110.0	92	24,963	
300CD-T	123 D30	7/81	date	7	ohc D5	2998	120[2]	3476	106.7	92		776
300TD-T	123 D30	11/79	date	10	ohc D5	2998	120[2]	3542	110.0	103		14,886
200	123 V20	7/75	date	1	ohc 4	1988/1997	94/109	3000	110.0	100/104	221,228	
200T	123 V20	5/80	date	10	ohc 4	1988/1997	94/109	3234	110.0	104		14,348
230	123 V23	7/75	10/81	1	ohc 4	2307	109	3000	110.0	106	196,185	
230E	123 E20	10/80	date	1	ohc 4	2299	136	3212	110.0	124	147,889	
230T	123 V23	2/78	4/80	10	ohc 4	2307	109	3234	110.0	106		6884
230TE	123 E23	10/79	date	10	ohc 4	2299	136	3245	110.0	112		16,462
230C	123 V23	11/76	6/80	7	ohc 4	2307	109	3025	106.7	106		18,675
230CE	123 V23	2/80	date	7	ohc 4	2299	136	3025	106.7	118		18,758
250	123 V25	12/75	date	1	ohc 6	2525	140	2992	110.0	113	116,561	
250T	123 E25	8/77	date	10	ohc 6	2525	140	3332	110.0	115		7696

[1] European model
[2] SAE

* 1 = 4 door sedan
2 = 4 door conv. sedan
3 = cabriolet 'A' (conv. cpe., 2 pass.)
4 = cabriolet 'B' (conv. cpe., 5 pass.)
5 = coupe
6 = roadster
7 = hardtop cpe., 2 door
8 = long sedan
9 = limousine
10 = wagon

model	chassis	production from	to	body styles*	engine type	cc	bhp DIN	weight (lbs)	wheelbase (in.)	top speed	production sedan	other
280	123 V28	7/75	7/81	1	dohc 6	2746	137-142²	3201	110.0	124	33,206	
280C	123 V28	12/76	4/80	7	dohc 6	2746	137-142²	3225	106.7	118		3704
280E	123 E28	7/75	date	1	dohc 6	2746	177	3212	110.0	131	110,199	
280TE	123 E28	10/77	date	10	dohc 6	2746	177	3400	110.0	124		13,420
280CE	123 E28	10/76	date	7	dohc 6	2746	177	3225	106.7	124		27,638
300SD	116 D30	2/77	10/80	1	ohc D5T	2998	110²	3850	112.8	103	28,634	
280S	116 V28	10/72	7/80	1	dohc 6	2746	130-160	3200	108.3	108-120	122,848	
280SE	116 E28	10/72	7/80	1	dohc 6	2746	185	3550	112.2	124	150,595	
280SEL	116 E28	4/74	12/80	8	dohc 6	2746	185	3800	116.7	120	7113	
350SE	116 E35	8/72	12/80	1	ohc V-8	3499	200	3685	112.2	127	51,140	
350SEL	116 E35	11/73	1/80	8	ohc V-8	3499	200	3750	116.7	127	4226	
450SE	116 E45	12/72	4/80	1	ohc V-8	4520	190-225	3950	112.2	125-130	41,604	
450SEL	116 E45	12/72	1/80	8	ohc V-8	4520	190-225	4050	116.7	125-130	59,578	
450SEL 6.9	116 E69	10/75	5/80	8	ohc V-8	6834	286	4250	116.7	140	7380	
280S	126 V28	4/79	date	1	dohc 6	2746	156	3432	115.6	124	22,630	
280SE	126 E28	2/79	date	1	dohc 6	2746	185	3432	115.6	130	73,208	
280SEL	126 E28	12/79	date	1	dohc 6	2746	185	3498	121.1	130	7128	
380SE	126 E38	5/79	date	1	ohc V-8	3818/3839	217/204	3400	115.6	134	24,049	
380SEL	126 E38	10/79	date	1	ohc V-8	3818/3839	217/204	3650	121.1	134	16,829	
380SEC	126 E38	8/80	date	7	ohc V-8	3839	204	3487	112.2	131		5298
380SL	107 E38	2/80	date	5	ohc V-8	3818/3839	204-217	3600	96.9	127		18,570
380SLC	107 E38	2/80	10/81	6	ohc V-8	3818	217	3650	111.1	140		3789
500SE	126 E50	4/79	date	1	ohc V-8	4973	240	3564	115.6	140	12,126	
500SEL	126 E50	10/79	date	8	ohc V-8	4973	240	3641	121.1	140	17,084	
500SL	107 E50	4/80	date	5	ohc V-8	4973	240	3388	96.9	140		2651
500SEC	126 E50	8/81	date	7	ohc V-8	4973	231	3542	112.2	140		4661
300SD	126 D30	12/79	date	1	ohc D5	2998	120²	3751	115.6	106	39,474	
190¹	201 V20	2/82	date	1	ohc 4	1997	90	2376	104.9	109	1665	
190E¹	201 E20	2/82	date	1	ohc 4	1997	122	2420	104.9	121	3099	
190D¹	201 D20	8/82	date	1	ohc D4	1997	72	2442	104.9	100	140	

[1] European model
[2] SAE

* 1 = 4 door sedan
2 = 4 door conv. sedan
3 = cabriolet 'A' (conv. cpe., 2 pass.)
4 = cabriolet 'B' (conv. cpe., 5 pass.)
5 = coupe

6 = roadster
7 = hardtop cpe., 2 door
8 = long sedan
9 = limousine
10 = wagon

INDEX